ARTISTS of the SPIRIT

New Prophets in Art and Mysticism

by

Mary Carroll Nelson

Arcus Publishing Company
752 Broadway/P.O. Box 228
Sonoma, CA 95476

Art works:

The Secret by Michael Naranjo. *The Return of the Goddess* by Peter Rogers. *Nature Mandala* by Richard Newman. *Wisdom* by Meinrad Craighead. *Another Song—Innocence* by Melissa Zink. *Barren Storm Diverted* by Pat Musick. The *Suicide* and *Sky Disk* by Bruce Lowney. *Toward the Source of Triangulation* by Gilah Yelin Hirsch.

Photo Credits:

He Who Sleeps at the Foot of the Horse by Cynthia Ploski; Richard Newman by David Oxton; Gilah Yelin Hirsch by Hella Hammid; Peter Rogers by Tony Vinella; Michael Naranjo by Terry Ketler; Alexander Nepote by Hanne-Lore Nepote.

Printing coordinated by Global Interprint, Inc.
Printed in the U.S.A.
Distributed by The Talman Company
131 Spring Street
New York, NY 10012

Library of Congress Cataloging-in-Publication Data

Nelson, Mary Carroll.
    Artists of the spirit : new prophets in art and mysticism / by Mary Carroll Nelson
        p. cm.
    Includes bibliographical references.
    ISBN 0-916955-14-1
    1. Religious biography. 2. Artists--Religious life. 3. Art and religion--Case studies. 4. Mysticism and art--Case studies. 5. Creative ability--Religious aspects--Case studies. 6. Prophecy--Miscellanea--Case studies.   I. Title
    BL72.N45 1994
    291.1'75--dc20   94-10117
                                                      CIP

A C K N O W L E D G M E N T S

I want to thank the Artists of the Spirit for sharing their stories and their wisdom.

I am deeply grateful to my husband, Edwin Blakely Nelson, my daughter Patricia Ann Nelson-Parker, my son Edwin Blakely Nelson, Jr. and his wife Debra, for their loving encouragement.

Along the way, my understanding was deepened by the insight of these companions: Suzanne Dunbar Caldwell, Emilie Dempsey, Francesca Broward, Michelle Lusson, Dorothee L. Mella, Marsha Melnick, Kimn Neilson, Hanne-Lore Nepote, Cynthia Ploski, Betty Rice and Doris Steider.

It has been my good fortune to work with Anne and Peggy Mackenzie of Arcus Publishing Company. They have brought this book into being with an empathy and creativity that vastly enrich my life and add another layer to our shared project.

This book is dedicated to

Grey Burchfield Parker

and

Clare Elise Parker

TABLE OF CONTENTS

MARY CARROLL NELSON
lives in Albuquerque, New Mexico, and has
successfully integrated the three goals she
established for herself early in life: to be an
artist, to be a writer and to be a teacher. The
author of over eleven books including *The
Legendary Artists of Taos* and *Connecting: the
Art of Beth Ames Swartz*, Nelson has also spent
over twenty years as a teacher. Her artworks
are mixed media, dimensional shrines of
transparent plexiglas™ which are often
illuminated. Founder of the Society of Layerists
in Multi Media (SLMM) in 1982 and educated at
Barnard College (B.A. 1950) and the University
of New Mexico (M.A. 1963), Nelson is deeply
committed to the holistic movement.

*his book is a record of the events,
almost entirely mental and emotional, that
transformed the lives of people I think of as
prophets. Among them are visual artists,
healers, channelers and shamans whose
creative breakthroughs were fueled by
upwelling changes in consciousness. My
thesis is that there is a close connection
between visual artists who express
metaphysical insights in their art and seers
who behave like artists in the structured
way they express their metaphysical
knowledge. This connection is their gift of
prophecy. I call these visionaries
artists of the spirit.*

*None of us can learn all we want to
know from personal experience alone.
Collecting the biographies of gifted
visionaries has expanded my own awareness of a multidimensional reality. I have
benefited from reading psychological
studies of the psychic and creative modes
of consciousness, but my perspective is
that of an artist and art observer.*

SINCE THE EARLY 1970s, I have interviewed many artists for books and articles. Some of them described having visions that left them with a feeling of universal connectedness. In each case, their worldviews were holistic, a philosophical viewpoint with which I felt in accord. Our conversations forced a change in the kind of questions I addressed to other artists who I sensed were also expressing a holistic perspective.

Creating art, reading art history and contemporary criticism, viewing art shows and networking with artists are my professional activities, but art alone does not define my interests. Searching for metaphysical knowledge by going to workshops and lectures, and through sustained reading also has been a lifelong private pursuit of mine. My network, therefore, includes people with exceptional psychic abilities who have disclosed, during interviews, their holistic worldview. The responses they have made to lightning flashes of intuition are as creative as those made by artists. It is upon this basis that I postulate a kinship, based in creativity and the imagination, between artists and psychics.

In this book I use artist and seer as synonyms because I see no fundamental difference in their experiences, and I view them all as artists. Psychologist James Hillman suggests that artists, instead of trying to process out their traumatic experiences through therapy, use them as "ore" from which to make their art. His discussion with Michael Ventura is relevant to my premise that the lives of creative people hold lessons for the rest of us. Hillman, speaking of artists, said, "Wounds and scars are the stuff of character." Ventura questions him, saying that we cannot all be artists. Hillman's response lends authoritative support to my premises. "It isn't to be literal about artists . . . Artists are simply models of people who turn to the imagination to work with things. That's why one needs to read the biographies of artists, because biographies show what they did with their traumas; they show what can be done—not what they did but what can be done—by the imagination with hatred, with resentment, with bitterness, with feelings of being useless and inferior and worthless." (Excerpted from *We've Had a Hundred Years of Psychotherapy and the World's Getting Worse,* in *New Age Journal,* June 1992, p. 137.)

I have found that artists and psychics seem to experience more anomalies than most, possibly because they are open to them. They work their imagination like a muscle and practice entering into their deeper layers of consciousness to draw upon them for inspiration. By the nature of their work, artists and psychics become athletes of consciousness.

From repeated discussions with creative personalities, I intuit that an emergent prophetic insight has permanently altered their worldviews. Emergence is a term used by neuroscientist Roger Sperry to describe "the appearance of new laws and properties at every level of organization in nature and the interaction of these laws and properties with all those that had previously evolved." (Erika Erdmann and David Stover, *Beyond a World*

Divided: Human Values in the Brain-Mind Science of Roger Sperry, p. 44.) In Sperry's theory, emergent properties represent evolutionary steps. I believe the prophets among us represent a prodigious step forward in evolution. They not only look ahead, they serve as causative agents of change in others.

Former astronaut Edwin Mitchell, on returning from a mission, decided our consciousness, rather than space, is the new frontier. During his historic flight, he was bombarded with psychic insights. He retired from military service and, in 1973, founded the Institute of Noetic Sciences (IONS) to "study the mind and its diverse ways of knowing in a truly interdisciplinary fashion." The IONS has focused on extraordinary feats of consciousness that could have beneficial effects were they made accessible to more people. For example, they have documented and analyzed cases of spontaneous remission of diseases. They have addressed and supported the spread of altruism.

Willis Harman, president of the IONS, in arguing for an epistemology of consciousness, writes, " . . . In a holistic approach, the meanings of experiences may be understood by discovering their interconnections with other meaningful experiences." (*Noetic Sciences Review*, August 1993, p. 76.)

The Origin of Consciousness

Julian Jaynes' *The Origin of Consciousness in the Breakdown of the Bicameral Mind* furnished an essential component in my concept of evolutionary prophecy. He traces man's mental evolution by focusing on the history of Western culture in the Mediterranean area. By means of linguistic analysis, he discovered that in the *Iliad* there are no words for consciousness. "The characters of the *Iliad* do not sit down and think out what to do. They have no conscious minds such as we say we have, and certainly no introspections . . . The beginnings of action are not in conscious plans, reasons and motives; they are in the actions and speeches of god." (p. 72.) Jaynes asks, "Who then were these gods that pushed men about like robots and sang epics through their lips? They were the voices whose speech and directions could be as distinctly heard by the Iliadic heroes as voices are heard by certain epileptic and schizophrenic patients, or just as Joan of Arc heard her voices. The gods were organizations of the central nervous system . . . The god is a part of the man . . . " (p. 73-74.)

Jaynes writes, "After the Iliad, . . . The contrast with the *Iliad* [and the *Odyssey*] is astonishing. Both in word and deed and character, the *Odyssey* describes a new and different world inhabited by new and different beings. The bicameral gods of the *Iliad*, in crossing over to the *Odyssey*, have become defensive and feeble . . . As the gods decrease in their direction of human affairs, the preconscious hypostases take over some of their function, moving them closer to consciousness." (*The Origin . . . ,* p. 273-274.) Jaynes cites the increase in words related to consciousness in the *Odyssey*. He found corresponding language alterations in other examples of world literature dating from the same period. In this way, Jaynes dates the initial stages of conscious human thought to around 700 B.C. worldwide.

The hero of the *Iliad* lacks awareness of an "analog-I." He does not visualize himself as a separate individual. Instead, he hears the voices of the gods and acts upon their guidance. In his bicameral mind, hallucinated voices received in the right brain are transmitted to the left brain, prompting him to action. Jaynes speculates that the function of the right temporal lobe, which allowed the voices of the gods to be heard, atrophied as language centers in the left brain took over full responsibility for speech.

The bicameral mind gradually broke down as consciousness developed. The more conscious man grew, the further he was from his gods. When his source of authority withdrew, man became more cruel. Jaynes notes the emphasis on deceit and guile in the *Odyssey*, human traits that were undeveloped while men responded instantly to the gods' directions without reflection. Now self-conscious, the characters have the potential for making analytical decisions. They can plan treachery. Jaynes writes about this changed use of language and the portrait of emergent consciousness in the *Odyssey*, "Poetry, from describing external events objectively, is becoming subjectified into a poetry of personal conscious expression." (*The Origin . . . , p. 274.)

As Dion Fortune points out, thought grows from language, not the reverse. Consciousness and language have continued to evolve in favor of rational thinking to the detriment of intuition. Jaynes writes, "In the second millennium B.C., we stopped hearing the inner voices. In the first millennium B.C., those of us who still heard the voices, our oracles and prophets, they too died away." (*The Origin . . . , p. 436.) The process was slow. It was given a push by the invention of writing that encouraged the left brain's development of memory. When the oracles failed, priests became intercessors with the mute and absent gods.

Jaynes characterizes the entire process of history as a gradual retreat from the sacred. "The erosion of the religious view of man in these last years of the second millennium is still a part of the breakdown of the bicameral mind." (*The Origin . . . , p. 439.) We are engaged, he believes, in a great search for authorization to replace our lost gods. In the final pages of his book he leaves open the possibility that, on the spiral of evolution and consciousness, mind is still developing.

Jaynes' conclusion led me to the speculation that once again we are engaged in transformation, so there should be forerunners already living on earth who embody expanded mental abilities just as there were when consciousness began to accelerate. I propose that the individuals I call *artists of the spirit* are among these harbingers of the future. They are attuned to an inner voice, either literally or through their intuition. Neither schizophrenic nor deluded, they operate in the world fully in command of their faculties, but their faculties are more versatile than average. They demonstrate a bicameral ability to use their intuition in harmony with their rational, conscious mind, with notably creative increases in the range of their perception. Such abilities seem prodigious to us now, but I believe they anticipate the normal capabilities of twenty-first century humans.

Re-imaging God

Richard Heinberg (*New Sense Bulletin*, January 1992) lists the necessary components for a "new revelation" which humankind might now be receiving. I have explored his list which includes these three elements:

To help heal the Earth, we need a balance of masculine and feminine values.

There must be encouragement of growth in knowledge.

We require a compelling cosmology with mechanisms for change and a "vision of God that is loving, supportive and *accessible to every person*."

The holistic movement embodies Heinberg's criteria for a new revelation. It reflects a momentous human effort to re-image God as an embodiment of wholeness—androgynous, nonpersonalized, nondualistic, a pervasive creative force animating an organic, living universe.

Like scouts pointing the way, *artists of the spirit* are in the forefront of this re-imaging activity. Among the prophetic voices in this book is Mary-Margaret Moore, who is a medium for the energy known as Bartholomew. Moore is contributing to a new revelation of God as one who is accessible within us and shares responsibility for creation with us.

Meinrad Craighead's name has soared into public consciousness from her writing and paintings devoted to God as Mother; yet she spent fourteen years in a cloister as a Catholic nun, and she has not disavowed her love of God as Father. Her vision is of a holistic, all-encompassing Divinity. She writes, "The symbolic dual being in whom the opposing energies are united is a sign of Divine creative life. Each of us experiences this polarity in striving for our own completeness and equilibrium. It is the sign of the Mother-Father creative spirit within, and in each soul these energies are uniquely reconciled." (*The Litany of the Great River*, p. 58.)

Matthew Fox, the priest who was exiled from the Dominican order, calls for renewal of the mystic tradition in Christianity. He sees the artist as the agent of transformation from patriarchy to creation spirituality. He writes, "The artist's task is awakening awe and providing vehicles of expression so that we can express our awe and wonder at existence. There is an artist in each one of us, and so the artist's task belongs to us all." (*The Coming of the Cosmic Christ*, p. 199.)

"If it is true that human beings have projected 'God' in their own image," Mary Daly writes ("Why Speak About God?" *Womanspirit Rising*, edited by Carol P. Christ and Judith Plaskow), "it is also true that we can evolve beyond the projections of earlier stages of consciousness. It is the creative potential itself in human beings that is the image of God."

She refers to the ontological experience of acting out of our deepest hope; a hope that is creative, dynamic and communal. "Ontological communal hope . . . is cosmic. Its essential dynamic is directed to the universal community." Daly pleads for an unfolding God of being, a verb rather than a noun. "The anthropomorphic symbols for God may be intended to convey personality, but they fail to convey that God is Be-ing." Daly's perspective is that of a feminist theologian; however, her vision extends beyond gender. "What is at stake is a real leap in human evolution, initiated by women. The ground of its creative hope is an intuition of being . . . an intuition of human integrity or of androgynous being." (p. 210-216.)

Daly's intellectual and feeling-based concepts support my belief that the leap in human evolution can only come from the simultaneous rise of feminine or yin-consciousness in all of us, men and women. Balancing the feminine and masculine consciousness is vital to a whole or healthy human psyche, and consequently to the whole human culture. The balancing process, to redress the out-of-kilter patriarchal society we have had for over 5,000 years, has already begun.

Psychologist Carl G. Jung differentiated the innate psychic components of men and women and also theorized the interrelatedness of the masculine and feminine in human personality. "Men are used to thinking of themselves only as men, and women think of themselves as women, but the psychological facts indicate that every human being is androgynous," explains Jungian analyst John A. Sanford (*Invisible Partners: How the Male and Female in Each of Us Affects Our Relationships,* p. 3.)

Emma Jung, in her essays on *Animus and Anima,* wrote of the "two archetypal figures," the feminine and the masculine, saying they belong to both individual consciousness and the collective unconsciousness. She summarized, "When the anima [the feminine personality components of the man] is recognized and integrated a change of attitude occurs toward the feminine generally. This new evaluation of the feminine principle brings with it a due reverence for nature, too; whereas the intellectual viewpoint dominant in an era of science and technology leads to utilizing and even exploiting nature, rather than honoring her . . . Life is founded on the harmonious interplay of masculine and feminine forces, within the individual human being as well as without." (p. 87.) Emma Jung reminds us that second sight and the art of prophecy are "ascribed to woman" because she is "more open to the unconscious than man. Receptivity is a feminine attitude, presupposing openness and emptiness, wherefore Jung has termed it the great secret of femininity." (p. 55.)

Each person represented in this book has become conscious of the inner yin and yang aspects of his or her nature. Tradition assigns to yin these aspects as related to the feminine: body, flesh, matter, chaos, nature, unconscious, passive, receptive, hidden, intuitive, immanent, irrational, subjective, of dreams, the soul, the moon and the dark. Masculine yang aspects relate to: the outer world of action, order, the intellectual, the objective, conscious, aggressive, creative, overt, transcendent, spiritual, the sun and the light.

The feminine anima, in different guises, has appeared to artists Richard Newman and Peter Rogers, and to the shaman He Who Sleeps at the Foot of the Horse. For Rogers, she is the Virgin, the bringer of truth. For Newman, she is the old woman, the reminder of death. To He Who Sleeps, she was a devouring bird of prey who killed him in order for him to be initiated into shamanism.

Morris Berman, whose writing reveals him to be comfortable with the yin in his own nature, reviews Western history in *Coming to Our Senses* (p. 136-155.) as a pattern of gnostic illumination repeatedly erupting as heresies against the dominant rational system. He posits that the hidden wisdom passed down from one century to another among initiates is a body practice leading to the direct experience of God/light. With the theory of the five subtle bodies, he describes multiple levels of consciousness. "The central issue is that there is a somatic and experiential bridge strung, like a rope ladder, across . . . transitional space." He uses the word gap to describe the transitional space between me and not-me, Self and Other. The subtle bodies (five or more) begin with the second body, the mind, the aura or force field around the physical body. The third body is the unconscious, the astral body, or the Higher Self, operant in dreams. The fourth body is the magical, capable of mastering matter, walking on coals, dematerializing objects and rematerializing or altering them, such as turning water into wine. "The fifth level is that of the spiritual body." The practitioner learns techniques to activate the five bodies at once and create a sensation of kundalini energy rising, or a sudden illumination. Such happenings can also occur spontaneously when the five subtle bodies fuse and the person experiences ecstatic union with the universe. This is the ascent, and it is essentially a description of what a shaman undergoes in initiation. Importantly, it is a nonintellectual, spiritual/body practice. Reading Berman as I did years after formulating my thoughts about artists and seers, I had a pang of recognition that the linkage I have intuited among those with exceptional consciousness is related to the five subtle body theory. Their experiences are somatic, gnostic, personal and illuminating.

Shamanism

In current art writing, it is fashionable to discuss the shamanic role of the artist. Not only is the artist a shaman, the shaman is an artist. Mircea Eliade speaks of shamanism as the *technique of ecstasy*. "The shaman is the great specialist in the human soul; he alone 'sees' it, for he knows its form and destiny." (*Shamanism, Archaic Techniques of Ecstasy,* p. 8.) Angeles Arrien, speaking from her position as a cultural anthropologist, says, "Shamanism basically is using outer nature as a mirror of your own internal nature. It's really a way of connecting to Mother Earth . . . It's the reclamation of self, and there are multiple doorways for the reclamation of self." (Angeles Arrien, "The Bridge of Healing: Discovering the Universal Themes of Human Culture," *Magical Blend*, issue 28,

October 1990.)

In order to understand, at least rudimentarily, the experience of shamanic practice, I took courses from Dr. Serge King in Huna, the shamanic tradition of Hawaii. King taught, "Shamanism is a craft, not a religion." (*Urban Shaman*, p. 14.) If I take the time to practice Huna methods, I experience a sense of effortless flow. Through exercises in mind control, I can transcend my daily reality to reach a place in the imagination that feels connected to an indefinable space-time of a different nature from the three-dimensional world.

Physicist Fred Alan Wolf lists nine hypotheses dealing with the relationship between modern physics and shamanic practice, which I will paraphrase from his book, *The Eagle's Quest*.

1. All shamans see the universe as made from vibrations.
2. Shamans see the world in terms of mythic reality. They are able to perceive the past and the future.
3. Shamans perceive reality in an altered state of consciousness.
4. Shamans alter a patient's belief about reality. Seeing is believing. Believing is seeing.
5. Shamans see all events as universally connected, in relationship.
6. Shamans enter parallel worlds.
7. Shamans work with a sense of higher power, the great universe-mother.
8. Shamans practice male and female medicine, using love as healing energy. Wolf believes the magic aspect of quantum physics is that love is a photon inclusion, an aspect of light.
9. Shamans enter the death world to alter their perceptions of reality. (p. 30.)

Michael Harner says that "Shamanism represents the most widespread and ancient methodological system of mind-body healing known to humanity." (*The Way of the Shaman*, p. 40.) He refers to the shaman as the guardian of the psychic and the see-er. King and Harner relate the shamanic tradition to the modern, urban condition. "Both shamans and scientists personally pursue research into the mysteries of the universe, and both believe that the underlying causal processes of that universe are hidden from ordinary view," Harner contends. "The shaman is an empiricist. One of the definitions of empiricism is 'the practice of emphasizing experience, especially of the senses.'" (p. 45.)

King writes, "The outstanding quality of the shaman, regardless of culture, is the inclination toward engagement, or creative activity." (*Urban Shaman,* p. 14.) It is in these areas of empiricism and creativity that I believe both the psychically and artistically gifted have the ability to move into what Harner calls SSC, the shamanic state of consciousness.

Channeling

Otto Rank speaks to the connection between the artist and the age in which he lives in his revolutionary *Art and Artist:* "The general ideology of the culture, which determines its religion, morals, and society as well as its art, is again only the expression of the human types of the age, and of this the artist and the creative personality are the most definite crystallization . . . We cannot possibly understand the change and growth of artforms without following the change of the idea of the soul in human history . . . The main task . . . is to expound the *development and change in meaning of artforms from similar changes in the idea of the soul.* The aesthetic history of the idea of the beautiful is probably no more than a reflection of the changes in the idea of the soul under the influence of increasing knowledge." (p. 7-12.)

For psychically and artistically gifted people, traumatic encounters with loss, illness, death, fear and psychic events often function as gates to increasing knowledge. *Artists of the spirit* have translated their knowledge into prophecies of a changing worldview. Unfortunately, they threaten many fervent believers in traditional religious prophecy. As a result of societal rejection, some of our current messengers have endured initiations of suffering and self-doubt before reaching a state of personal acceptance and responsibility for their gift. Acceptance of new prophecy is resisted by the general population, which is conditioned to fear, yet channelers who serve as modern prophets are proliferating.

A few of the people featured in this book find the word channeling to be an unwelcome description of their experience with awakening, but it fits some of them very well. Dr. Frank Alper, Barbara Hand Clow and Mary-Margaret Moore are acknowledged channelers of depth and vision. Linda Tellington-Jones, a healer of animals, and Patricia Brown, a clinical psychologist, have been recipients of creative expressions, all at once, complete without editing. Michael Naranjo, who is totally blind, can see his sculptures completed in his mind. Miguel Angel Ruiz and He Who Sleeps at the Foot of the Horse, both healing shamans, can see and hear the discarnate entities who assist them in knowing what their clients need.

Arthur Hastings, in *With the Tongues of Men and Angels,* says channeling "refers to a process in which a person transmits information or artistic expression that he or she receives mentally or physically and which appears to come from a personality source outside the conscious mind. The message is directed toward an audience and is purposeful." (p. 4.)

Channeling is a talent, a gift of the Spirit, as described in these Biblical passages: *Corinthians, 12:10-11,* "Through this one Spirit; one, the power of miracles; another, prophecy . . . All these are the work of one and the same Spirit, who distributes different gifts to different people just as he chooses." *Corinthians I4:4 ,* "The one with the gift of tongues talks for his own benefit, but the man who prophesies does so for the benefit of the community."

Creativity, Leadership and Holism

We are at the dawn of a new stage in human history. Warriors, priests, kings and statesmen have taken their turn leading the world, each competitively grasping for power. Now, we require new leadership. Due to the nature of their mental processes, creative people could provide insightful leadership for the greater society. Though individual artists can be as viciously competitive as anyone else, they are practiced in solving problems holistically. To achieve a harmonious artwork, artists must withhold closure, accept preliminary chaos and observe open-mindedly the whole pattern of their work as it evolves. Instead of making an analytical search for a single solution to an aesthetic problem, many artists customarily practice what Edward De Bono calls horizontal thinking: they consider a variety of possible solutions and synthesize them.

Reliance upon synthesis suggests a vitally needed alternative to the adversarial confrontation that is clearly failing on a global scale. Compromise among many possible courses of action is a way to create the win-win solutions that lead to cooperation. Paying heed to those whose vision widens our choices can lead us through the chaos we have helped to create. We need prophets to help answer the questions: How do we heal our stricken planet? How do we heal ourselves? Our imaginers—our shamans—are our prophets. I propose that *artists of the spirit* are not only prophetic; they are potential leaders for a global turning toward holism.

Both ancient and new prophecies predict the time of chaos we are now undergoing will be replaced by a harmonious, lasting period of peace in the next millennium. A forerunner of that peace is the spread of holistic consciousness, whose most important by-product is the reduction of polarities. Anna F. Lembkow writes that "What is especially appealing and significant . . . about the nondualistic perspective is that it can *conciliate and embrace all differences*—and do so by affirming rather than eliminating multiplicity, variety and distinctions." (*The Wholeness Principle*, p. 29.)

Becoming aware of prophetically gifted people was a spiritual gift in my life—one I felt obligated to accept, ponder and bring into form. In planning this book, I felt at first that I should make a strenuous effort to find creative prophets in all areas of the country in order to force the point that they can be found everywhere, but I decided to follow the discovery of them as it unfolded for me. From the first inkling of an inspiration, synchronistic "coincidences" have guided my progress to such an extent that I finally just let go and trusted my source, whatever it may be. Consequently, I have drawn upon my own experience with people whose lives have naturally touched mine. New Mexico, where I live, attracts artists as well as spiritual seekers, but my work brings me into contact with people throughout the country; there are no fast borders in this selection.

Sixteen life stories comprise the body of this book. My purpose in telling them is to alert readers in two ways: that they might notice signs of expansion in their own consciousness, and that they might recognize the prophets in their lives.

I am comfortable with mystical language. If someone describes an "ecstatic moment" or a vision or speaks of a "spiritual dimension," I have no problem accepting the validity of the statement. Among the featured biographees in this book are those whose vocabulary is more neutral, more academic or intellectual than mine. Artists Pat Musick, Richard Newman, Gilah Yelin Hirsch and Melissa Zink tell their stories objectively, with restraint. They prefer not to be associated with a spiritualistic interpretation, although each has gone through an initiatory process involving trauma. Serge King and Frank Alper structure their shamanic knowledge without recourse to a special vocabulary. I value these distinctions, and I attempt to honor them by reflecting the language each person in the book has chosen. Actually, the direct way these gifted people told their stories was persuasive to me, and it influenced my choices.

The *artists of the spirit* I have selected do not describe themselves as prophets. Bruce Lowney wrote an articulate letter to me a number of years ago when I was just beginning this project, to say he could not see himself as prophetic. Yet these artists and shamans have served as prophets to me and to others. My criteria were that they have accepted responsibility for their gift, given form to it and shared it openly with an altruistic spirit. In effect, their life stories are a tool for transformation. From knowing the cataclysms in their lives, we are better prepared to understand our own. Retelling their stories has deepened my conviction that the universe mirrors not only the responsive connections within a single mind, but also the creative vibration of one mind connecting with another. The role I have chosen for myself, however briefly, is to hold the mirror.

MATURITY has a singular virtue: it provides us with a long view backwards to those pivotal encounters that direct our curiosity. Curiosity, in turn, controls the focus of our attention. Attention determines what we learn.

Why were we born? What happens to us when we die? Most of us struggle with those questions or flee from them in fear. Whatever our talents, wherever we find ourselves, we can search for answers and fully participate in the unfolding we see around us. All fields of inquiry are possible doorways to philosophy.

A Search for Perennial Wisdom

Since childhood, I have been lured by mysticism and the unexplained. Although our culture plays down mysticism in science, government, and education, access to a dimension beyond the tangible has always been available. As a Catholic child, I knew the mystery of the mass, miracles, the Virgin Mary, Lourdes, Fatima and the comforting protection of a personal guardian angel. I was exposed at a young age to the sacraments, the liturgy, incense, grace, sacred music, holy days, saints and the belief that anything can be blessed through our own intention. Growing up with beliefs in the Annunciation, the Virgin Birth and the Resurrection sensitized me to expect the miraculous. I am saturated with Catholic patterning and well-worn prayers arrive unbidden in my inner ear. Yet even as a youngster of five, I argued with dogma. I have never reconciled my innate sense of wholeness with dualistic church doctrine. Torn between loyalty to the ritual of the mass and doubt, I eventually became outraged at the patriarchy's systematic exclusion of the feminine.

It was a long wait, but today there are voices pleading for holism, for healing the many splits caused by the unyielding masculinity of the Judeo-Christian worldview. Matthew Fox is the former Dominican priest who was silenced by the hierarchy for admonishing the church in *Original Blessing* and *The Coming of the Cosmic Christ*, and other writings. He is the inspiration behind Creation Spirituality, a revisioning of the Christ as a universal, androgynous and cosmic creator/source. Matricide, Fox says, is the "reigning dis-ease of our time," dating from 4500 B.C. to the present. (*Cosmic Christ*, p. 34.)

Fox defines mysticism in twenty-one ways, many of which could be applied to the experience of those I refer to as *artists of the spirit*. Mysticism is experiential, compassionate, connection-making, affirmative of the world as a whole, feminist, image-making, prophetic. "A prophet is a mystic in action." (*Cosmic Christ,* p. 63.)

While waiting for Fox's creation-centered vision to become the guiding one in a future church, I've made a search for perennial wisdom in areas that are independent of an organization. Anna F. Lemkow uses these key words and phrases to summarize the perennial philosophy:

1) Concerning the universe: nondualistic, oneness, unity, multidimensional, dynamic, living, ordered, and consistent.
2) Concerning human beings: divine in their innermost nature, potentialities limitless, creators of human destiny.
3) Concerning terrestrial life: incipient in so-called inanimate life, matter and con sciousness inseparable, all life interdependent, interpenetrating.

"The universe as a whole, terrestrial life, and man . . . are homologous in their hierarchical structure wherein each dimension or state of being includes but transcends all 'lower' or less inclusive levels or dimensions. Higher levels can explain lower levels but not vice versa." (*Wholeness Principle*, p. 38-40.)

Geneticists and psychologists suggest that our cells inherit the memory of prior human experience. Cellular memory is a premise that substantiates the esoteric idea that the soul incarnates with a heritage of knowledge acquired in former human experience. Prophets have a demonstrable ability to access their cellular or soul source of wisdom. It follows that we are all equipped to tap into this matrix.

As a displaced person within the Catholic Church, I discovered in myself elements of belief originating far back in time within the mother culture from which traditional religions evolved. Since I first encountered the concept of reincarnation, I have accepted it as an explanation for the great disparities in our fate, and also for our frequent feelings of déjà vu. Through some repetitive process, our spiritual essence experiences life over and over again. We incarnate to learn in this earthly school. We depart to evaluate our soul's progress, and incarnate once again.

Reincarnation: The Phoenix Fire Mystery (edited by Joseph Head and S. L. Cranston) is a compilation of essays and research into this recurring idea found in Eastern and Western religions, literature and philosophy. *Reincarnation: A New Horizon in Science, Religion and Society* (by Cranston and Carey Williams) is a book that challenges contemporary interpretations of the Bible. Both books are objective, historical resources on this subject.

Today, something new has been added or reworded, in the perennial understanding that everything is connected. On all sides are people with the talent for prophecy who tell us there is divinity within each of us, man and woman. We are cocreators, responsible for this planet and our own evolution, and it is time to claim our own empowerment. This is a different message from those that posit a distant god in judgment over his flawed creation. New prophets say we can heal our stricken planet, but first we have to discover the way into our intuitive wisdom.

George Leonard, in this beautiful passage from *The Silent Pulse*, envisions holistic energy as music of the spheres: "At the heart of each of us, whatever our imperfections, there exists a silent pulse of perfect rhythm, a complex of wave forms and resonances, which is absolutely individual and unique, and yet which connects us to everything in the universe. The act of getting in touch with this pulse can transform our personal experience and in some way alter the world around us." (p. xii.) Although I have not met him, I feel Leonard's influence. He taught me to value my personal experience and insight.

On a Path of Books

Marilyn Ferguson, in *The Aquarian Conspiracy*, speaks of an entry point into the transformation of one's thinking. Each of us has such an entry point; mine is books. I do not intend to belabor personal issues on my journey to mysticism, but I will set forth the influences on my thinking. What I find meaningful has made me alert to the inner experiences of some extraordinary people. Had I been absorbed by scholastic boundaries and rhetorical concepts, I believe I would have missed the prophetic nature of their lives. Beginning with the fairy tales, read to me by my mother and then by myself, which stimulated my connection with a fantasy world where little people and angels hold sway, the right book has consistently fallen into my hands. College, in retrospect, was a four-year, self-guided tour of books. One that imprinted itself in my memory was Antoine de Saint-Exupery's *The Little Prince*. From it came the cherished line, "Only the children know what they are looking for," which I later wrote on my daughter and son's toy trunk. I taught little children for twenty-one years. I am certain that for a few years every child can still remember the mysterious state of prebirth.

The word "children" still beckons me in these resonant Biblical passages: "Anyone who welcomes one of these children in my name, welcomes me." And, "I tell you solemnly, unless you change and become like little children you will never enter the kingdom of heaven." One of my unstated goals has always been, no matter what the odds, to retain a sense of childlike wonder.

I graduated from college in 1950 unhappily convinced that an unbridgeable gap separates the world of faith from that of academicism. The gap closed somewhat when I read Lecomte du Nouy's *Human Destiny*. Du Nouy tried to prove that no essential conflict divides the revealed wisdom of the Judeo-Christian tradition based on prophecy and the discoveries of contemporary science based upon experimentation and controlled observation of the universe. I relished his inclusiveness, so opposite to the categorization of academic disciplines. In the conformist period of the early 1950s, he challenged the church and science to reach a consensus. That was a daring act.

The Feminine and the Mystic

Like Du Nouy, Pierre Teilhard de Chardin espoused a theory that grew from his lifelong devotion to science and Christianity. A Jesuit priest and archaeologist who described himself as a naturalist, de Chardin had one of the noblest minds of the twentieth century. His seminal work, *The Phenomenon of Man*, contains his vision of mankind's upward evolution through the moral level, and onward to the Omega point of spiritual reunification with God. The Catholic Church refused to sanction Teilhard's ideas and his book was not published in France until after his death in 1955. When I read the American edition in the early I960s, I seized upon Teilhard's theory of the noosphere—that envelope of consciousness encircling the earth in which all human thought reverberates.

I read Teilhard's work and Betty Friedan's *The Feminine Mystique* at nearly the same time, a coincidence that still seems significant to me. In 1963, Friedan called upon women to be fully independent persons, not simply adjuncts to men. Teilhard and Friedan qualified each other. Their insights provoked an inner dialogue that I had to face—and this dealt with the nature of God and the place of the feminine. Within the noosphere, the exigent feminine principle was demanding to be acknowledged, by the Church and society perhaps, but surely by me and other women.

There comes a time when you realize that you read in order to confirm what you intuitively feel is true. Teilhard and Friedan instigated my long search for responsive acknowledgment of the feminine coupled with divinity. *Womanspirit Rising* (edited by Carol P. Christ and Judith Plaskow) soothed the feeling of being alone in this search. The voices in their book dare to criticize. They are scandalized by women's ostracism from decisive roles in religion, theology and the greater society. Most importantly, they underscore their conclusions with scholarly and articulate research.

A Time Without a Myth

Second only to Teilhard, Joseph Campbell has most deeply affected my thinking. In my favorite of his books, *The Inner Reaches of Outer Space: Metaphor as Myth and as Religion*, Campbell writes that the prevailing Christian myth is " . . . addressed in all seriousness to a named and defined masculine personality inhabiting a local piece of sky a short flight beyond the moon." Our Western myth, a tribal one, local to the Middle East desert area, does not accommodate the vastly expanded modern sense of the unexplored depths of our inner space and the infinite vastness of outer space that our microscopes and telescopes have revealed to us. Essentially, we inhabit a different reality from that of the original creators of our myth. It no longer fits. Asian myths do not account for our contemporary knowledge either.

Under Campbell's tutelage, I was able to take a more objective, though affectionate, look at my inherited myth and to grant myself a long-delayed freedom from grieving that the religious structure of my childhood could not sustain me for life. Two strands of mental fiber, the one called religiosity and the other spirituality, separated themselves in my mind, giving me the opportunity to reweave them at will.

The Portable Jung, edited by Joseph Campbell, is my source for studying the concepts of anima/animus, archetypes, the collective unconscious and dream interpretation, not as projected by popularized usage, but as defined in these selected writings by Carl G. Jung. Particularly comforting to me is his observation that modern religions are so exoteric, of the outer world, they no longer express our esoteric or psychic life. Jung's Man and His Symbols, Modern Man in Search of a Soul, and The Undiscovered Self prophesied the wasteland of a civilization trapped in rationalism.

William Barrett philosophizes in Irrational Man that rational thinking carried to extremes is insane. By excluding information from his intuitive self, the modern person is out of balance. From Barrett's and Jung's gray pictures of contemporary angst, I turned to other writers who perceive a present day return to the sacred. Two that stand out are Frances Huxley's The Way of the Sacred and David Spangler's Emergence: The Rebirth of the Sacred.

Spangler bridges Christian and Eastern traditions in his prophecy that the world is infused and energized by Spirit. Revelation: The Birth of a New Age is his early vision of the transformation in consciousness he believed to be already in process. He visualized human society dividing. In one camp are the entrenched fundamentalists around the earth who cling to old patterns, be they religious, xenophobic, scientific or political; and in an opposing camp are those who avidly accept new creative principles. Though he does not like the term, Spangler is a psychic channel in contact with an energy source he calls John or Limitless Love and Truth. He says frankly that he has always been conscious of two aspects of reality—the normal world and the spiritual or mystic dimension. From this other perspective he sees that we have an "essential Identity within us each, which in turn resonates with and is part of an essential Identity within the universe . . . This essence can be focused, and the lesson of individuality is to learn how to skillfully exercise such a focus: how to be a unique, discrete entity. This essence can also be expanded, and this is the lesson of universality, of coming into resonance with the world around us . . . " (p. 49.)

Dorothy Maclean, a co-founder of Findhorn and one of the personalities featured in The Findhorn Garden, relates her day to day communication with the devas, who are " . . . the overlighting intelligence and spirit . . . for each plant species." The devas taught her how to nourish the garden. On May 1, 1972, the message was, "Just tune into nature until you feel the love flow . . . Always it is your state that the nature world responds to, not what you say, not what you do, but what you are." (p. 79.)

In The Secret Life of Plants, Peter Tompkins and Christopher Bird suggest plants have a primal nervous system that reacts to human emotions, other plants and to pain. Their descriptions of experiments with plants and the Maclean material were early indications to me that the biosphere is alive and aware. Perhaps we have looked in the wrong place for a myth relevant to our time; maybe it begins with the philodendron on the windowsill.

Trigger Words

Certain words demanding instant attention are what I call trigger words. From years of interviewing, I find others share my trigger words: Lemuria, Atlantis, Tibet, Ancient Egypt, Kabbalah, chakra, reincarnation, Macchu Picchu, angel, deva, fairy, avatar and also Jung's word, archetype. One afternoon I noticed a story about Atlantis in *The National Enquirer*. Though I have "an inquiring mind and want to know," I usually just ogle the headlines at the supermarket, but this was too alluring. I bought the paper and read that Charles Berlitz was hiring a mini-sub to explore a stepped pyramid, possibly Atlantean, discovered by sonar in the water off Bimini. When I showed the illustration to my first grade students who were in the midst of a month-long study unit on Ancient Egypt, the clipping excited them. One said, "That's in the Bermuda Triangle." Another child called out, "It's a machine that sends out electricity and makes boats and airplanes sink into the water. It's like a magnet." And a third argued, "No, it's beaming power out and it makes airplanes and boats rise up and disappear." We tacked the picture to the bulletin board.

Unknowingly I had initiated a major juncture in my book path. At the end of the month I changed the board and put the clipping in my purse. On the way home, I stopped at a metaphysical bookstore where an oversized book was prominently displayed on a table. It was opened to a watercolor illustration of Atlantis with a stepped pyramid in its center, nearly identical in form to the drawing from the tabloid. *The Secret Teachings of All Ages: An Encyclopedia of Masonic, Hermetic, Qabbalistic and Rosicrucian Philosophy* (1975) by Manly P. Hall, was republished in honor of its fiftieth anniversary. I ordered a copy, and found myself with a lifetime source of esoteric information. Henry L. Drake, in his foreword, wrote, "The science of life is . . . the supreme science, and the art of living, the finest of the arts . . . Human ambition may produce the tyrant; divine aspiration will produce the adept." I added adept to my trigger word list.

Atlantis, Imaginary and Concrete

Atlantis was, in my opinion, a fact that became a myth. According to legend and channeled information, it was the site of an advanced culture whose technology was based on a power derived from or enhanced by crystals. Atlanteans could fly and had submergible craft. The version of the story I subscribe to is that Atlantis was an island continent in the Atlantic Ocean, filling a space as far south as the Caribbean, north to Iceland, east to beyond the Azores, and west to the Bahama Islands.

Taylor Caldwell channeled *The Romance of Atlantis* at the age of twelve. Through the efforts of Jess Stearn it was published decades later in 1975 bearing both their names. The love story is filled with technical details of how life was lived in Atlantis. William Irwin Thompson painted a melancholy view of the technology-ridden Atlantean theocracy in its last days in *Islands Out of Time,* which is termed a "metafiction." Thompson's imaginary staging of the story is so convincing in its description that *Time* magazine described him as "some kind of magus."

Of all the rationales that explain the existence and subsequent destruction of Atlantis, I prefer that of Otto Muck, German author of the deceptively titled *The Secret of Atlantis* (German, *Alles Uber Atlantis*). Despite its title, Muck's book does not engage in secrets. He presents a take-it-or-leave-it geophysical speculation with ample supportive evidence he has put together from nature and from myth. I find it persuasive.

Muck says the Gulf Stream was formed during the cataclysmic destruction of Atlantis, a process that took a long time to complete. Before it was too late, Atlanteans explored the warming rivers of Europe and colonized. Cro-Magnons who appear suddenly in European prehistory were, Muck suggests, Atlanteans who took with them portions of their advanced civilization just as later Europeans brought elements of their civilization to the New World. Other Atlanteans went into the Yucatan peninsula and the Andes; still others reached Egypt as refugees. Wherever they went they retained and passed on the distant memory of Mount Atlas, a stepped volcanic mountain in central Atlantis. The practice of building a stepped structure that rises to a spire in the center, for sacred religious or burial purposes, is found worldwide. Pyramids are a relic of Atlantean culture.

The initial cause of Atlantean destruction, in Muck's theory, was the collision of an asteroid with the earth. A violent tearing of the crust off the Carolina coast of North America was followed by multiple explosions of magma and continued volcanic and earthquake activity at a level unknown in modern times. Muck cites references in world literature to confirm that the amount of material emitted by the volcanic eruptions caused the skies of the northern hemisphere to darken for over 2,000 years. He maps the loess belt, an alluvial deposit of clay, ochre or gray in color, found extensively in Europe and Asia, which he thinks was carried by the Great Flood recorded in the Bible and all major religious traditions. The flood, he says, was caused by the subsidence of Atlantis. He goes so far as to date the cataclysm to precisely June 5, 8498 B.C., a date related to the Mayan calendar. He also makes reference to Genesis and other sacred creation stories. Muck is a physicist, engineer and inventor with over 2,000 patents. His book makes a logical, supportable hypothesis for Atlantis.

Many new prophets accept the reality of Atlantis. Dr. Frank Alper's channeling is primarily devoted to the lessons of this lost civilization. He believes many people alive today were also incarnated in Atlantean times, and their challenge is to help humanity avoid the destructive use of technology which caused the decadence of Atlantean civilization around the time of its disappearance. The Toltec nagual (healer) Miguel Angel Ruiz thinks that inner city children are former Atlanteans who are living sacrificial lives in order to force our society to change. Somehow, the destruction of Atlantis seems relevant to this period. The medium Edgar Cayce predicted that parts of Atlantis would reemerge in the latter part of this century. Occasional reports of organized searches for Atlantean artifacts off the coast of Florida, where some possibly human-crafted architectural elements have been spotted underwater, have been published by the Cayce foundation's Association for Research and Enlightenment in Virginia Beach. The A.R.E. has funded these explorations as well as others in Egypt.

The Kabbalah

Manley P. Hall devotes four chapters of *The Secret Teachings of All Ages* to the Kabbalah (Qabbalah), which is another siren call to me. In a course in Christian iconography, art historian and artist Sister Giotto Moots traced the sources of symbolism in European paintings to the Tarot and the Kabbalah, thereby shedding a more penetrating light on the intention of the artists than the erudite, totally academic analysis offered by my college art history professors. Temperamentally, I have always felt distanced from academicism for many of the same reasons I am alienated from religiosity. In both institutionalized systems, the actual experience of body, mind and spirit is overlooked in favor of arbitrary categories and verbiage. Giotto speculated about the spiritual/psychic/aesthetic linkages in the artists' minds. She offered a mystic corrective to scholasticism, and her classes opened new areas to pursue far beyond her ostensible subject—and she was a major teacher in my life.

Beth Ames Swartz, a visionary artist, read an article on Sister Giotto that I wrote for *American Artist*. She contacted me and a friendship grew between us that led to my writing her biography, *Connecting: The Art of Beth Ames Swartz* for Northland Press. Our mutual interest in the Kabbalah is reflected in my text. We began recommending books to one another. Beth praised Edmund W. Sinnott's *The Biology of the Spirit,* a thesis similar to Chardin's *The Phenomenon of Man* minus the derivation from Christianity. Sinnott explains "spirit" as an outgrowth of biological evolution in a Universalist context. He writes, "[Spirit] . . . is the supreme manifestation of the organizing power in nature." I, in turn, recommended *The Thirteen Petalled Rose* by Adin Steinsaltz. Steinsaltz begins his poetic exposition of the Kabbalah by stating: "The physical world in which we live, the objectively observed universe around us, is only a part of an inconceivably vast system of worlds. Most of these worlds are spiritual in their essence; they are of a different order from our known world. Which does not necessarily mean that they exist somewhere else, but means rather that they exist in different dimensions of being." (p. 3.)

The Kabbalah is a philosophical-psychological-mystical construct, a paradoxically concrete structure applied to that which cannot be known. In my small library on the

Kabbalah is Z'ev ben Shimon Halevi's *Kabbalah: Tradition of Hidden Knowledge.* He writes, "Kabbalah is the inner and mystical aspect of Judaism. It is the perennial Teaching about the Attributes of the Divine, the nature of the universe and the destiny of man, in Judaic terms."

Halevi's brief text, diagrams and color plates are a succinct introduction to the central Kabbalistic symbol, the Tree of Life, which encompasses the macrocosm and microcosm, the Divine and the human, exemplifying the esoteric adage, "As above, so below." Kabbalists affirm the Shekhinah as the Feminine Aspect of God and also as the Presence of God in matter. Like so many women today, I identify with her. Between my daily life and this ancient hermetic system, I find endless relationships that feed my artwork.

Dion Fortune, in *The Mystical Qabbalah*, says "The Christian races owe their religion to the Jewish culture as surely as the Buddhist races of the East owe theirs to the Hindu . . . The mysticism of Israel supplies the foundation of modern Western occultism." (p. 2.) Fortune considers the Kabbalah "the Yoga of the West," and she writes, "The Qabbalah is essentially monotheistic; the potencies it classifies are always regarded as the messengers of God and not His fellow workers. This principle enforces the concept of a centralized government of the Cosmos and of the grip of the Divine Law upon the whole of the manifestation . . . " (p. 12.)

Kabbalists, Fortune tells us, believe the origin of their esoteric tradition came from angels, not of this world. Almost all traditions say that hidden wisdom was originally given to mankind and then carried forward in myths and legends.

Symbolism and the Goddess

The Dictionary of Symbols by J. E. Cirlot is an old war-horse first published in 1962. I bought it for Giotto's class. Fred Gettings' *Dictionary of Occult, Hermetic and Alchemical Sigals*, is a hand-typed, hand-lettered assembly of historic alphabets devoted to encoding hidden knowledge. Dion Fortune refers to these graphic devices as "sacred glyphs" and remarks, "It is well known to mystics that if a man meditates upon a symbol around which certain ideas have been associated by past meditation, he will obtain access to those ideas even if the glyph has never been elucidated to him by those who have received the oral tradition 'by mouth to ear.'" Symbols that are legible to initiates can also resonate at a level below cognition, acting as catalysts to more awareness for lay persons.

The Woman's Encyclopedia of Myths and Secrets and *The Woman's Dictionary of Symbols and Sacred Objects* by Barbara G. Walker are illustrated references to symbols that I have used during the conjuring stage of a new artwork.

A cluster of recent "Goddess" books provides a basis for a revisionist view of history. *The Language of the Goddess* by Marija Gimbutas is basic research. In his foreword, Joseph Campbell compares her work to the Rosetta Stone, saying she has prepared a

" . . . fundamental glossary of pictorial motifs as keys to a mythology of that otherwise undocumented era" from around 7000 to 3500 B.C. in which there was a religion in " . . . veneration, both of the universe as the living body of a Goddess-Mother Creator, and of all the living things within it as partaking of her divinity . . . " (p. xiii.)

Like branches on the Gimbutas tree are other notable books, particularly *The Chalice and the Blade* by Riane Eisler, who extrapolates from the research a picture of a partnership society in the ancient Mediterranean world that was destroyed by an invasion of warriors. Eisler suggests that we are once again at a point of decision. "The lethal power of the Blade . . . threatens to put an end to all human culture . . . " (p. xviii.) I believe Eisler is a modern prophet, pointing the way forward by discovering a treasure we have lost. Elinor W. Gadon, in *The Once and Future Goddess,* reviews the past and searches the present for signs of the Goddess reemerging through art and culture. Well after beginning my work on this book, I was gratified to read in her chapter "Reclaiming Her Sacred Iconography: The Artist as Prophet," this relevant insight: "Artists are prescient, that is, acutely sensitive to changing culture, often expressing in both subject and style underlying currents not yet recognized by the culture at large."

Channelers

Betty White was a medium who channeled visions of beings living invisibly side-by-side with us at a higher vibrational level. They move amid glorious colors and tinkling sounds. She described their meeting on Mt. Shasta, a picture as clear to me as my memory of spending the night within view of that perfect mountain. When Betty died, her husband Stewart Edward White wrote her revelations in *The Betty Book* and *The Unobstructed Universe.* I read them in the late 1960s.

Years later, I came upon this passage in physicist Fred Alan Wolf's *Parallel Universes: The Search for Other Worlds:* "Whole universes . . . overlap . . . as if they were nested together like Chinese boxes one inside of the other. The only difference is that the boxes are all the same size.

"An object in any space exists in all of the spaces at the same time in the same way that an electron in an atom exists at an infinite number of points at the same time but only occupies a single point any time it is observed. Objects in each space pass through the other spaces like ghosts in the night." (*Parallel . . . ,* p. 88-89.) The idea of parallel universes inhabiting our own space, as Wolf suggests they do, makes mediumship and higher dimensions plausible.

Dr. Shafica Karagulla, a neuro-psychiatrist, was well ahead of the New Age in her study of uncommonly able psychics living normally in society. In her book, *Breakthrough to Creativity*, one of the psychics described her nightly visits to an esoteric, noncorporeal school set in the open among classic columns, a word-picture that was startlingly familiar to me. Instructors in this school included famed discarnates whose teaching was both mind-expanding and of practical benefit to the dreamer. Karagulla traced in her subjects' experiences what she called their Higher Sense Perception, and she made the suggestion that we all might have extrasensory talent.

There Is a River by Thomas Sugrue introduced me to the life of trance medium Edgar Cayce, surely the most recognized twentieth-century psychic. Gina Cerminara's *Many Mansions* is an exposition of ideas Cayce channeled. Jess Stearn wrote a highly readable biography, *Edgar Cayce: The Sleeping Prophet.* I collected and read almost every paperback devoted to the thousands of readings he did for people who often were far away and unknown to him. All of his readings were recorded and are the subject of continuing research. Cayce was able to extract information from the akashic records, a cosmic memory bank where all knowledge of human lives is said to be retained. I was taken by the fact that Cayce was an American whose lifetime had extended well into mine. His practical application of unexplained knowledge appealed to me, and still does. For twenty years, I was a member of the Association of Research and Enlightenment, based in Virginia Beach, which is devoted to Cayce's work. A benefit of associate membership is the bimonthly journal *Venture Inward.*

Cayce insisted upon the linkage of mind, body, spirit. "Mind is the builder" is the core of what he said. What we think affects not only us but *All There Is.* Thinking is creative. It is the source of our health or disease. The cures he suggested come from natural products. Since reading Cayce, castor oil became a part of my medicine chest. When used as an external ointment, castor oil fades bruises, dries up warts and soothes aches. Castor oil packs reduce inflammation and stimulate healing. Since his remedies work, I thought maybe his prophecies were valid. Cayce made prophecy almost folksy.

Fred Alan Wolf, in developing his thesis of parallel universes, addresses the notion that the future sends us messages, just as the present sends messages to the past. "Events that have passed must still be around. Events that will be must exist like boulders behind blind corners of the roads of life. And if both the future and the past exist now, then quantum physics implies that devices must exist that enable us to tune in on the future and resonate with the past. These devices may be our own brains." (*Parallel Universes: The Search for Other Worlds,* p. 222.)

Messages from the future, Wolf says, come in quantum waves. If these waves match those we are sending forward, a strong probability is generated. "It is quite possible that visionaries are those who successfully marry streams coming from far time-distant sources," he writes. (*Parallel . . . ,* p. 223.)

With the exception of Edgar Cayce, one of the most widely read channelers is Jane Roberts, who channeled *The Seth Material.* Roberts' husband, artist Robert Butts, recorded Jane's channeling sessions and helped compile the Seth books. Reduced to its essence, Seth's central theme is that we cocreate the universe. Prior to each birth, we choose our family and all our challenges for the life ahead. Roberts left a legacy of creative writing as well, including *The Education of Oversoul Seven,* a warm, funny narrative illustrating Seth's description of "aspects" of an Oversoul. Seth/Roberts' portrait of universal reality is one in which each of us is linked through an Oversoul to many other aspects of one Self, living other lives, in other eras, that may impinge psychically upon ours. She stressed that everyone has psychic ability. Our dreams give us information about other aspects of our source Self. Even our imagined lives are possible aspects of Being. Some of Roberts' trance work was published posthumously by Robert Butts.

I corresponded briefly with Roberts and Butts, and was moved when they sent me an inscribed, hot-off-the-press copy of *The World View of Paul Cezanne: A Psychic Interpretation,* one of the most insightful art books I have read, written by Roberts during conscious trance as a gift for Robert Butts.

Seth's work was enormously popular and many of her readers were so affected by it they opened to their own esoteric experiences. Her exceptional sensibilities were possibly enhanced by living near the Finger Lakes in Elmira, New York. Through her channeled knowledge, she cited certain places on earth as magnetic vortexes where energy/information from a higher vibrational dimension more easily penetrates the denser level in which we live. The Finger Lake region is on her list, and so is the Southwestern part of the United States. Since that is where I live, I'm inclined to believe her theory. People claim that this area attracts and sustains a mystical turn of mind.

Paperbacks written by mediums were easily available in the supermarkets during the 1970s. The first book I read by Ruth Montgomery on an esoteric subject was *A Gift of Prophecy*, the story of Jeanne Dixon. Montgomery, who describes herself as a former skeptic, sat down at her typewriter one day and found herself typing a book dictated by the medium Arthur Ford after his death. Ford described his post-death experience, making it sound amazingly lively as a state in which a person continues learning. Montgomery was the medium for a number of guides who provided the idea for what she calls "walk-ins." In this theory, if people have a strong desire to end their lives, discarnates can "walk in" to their bodies in order to carry out a special mission. The original soul is free to leave. A walk-in may appear to be enlightened beyond the capability of the first inhabitant of the body.

For several years before his death, I was a friend of David Paladin, whom Montgomery described as a walk-in. He neither agreed nor disagreed with her theory, he simply stated her right to hold it. His porous, allowing attitude toward other people's ideas is a trait that I admire.

In Paladin's legend, he had almost no advantages in childhood and very little formal education. He suffered severely in Germany as a prisoner of war during World War II. After American soldiers found him unconscious in a pile of bodies, he was sent to a hospital in the United States and remained in coma for thirty months. When he awakened he spoke

Russian, knew musical theory and began painting in an abstract style like that of Kandinsky. Paladin had an excellent vocabulary and was knowledgeable on many subjects. He was a creative, original artist and a recognized shaman with many followers who took his workshops and sought his counsel. His story is only one of the many Montgomery told in her widely read books.

Historically, the fact that one can buy eggs and a book about the afterlife in the supermarket might be looked upon in the future as a pivotal moment. The invention of the Gutenberg press is considered a major factor in the Protestant movement because it made the Bible available to anyone. Surely, the wide distribution of affordable paperbacks that describe in detail an opening from this reality to another is also a turning point because of its effect on readers' imaginations.

In *Aliens Among Us*, Montgomery says nonearthborn beings are incarnating to assist us as we awaken to a greater reality. That book preceded the plethora of contact stories such as *Communion* by Whitley Strieber. Steven Spielberg's *Close Encounters of the Third Kind* and *E.T.* and George Lucas' *Star Wars* series contribute to an enormous sweep of mythmaking, miracle-based imagery that is changing our sense of the possible.

What is the effect in the minds of our young children who have seen these films? As a child, I was enthralled by the serial *Buck Rogers*. As an adult I watched Americans walking on the moon. To me, those two facts are connected. The future is being shaped in the imaginations of children throughout the world by popular books and films as much as it is in laboratories. In fact, the impressionable mind of ordinary people is the only laboratory that counts in human evolution. The poetic possibilities projected by Roberts and Montgomery affect reality by way of our imagination.

I was teased for years for my shelf of UFO books. I still read journals and attend lectures about the phenomena. Contemporary prophets tell us "others" have always visited the earth, but contact with them depends upon an individual's perception. We are not surprised by singers with an extraordinary range in their voice. Perhaps those who see the UFOs and their occupants are perceiving at a higher level of vibration than normal.

Jon Klimo, in *Channeling: Investigations on Receiving Information from Paranormal Sources*, and authors Sanaya Roman and Duane Packer, in their *Opening to Channel: How to Connect with Your Guide*, teach their readers how to channel. They compare the process to learning to meditate, becoming an artist or developing skill in a sport. Channeling is a latent ability that we can all practice and improve. Prophets, however, are prodigies, born with an exceptional ability to perceive the ineffable. Their gift demands that they practice to gain control over their perceptions and to focus their intention.

The Lusson Twins

I met two psychic prodigies as a result of severe back pain in 1980. I took my problem to Dr. Lyman Atchley, a healing chiropractor, and a few days later he hosted an evening talk at his clinic. Dorothee (Dottee) L. Mella introduced her visiting twin sister, Reverend Michelle Lusson, who gave her view of the future. The women are fraternal twins who look very much alike—blonde, brown-eyed and stylish. They are in frequent contact.

Through Domel Color Consultants in Albuquerque, Dottee advises clients on the effects of color in schoolrooms, prisons, bank exteriors and even on what color tie to wear when running for office. An artist and former painting instructor in Washington, D.C., Dottee observed and intuited health-related influences of colors which she tested on her students. She then formulated the Self-Image Color Analysis (SICA), a test based on an individual's response to color questions. I took the test in 1981. After her analysis, she told me to wear red as a protective color whenever a situation was nervewracking or confrontational. She also said to stop wearing so much lavender and purple in order to shield myself from other people's problems and moods. SICA is now available for self-administering in Dottee's book *The Language of Color*. My interest in the color energy of semiprecious and gem stones was enlarged by working with Dottee and from her book *Stone Power II*.

While preparing for this book I interviewed Dottee's twin, Michelle Lusson, at her headquarters in Reston, Virginia. She runs it like a doctor's office. For the past two decades she has maintained the records of her clients, now totalling more than 18,000. Through her intuitive observations of people who came to her for help with stress management, she devised the holistic health plan that she presents in her book *Creative Wellness*. She has tested and refined Creative Wellness in clinical settings. In the late 1970s, she identified fourteen personality types with a god or goddess persona. Michelle's thesis is that we can reach optimum weight and good health by following a program keyed to our nature. Her descriptions of the characteristics of these fourteen basic natures are so clear it is easy to identify oneself among them and find the appropriate sections on stress, exercise, nutrition, color and gem stones.

In light trance Michelle gave me a past lives reading, not when we were together, but in the presence of her secretary who recorded the information in shorthand as she spoke. I received a tape and Michelle stored the hard copy. The overview of my soul path that she received by channeling The Nine, her source, is as practical as Dottee's SICA. Her seamless account of my life upon life feels entirely plausible and relates to my present life, about which she was not informed ahead of time, or since.

Michelle wrote about channeling in a pamphlet, "What Is Wholism?" that she published in 1982. "In the current pursuit of scientific advancement, those searching for knowledge enter all fields of endeavor, including those areas outside the boundaries of human consciousness. It is into these uncharted depths, these outward boundaries, that a channel attempts to go in order to locate and interpret patterns of a multidimensional nature that can shed light on the material reality of human consciousness."

The twins, whose maiden name is Lusson (French for light) were raised in Florida, and were descended from a noble French family in which the psychic gift appeared in earlier generations. Each of them has faced traumas and had visions. They have a clear understanding that they are meant to help others reach higher awareness. In keeping with my thesis of a relationship between artist and prophet, the Lusson twins combine creativity with a gift for prophecy. They are both working on further books of their own.

Following the Ley Lines

Gifted psychics vary in their expertise. Dowsers apparently feel the presence of water. Subtle emanations have been sensed by certain people for eons. Geomancy is the esoteric art of detecting and plotting the subtle energies of the earth in a planetary grid comparable to a human nervous system.

F. W. Holiday, in his book titled in England *The Dragon and the Disc* (peddled in the United States as *Creatures From the Inner Sphere*), tells of Alfred Watkins, a retired Hereford merchant, who amassed dozens of maps of England and found a network of alignments between menhirs, churches and Bronze Age monuments whose placement suggested a route. Watkins gave the word "ley lines" to these pathways. Holiday quotes Watkins' preface to his book, *The Old Straight Track:* "What really matters is whether it is a humanly designed fact, an accidental coincidence or a 'mare's nest,' that mounds, moats, beacons and mark stones fall into straight lines throughout Britain, with fragmentary evidence of trackways on the alignments." (Interestingly, crop formations found recently in England and other countries follow ley lines.) Holiday traces his interest in Bronze Age linemakers to the findings of Alexander Thom who said the people of that age were astronomers. Holiday then refers to the discovery by Aime Michel (*The Truth About Flying Saucers*) that sightings of UFOs in France also follow straight lines. Holiday believes ley lines form triangular figures related to an ancient "disc" culture whose artifacts frequently depict dragons. Peter Devereux, a modern researcher, has founded the Dragon Project to measure geomantic energies along ley lines, from ancient stones and even from crop circles. Holiday does not claim to know why ley lines were connected with the dragon throughout England, but his book, along with many others, implants the idea that the ancients were sensitive to forces on earth that we, with our instruments, are just beginning to measure. To find out if a book has any value, I always check the bibliography and the index. Holiday lists credible sources.

In 1992, I had a lesson in how to dowse for ley lines in Wiltshire from English medium Isabelle Kingston, who led us on a tour of Avebury and nearby crop formations. Walking the old straight track vivified what had been just a theoretical exercise. Kingston is also a prophet and channeler. A chapter about her predictions is included in *Crop Circles-Harbingers of World Change*.

Popular Revelation

Shirley MacLaine, by reporting the paranormal events in her life straightforwardly in *Out On a Limb* and other books, has stimulated many people to speculate about the nature of reality. Her New Age approach to life promotes the notion that anyone can dance in the light. I think life is tougher, darker and harder than that. Yet, I respect her courage in sharing her story and making herself vulnerable to cynical ridicule.

Erich Von Däniken's *Chariots of the Gods!* hit the racks in 1970 and sold millions of copies worldwide in several languages. Von Däniken made bold, often unsubstantiated, links between seemingly unrelated facts; but in doing so he created interest in relatively unknown mysteries. He brought the figures drawn on the Plain of Nazca in Peru to world attention, citing them as "evidence" of a former time when aerial flight was commonplace, which jibes with Atlantean legends. He proposed that aliens have visited the planet before and perhaps came to seed the human race, a viewpoint espoused on television by one of the Apollo astronauts. Seeding the earth by civilizations elsewhere in the universe is given detailed coverage in *The Only Planet of Choice*, by Phyllis V. Schlemmer and Palden Jenkins.

A television documentary of sites Von Däniken mentioned created a lasting impression in people's memory, so his thinking has effected our collective imagination. His effect was global because his books were printed in many languages, and his documentary was shown internationally.

To live today and not know of these ideas that are percolating in the minds of people all around us is, I think, to miss something vital. If you want to test the winds of change you do not go to academic sources rooted in the acceptable, proven safety of the past. You go to the free places where minds roam unhampered.

East Meets West

I have been aware of the Hindu-Buddhist chakra system for so long I no longer remember learning the sequence of the seven colors and energy vortexes most often cited: red at the base of the spine, orange at the genitals, yellow at the solar plexus, green at the heart, pale blue at the throat, deep indigo at the forehead and lavender to white at the crown. This information has become a fixture in my mind. I use the chakras in a form of mental self-healing that I learned from Reverend Georgina Regan, a British "Spiritual Colour Healer" who travels the world teaching healing workshops based on the chakras.

Such concentrated experiences, as well as academic study of Oriental art, made me minimally conversant with some Eastern philosophies. Upon that background I read *The Tao of Physics* by Fritjof Capra, in which he created a mirror image of science and metaphysics. Capra gave me access to physics through his imaginative approach, despite my lack of education in higher mathematics. In *The Turning Point*, he describes a worldwide change toward a more holistic paradigm.

Capra, in his lectures, uses the term Ecological Paradigm to describe the holistic model of the universe that is transforming all major segments of our culture. I traveled to San Diego in 1986 expressly to hear him speak about "Bootstrap Physics," the edge theories of Geoffrey Chew and his colleagues at Berkeley. Chew's team was ready, Capra said, to suggest a very basic possibility, carefully hedged in speculative language, that the direction an electron takes when hit by an incoming photon might be intentional—hinting that a Cosmic Mind guides the evolution of matter.

Capra's work led me to read what other modern physicists are thinking. Fred Alan Wolf, in *Star Wave: Mind, Consciousness and Quantum Physics,* speculates that the basic form of energy in the cosmos is akin to thought. Wolf has become lionized in the "new frontiers of consciousness movement" based in California. Rudy Rucker's thesis in *The Fourth Dimension: Toward a Geometry of Higher Reality* is that thought is the fourth dimension. In *Einstein's Space and Van Gogh's Sky: Physical Reality and Beyond,* psychologist Lawrence LeShan and physicist Henry Margenau define parallels between their two fields. An earlier book by LeShan, *The Medium, the Mystic, and the Physicist,* is also about correspondences between disciplines. In *Alternate Realities,* LeShan put forth ideas about stretching one's focus and choosing "realities" from a fluid field of possibilities.

The Gaia theory, named for the Earth Goddess and conceived by J. E. Lovelock, has been popularized as a model of the Earth as a single living system, although the author himself disavows such a definite interpretation. Lovelock proposes that evolution of life on this planet follows a definite direction, rather than random selection. Recent tests of this theory upon bacteria imply the possibility that mutation is a deliberately chosen option. (*Science*, September l6, 1988, p. 1431.)

A fusion of philosophical and scientific thought is strengthening the sense of wonder and awe we used to associate with religion. In *God and the New Physics,* Paul Davies writes, "It would be foolish to deny that many of the traditional religious ideas about God, man and the nature of the universe have been swept away by the new physics. But our search has turned up many positive signs too. The existence of mind, for example, as an abstract, holistic, organizational pattern, capable even of disembodiments, refutes the reductionist philosophy that we are all nothing but moving mounds of atoms . . . It is my deep conviction that only by understanding the world in forces, fields and particles as well as through good and evil—that we will come to understand ourselves and the meaning behind this universe, our home." (p. 229.)

Einstein affected my understanding of art. I speculate that the turbulent innovations in twentieth-century art have been synchronistic responses to the ideas making their way into the noosphere, ideas that affect both artists and scientists. Had Einstein or some other physicist not proposed the theory of relativity, would artists have begun fragmenting reality in their artwork? Would they have made works in which seemingly random elements are related? In my view, these developments were inevitable because, early in the century, artists and scientists were acting separately upon similar inspirations. A dynamic idea percolating in the noosphere affects all of us, whether we are scientifically trained or not. Today Einstein's discoveries have long since reached the level of popularly held, even if not entirely understood, ideas. I believe in these late years of the century a process of synchronistic understanding can still be found among artists and scientists.

Leonard Shlain, M.D., in *Art and Physics: Parallel Visions in Space, Time and Light*, has developed this thesis in a most welcome and inspired manner. From a moment of epiphany when he sensed a " . . . connection between the inscrutability of modern art and the impenetrability of the new physics," Shlain, a surgeon, set himself the task of studying art and physics in history. As a true amateur, one whose scholarship comes from a love of the subject, Shlain is a superb writer. He begins with the observation that physics and art are both involved with nature. Each is at the forefront in developing our worldview. "In the case of the visual arts, in addition to illuminating, imitating and interpreting reality, a few artists create a language of symbols for things for which there are yet to be words." (p. 17.)

Regarding our century, Shlain lists the principles in Einstein's special theory of relativity which we have had to integrate into our worldview: space and time are relative, not constant, absolute and separate. Together they form the spacetime continuum, the next higher dimension. There is no such thing as a favored point of view. A universal present moment does not exist. Observations about reality are observer-dependent, implying subjectivity.

"As radical as all of these principles were," Shlain writes, "artists anticipated each and every one without any knowledge of this theory of science. With sibylline accuracy, revolutionary artists incorporated all these new perceptions of reality into the picture plane of their art . . . It was these very innovations that brought down upon their heads the scorn and ridicule of the public and critics alike, who could not know that they had been privileged to be the first to glimpse the shape of the future." (*Art* . . . , p. 137.)

We are again at an edge in history when our worldview is becoming even more rooted within the subjective experience, a product of our minds. In Shlain's view, the coming change will emerge from our absorption of spacetime consciousness as a holistic awareness. Again, he believes artists will be harbingers. "It most likely issues forth from the right hemisphere, since the artists and mystics, expressing themselves in images and poetry, are more attuned to this type of consciousness." (*Art* . . . , p. 427.)

New Paradigm

Fritjof Capra and Marilyn Ferguson both speak of the "new paradigm" and the "paradigm shift" credited to Thomas Kuhn's book, *The Structure of Scientific Revolutions*. Kuhn wrote that scientific revolutions involve a change in the basic assumptions by which science models the universe. Ferguson is a pulse-taker of society. Her book *The Aquarian Conspiracy* is a multifocused observation of perceivable changes sweeping through our civilization, moving us toward a synthesis of disciplines and a holistic worldview. Ferguson calls upon the reader to act in concert with the transformation to planetary awareness and to grasp the idea that actions taken anywhere affect the whole planet. Our century has been subjected to repeated scientific revolutions. Each one has dislocated the prior theory and caused a change or reevaluation of what is considered fact. Likewise, our century has seen successive art revolutions, each one an outgrowth of what preceded it.

I am interested in the trickle-down effect of scientific revolutions as they enter our daily language and our imagination. Philosophical speculations evolve along with our changing picture of the structure of the universe. In the new paradigm, the universe is closer to a hologram than to a machine. The part reflects the whole; the whole is in the part. The general population has become aware that there is no such thing as an objective observer. We affect the universe just as it affects us.

If the cosmos is a mind and everything in it is connected, what happens to our consciousness when we die? Where would one experience an afterlife? For answers, we are turning in many directions at once: to science, to the hidden wisdom of the past and to human experience.

The Veil of Death Is Lifting

Knowledge of death, life after death, out of body experiences (OBE) and near-death experiences (NDE) are coming into the public mind through the brave efforts of a few courageous people who defy our cultural taboo against the discussion of death. A picture of the death experience is emerging, with consistent components. Those who have just died encounter loved ones who are in spirit form. There is an awareness of a compellingly bright light, a feeling of motion upward through a tunnel toward a Divine being, accompanied by a life review. The mysterious nature of this final passage is being revealed by those who have partially gone through it and returned to describe it or witnessed the return of others and recorded it. They tell of an adjacent dimension beyond visible reality.

Raymond A. Moody, Jr. describes his out of body adventure in *Life After Life*. Elisabeth Kubler-Ross's *On Death and Dying* is a loving, hopeful work in the near-death field, by a pioneer who has sat at the bedsides of terminally ill children. Robert A. Monroe, founder of the Monroe Institute in Virginia, describes his own experiments in *Journeys Out of the Body*. These books offer Westerners solace and a stimulus to the imagination about the most awesome adventure any of us will ever have—death itself. Hermann Hesse, in *Narcissus and Goldmund,* stresses that the fruits of creativity, be they art or scientific theory, survive death.

Lewis Hyde, in *The Gift: Imagination and the Erotic Life of Property,* addresses the embodied gift residing in the artist's work of art. "It is when someone's gifts stir us that we are brought close, and what moves us, beyond the gift itself, is the promise (or the fact) of transformation, friendship, and love." (p. 68.) Hyde stresses the responsibility of the gift. The gift received (such as an innate talent) is to be passed on. It is not a possession, but it implies a duty. I have observed the effect within an artist of this inchoate belief. The ego is bypassed, despite its insistence, and the artist arrives at an altruistic state of mind. Fame, fortune and critical acceptance are no longer the determining goals of such an artist whose inspiration is to make art as a gift returned. "The artist's gift refines the materials of perception or intuition that have been bestowed upon him; to put it another way, if the artist is gifted, the gift increases in its passage through the self." (p. 191.)

Exploring the New Frontier

In the periodical *Brain/Mind and Common Sense* (*Brain/Mind Bulletin, New Sense Bulletin*), editor Marilyn Ferguson digests relevant scientific research and keeps her readers abreast of discoveries and new books. At the edge of science today, studies of the brain/mind indicate a limitless range of potential. Among its abilities is the self-healing of the body.

Ex-astronaut Edgar Mitchell founded the Institute of Noetic Sciences (IONS) to explore the frontier of consciousness. IONS espouses the idea that the paranormal will be rendered normal when it is explained. The organization sponsors deliberate study of those who are gifted with extraordinary qualities of mind. The effort is to pinpoint the valuable components of human consciousness on the supposition that they might be learned or developed by many more people. Altruism, spontaneous remission, exceptional creativity and channeling are among the mental capabilities under study.

Current president of IONS is Willis Harman, a man with a notable gift for clarity of language in essays about difficult concepts. He contributes to the *Noetic Science Review* and *Bulletin.* In *Higher Creativity,* Harman and Howard Rheingold dissect the process of advanced creative thought (inventions, discoveries, art) in terms of the computer. Input is necessary, but then one has to go "off line" and allow one's mental computer to do its work. Eventually, the mind connects various elements and comes up, seemingly all at once, with a creative idea. *Global Mind Change* is Harman's clear presentation of three metaphysical paradigms which have dominated science and philosophy, in their historical order: M-1, Materialistic Monism (Matter giving rise to mind); M-2, Dualism (Matter plus mind); M-3, transcendental Monism (Mind giving rise to matter). He says we are moving into M-3, the holistic paradigm in which the source of matter (reality) is mind.

Mind giving rise to matter is another way of saying that we are cocreators of the universe. Deepak Chopra, M.D., writing in *Unconditional Life: Mastering the Forces That*

Shape Personal Reality, makes reference to this point, "If we are all cocreators of reality, then our goal in life is not just to be bright, alert, or imaginative, but to shape existence itself." (p. 23.)

I propose that new prophets have already adopted M-3. Through experience, they have become holistic thinkers. In their stories, they have faced their fears and released their creative power to shape their own reality. If we are to follow our own paths with similar dedication, a first requirement is to shore up our independence of mind.

Until I had matured enough to become objective about my own background, I did not know how brainwashed I was by my religious heritage and my academic education, not to mention the limitations of being a white, middle-class person. It is a lifelong task to get past those structures of mind we have been given. I would like to share one of the tools I use to gain control over my own thought process, which is this meditation suggested by Dottee Mella:

"In the name of Light, I release all blocks in my conditioning that prevent me from being self-allowing, self-accepting and self-aware."

*I*n addition to a journey through books, art is my other way of knowing. Although I was not aware of it at first, I was searching in books and in art for a metaphysical resonance.

My field of undergraduate study was art history, which promoted looking at art and making up words to describe it. Since 1950 I have observed, written about and made art.

In 1961 my husband Ed, an army officer with a specialty in physics, was on orders to leave Livermore, California, and transfer to Sandia Base (now Kirtland Air Force Base) in Albuquerque, New Mexico. Thinking—erroneously—I was heading for a cultural wasteland, I made a ceremonious final trip with my children to the San Francisco Museum of Modern Art. Prophetically, as it turned out, I saw a black and white painting of a large boulder torn from a piece of paper and thoroughly integrated with the rest of the canvas. It had a powerful, tangible presence; but there was something else about this work that haunted me with the same sense of mystery as Stonehenge. The artist had expressed a connection between himself and the rock. He had invested his painting with meaning. The painting imbedded itself in my mind; and years later when I learned the artist's name was Alexander Nepote, it was like finding a treasure.

ALEXANDER NEPOTE

NEPOTE joined a growing list of my favorite artists, each of whom produces work that has a hidden dimension. All of them suggest a concern with universality, an awareness of ultimate connectedness and a reference to the spirit. At some point in the early 1970s, I began to review these artists and the impact they have made upon my growth as an artist and art appreciator.

Rainy Sunset by J. Francis Murphy, a National Academician working early in the twentieth century, hung in my family's home. In contrast to lighter landscapes in the house, this murky scene was mysteriously compelling. Nature as a brooding force, full of potential menace, is the message of this work. It is now on my own wall as a legacy from my mother's father, its original owner.

It was my privilege to take a Saturday morning watercolor class given by Dong Kingman at Columbia University. A man of bubbling good humor and infinite talent, Kingman added an extra ingredient of magic to his cityscapes. Everywhere you looked in his paintings were ghostly beings, often out of scale, like obscure evidence of another reality. He painted a demonstration of a tree on my watercolor pad and signed it for me as a wedding present. Lurking in the grass under this tree is his trademark cat staring up at a bird. I've always treasured this sample of Kingman's heavenly joy.

An artist I came to revere for a single painting is Pavel Tchelitchew. Class assignments required many visits to study work at the Museum of Modern Art where I usually sat a while staring at Tchelitchew's painting, *Hide and Seek*. It pictures a hand which is also a tree that reflects the four seasons: it's a pentagram, and a hiding place for embryos, toddlers and baby feet and hands, created in layers of oil as sheer as a whisper. I'm still mesmerized by the painting and its implication that all is one—human life, vegetable life, time and geometry.

While living in Massachusetts, I heard for the first time of the American watercolor master Charles Burchfield when a teacher said my paintings of the old houses in the area reminded her of his. That casual mention of his name became my compulsion to know more about Burchfield, and I collected a library of books devoted to his work. He is called America's great pantheist. For him, everything in nature, including the man-made, is alive. He invented a calligraphic equivalent for insect songs, wires humming, wind blowing and dark storms glowering. He treated old houses in Ohio and Buffalo, New York, as personalities who appear to have animated eyes and facial expressions. His paintings are layered with meaning and are sometimes densely painted and repainted. Time and space fuse in his work. It is too late for him to know one of the amazing facts of my life, given the preoccupation I have had with this artist: our grandchildren are Charles Burchfield's great-grandchildren.

A few years ago I discovered Louise Nevelson's complex, harmonious sculptures in museums and books. Created from boxes, crates, pieces of wood, newel posts, moldings and scraps, Nevelson's work is a grand symphony of light and shadow. Quotes of her trenchant remarks reveal that she was enlightened with a regard for the wholeness of the cosmos and very aware that her work connected her to this greater reality.

Gradually, I realized that I was engaged in an active search for a numinous quality of otherness in art, regardless of style or period. I began to insert probing questions in my interviews with certain artists to find the source of his or her philosophy. Over the space of a few years, I met several artists whose holistic philosophy and spiritual awareness are based in science and nature as well as metaphysics. They view separate objects and events as if, at some level, they are related. The art they make is quite different from one artist to the other, yet they quote the same authors, make similar statements in interviews and often express nearly identical thoughts.

Layering as Metaphor

Around 1975, my openly acknowledged way as artist and writer about art came together with the private journey of metaphysics. What had been hidden became more obvious, even to me, in my conversation, writing, artmaking and art-related activity. I became aware that other artists were creating images of holistic perceptions I had been developing in myself and my work.

One by one I discovered artists who make multireferential art by means of layers which they use metaphorically to project a feeling of oneness. Although their art is diverse in style and medium, there are some commonalties in their techniques. Overlapping transparencies, scratching through the surface to reveal what lies beneath and mixing materials and objects freely in seemingly incongruent juxtapositions are among their means for expressing a holistic worldview in which everything is connected with everything else. During my interviews I learned that these artists rely upon similar sources of knowledge for inspiration, such as contemporary physics, transpersonal psychology, world religions, metaphysics and a range of other scientific disciplines, particularly archaeology.

Internally for several years and then publicly, I referred to this special group of artists as layerists and their art as layering. It struck me that they share a perspective entirely in keeping with twentieth-century theories of relativity, holograms and ecological or global consciousness. Just as linear perspective perfectly coincided with the great age of exploration, the holistic perspective is synchronized with the image of our beautiful blue, white and green Earth floating in black space. This one image has changed our perspective so profoundly that our relationship with the earth is transforming. In our deepest awareness, we realize there are no borders on the planet except the ones we have invented. We all inhabit a single, isolated "spaceship" circling in a universe we are determined to explore.

Our initial probes of outer space are occurring at the same time that we are discovering more about the inner space of atoms, cells and consciousness.

Brian O'Leary, former professor of astronomy and physics, once a colleague of Carl Sagan, an ex-Apollo astronaut, now a futurist and a founder of the International Association for New Science, has made a moving personal statement about his encounters with unexplained psychic events and their effects on his life in *Exploring Inner and Outer Space*. His reaction, after years of suffering from a split between his knowledge and his experience, was to attempt to expand the modern boundaries of science. He writes, "In the new physics, mind meets matter, East meets West, yin meets yang, psychology meets physics, and mathematics meets mysticism." (p. 42.) O'Leary, who is also a composer, gives voice to a multireferential worldview.

To express inner and outer explorations, artists as well as scientists have invented a holistic perspective. I define the perspective in layered art as one that connects many moments of time at a single point in space and joins many points in space at a single moment of time.

Layering is not a style. It is a way of thinking about art. The metaphorical aspects of the work, the artists' intention to convey meaning, are apparent in layered art despite the variation in style and materials. Also perceivable are the essentially spiritual references to eschatology, the sacred and the profane, life, death and rebirth.

In 1982 I founded the Society of Layerists in Multi Media (SLMM). At first we had less than ten members, but now I am in contact with nearly two hundred questing artists who express a holistic viewpoint. Of course, most artists who create layered art are not members of this network. SLMM is but a modest indicator of a major change in consciousness among artists which, in turn, reflects the transformation sweeping the collective human mind.

I began using the word *layering* in my feature articles about certain artists, tentatively at first, but then more assertively. The word gained more currency in 1985, when the show I curated for Albuquerque Museum, "Layering: An Art of Time and Space," was exhibited with the work of thirty-one artists. Half of them joined SLMM.

The description of layering was not just an intellectual interest for me; it grew viscerally from my own artmaking. In the early years of work on the layering project, my life was markedly changed by the death of my father, the birth of our first grandchild and the increasing responsibility for my grieving mother. These encounters with birth, death and my mother's despair had a tremendous effect on my art, which had already moved steadily away from watercolor into more complex mixed media.

By 1985 my art involved symbols related to death, inner wisdom, transitions and transformations. I was engrossed by spirits, spirals, chakras and the double helix of DNA. Over the next half-decade, I made shrines or images of the sacred, usually related to the feminine. I stopped painting on paper and worked mainly on sheet acrylic, constructed into boxes or dimensional wall pieces.

I respond spontaneously to works of art that feed my soul and mind, illuminate a path, and lead me to others whose vision amplifies my own. Making art and writing are my alternate creative expressions. Both reflect my commitment to a holistic worldview, and both derive from the same insight that led me to notice the connection between the artists and seers I think of as *artists of the spirit*.

Alexander Nepote, The Mystery of Continuous Change

First among layerists and *artists of the spirit* is the late Alexander Nepote. Twenty years after seeing his collaged painting of the rock, I finally met him at Suzanne Brown's Gallery in Scottsdale, Arizona, on the night of his opening in March 1981. He recognized my name from my writing. When I asked if he would be interested in a proposed project dealing with the idea of "layering," his eyes twinkled in delight and he seemed to understand what I meant without explanation. For the next few years, he was a staunch supporter and enthusiastic researcher who suggested articles to read, people to contact and artists he considered to be layerists. He was serving as president of SLMM when he died.

Our friendship grew by correspondence and interviews. He sent this statement from one of his show invitations: "It is not my intention to describe a parcel of landscape which may interest me, but to suggest the inner spirit which is felt and experienced at a particular place."

Nepote was born in Stockton, California, in 1913. His father, who came from Italy, was a farmer and a woodcarver. One of his aunts was a fine embroiderer. Nepote's art folio earned him a scholarship to the California College of Arts and Crafts in Oakland where he received his art diploma and a degree in art education.

Even as a student Alex taught classes, and his early watercolors established his reputation before he finished school. He earned a master's degree in art at Mills College in Oakland, paid for with a monetary James D. Phelan Award. After five years as a full-time teacher and administrator at his alma mater, CCAC, he joined the faculty of San Francisco State University and remained there for 27 years until he retired in 1977. Hanne-Lore Nepote, an artist and former pupil, and Alex were married in 1945. They had a daughter and a son.

In 1963, when a heart attack forced him to find a less arduous mode of painting than the seven-foot, heavily pigmented abstract expressionist landscapes he was known for, Nepote worked on the method that became his mature style: a meditative, slow build-up of collaged papers, glued, torn, sanded, and repainted in a radiant combination of acrylics, watercolors and pastels. The theme that preoccupied him was the cliff.

Perhaps this first brush with mortality encouraged Alex's natural tendency toward philosophy. Concurrent with his changing art, he pondered the basic question, "Who am I?" By the time we met, he had reached firm conclusions about the cosmos and the place of man, the place of art and the essential patterns of life. In retirement, he devoted himself to unifying his painting with its philosophical base. As an articulate man and a seeker with a habitually meditative cast of mind, he was exceptionally able to voice his worldview and relate it to art.

Talking with Alex was a joy for me, on the order of receiving food after years of starvation. He told me:

"After I became seriously interested in art, I asked myself and others, what is art? What makes a painting great? What does the artist try to express? And, deeper questions, such as, Why are we here on earth? What is the goal of the universe and All That IS?

"It is my personal belief that everything that forms the universe exists as a unity. All That IS is the ultimate wholeness. I use the term ISness which is somewhat related to Suchness, used by Eastern mystics. I believe ISness includes the transcendental and consciousness. If you believe in God, ISness includes God.

"You get in touch with ISness through meditation. When I am meditating, I can see/feel/imagine/be a part of x billion microscopic dots (which represent the particle/wave or consciousness) darting in and out of one another in constant activity and change. I feel that I no longer exist, yet I feel wholeness.

"Science tells us solid matter is not solid at all. Everything is scattered and space-filled. Empty space between parts at the atomic and subatomic levels is like the space between the planets and the stars. What is this empty area? I wonder if this unknown space, which is where the cosmic dance of constantly changing subatomic particles occurs, might not be where strange phenomena of the mind, consciousness, intelligence, extrasensory perception and the transcendent take place. Maybe this is where heaven is, in the emptiness, in the vastness. Humans too are almost empty. There is so much truth to the idea that spirit is within; it fills all the emptiness and joins with the soul of the universe.

"ISness includes the cosmic love Teilhard de Chardin proposed, in truth, wisdom, order and power. I'm trying to establish that truth and wisdom are not separate, but part of God or the Creative Force of the universe. People try to place truth and wisdom outside of ourselves, but I think we find all that we need inside. In my seminars I teach people to become alert, to become aware. Connecting with the Creative Force is done with prayer. I think art is love, order, truth, wisdom and power. The artist does not create art. Art already exists in human form as beauty, and in the environment, perhaps as a beautiful plant. It also exists in the beauty of erosion, in fallen leaves. Even in diseased elements of the human body, seen up close in magnified photographs of viruses, there is beauty of design. By being receptive, you grasp what art is, and then you put that in your own work."

"Do you think you channel art?" I asked.

"Yes," he said.

I was especially interested in Alex's ideas about connectedness and I asked him to explain his comment that everything exists as a unity, yet it is all connected. He told me, "Connecting brings me to another big word in my teaching—that is relationship. I've found George Leonard's book *The Silent Pulse* has helped me define my views about relationships in the universe. I accept his word identity. A large identity, say a panorama or an individual, has billions of smaller identities within it. All the identities form a whole. Between identities there is a reciprocal exchange of power in established relationships. We can feel this power. In Leonard's terminology, it is vibration. The universe, then, has these two characteristics: first, it is a whole, and second, it consists of identities connected by relationships."

How, I asked him, does the artist relate to the cosmos? Alex believed that he had a responsibility to get in sync with the vibrations between all that exists. He said, "Art, to me, is a structure of these relationships or vibrations that we experience." He concentrated for over twenty-five years on what he loved in nature: cliffs, caves, rocks, waterfalls, creeks, tree roots, shrubs, grasses, leaves, sand and weather effects of clouds and mists and snow. His favorite haunting grounds were the coastline, the high mountains and the desert. "I feel the vibrations from these areas and it makes me excited. I feel these relationships taking place around me and I feel I am part of them."

My questions were intended to lead Alex from his philosophy back into his art process and to tie these two together. Of all the artists I have interviewed, he was most comfortable in speaking of this linkage.

"The cliff was brought into being by the process of creation. Over time, it has developed its vibrations so that the cliff is what it vibrates now. Everything within, surrounding, and of the cliff is tied together in a set of relationships. My experience in front of the cliff—sketching, taking photos, just looking, comparing this cliff to all my experience with cliffness—is like drinking in the cliff. When I am there, consciously and unconsciously, what I see, what I know, what I feel emotionally and tactically, what I hear or smell or taste, the information stored in my memory, and my intuitive and mystical insights become part of my life of feelings. From my life of feelings come my art and my subject matter. The image of the cliff is the vehicle I use to convert the vibration/relationship that I felt on location into art. The painting becomes a symbolic expressive form in a structure of visual relationships which has a separate life. I create a new identity. A successful painting has a vibration of its own."

Alex made it clear that his symbolic expressive form did not just arrive as soon as he returned to his studio. He had to wait and meditate.

"Once in a while, the symbolic expressive form 'pops' whole into my consciousness, but most of the time it comes out of a fog in bits and pieces. It comes as partial insights which flash into my mind and excites my imagination like the many separate frames of a motion picture film. Some frames show the vibration of the cliff as a whole. In these, I see massiveness, weight and the mountain that supports the cliff. The mountain is part of the earth. The earth is part of the solar system. The solar system is part of the galaxy, the whole universe. In other frames that zero in on a small area of the cliff, I see the vibration of a segment of the exterior surface of the rock, the cracks, the rough etchings created by the weather, wind, water and ice. I see streaks of iron oxidation, stains from water and vegetation, mosses, lichen and grasses. At some point, I start sketching images. I try to become more attentive, open and aware, to be receptive to the content of my imagination. The ultimate vision comes from the unconscious, perhaps reaching all the way to the transcendent."

Alex demurred from the idea that he was actually in control of his process. He said, "The artist cannot will art." He relied upon a combination of his own effort and then letting go. Alex said:

"I accept Rollo May's idea that our intentionality gives meaning to our concept. We mean what we intend. Our intention shapes the process by sorting the vibrations and relationships that will make up the structure of the painting.

"I try to discover and express the foundation of the structure of relationships. The sketch is the concept layer and the physical layer. Eventually, I see and feel what could be significant, important or beautiful. With this vision, I start gluing paper to the canvas, masonite or watercolor board. I begin with dark fade-proof charcoal paper which I moisten, blot with newspaper and glue down. The dark represents the mystery in life, the unknown, the ultimate question, what happens to us after we die?"

Nepote imbedded this unfathomable darkness deeply into the work, furthest away in terms of time and space from the surface.

"The presence of the first layers is felt in the final structure. These layers have their own identity; their vibration is a relationship to the whole. This applies also to the thin, white, all rag torn shapes that I add next. I pin them to the ground, without gluing them, until I am sure what these shapes should be. The old adage, 'well begun is half done' is certainly true of my work. Sometimes I peel off paper to regain a shape, even if it is partially dry after gluing. Contrast, tension and resolution appear in the relationship of sizes, kind and position of shapes and in the interaction of lines and shapes."

Alex used the idea of contrast as a vital element in the expressive form, and also as an element of his philosophy. He often considered the mystery of polarities, the yin/yang symbol; and he liked a statement by Suzanne Langer that the vitality of a work of art depends upon tensions and resolutions.

The cliff was a metaphor for Alex's preoccupation with the universal rhythm of creation and destruction. Symbolically, he reenacted nature itself. He was conscious of doing it. His creative method was in symbiotic relationship with his philosophy of wholeness.

This statement by Nepote appeared in Edward Reep's book *The Content of Watercolor:* "I feel that man's existence in historical time is his greatest experience—his life. It is . . . my intention to . . . suggest that the transitory things of nature are not the real reality. The ultimate reality is the never-ending process in which things come into being, exist and pass away—the mystery of continuous change."

Alex Nepote died on March 12, 1986, moving on into the mystery of continuous change. He left behind a metaphorical road map that I take out to study now and then by reading his letters. I miss him and his mentorship—and his prophetic insight into the link between art and idea. I can't help but wonder if he has guided me toward other *artists of the spirit.*

PLATE 1

"The Secret"
Michael Naranjo

S pirit, *a 20" bronze sculpture, caught my eye on a gallery tour in 1972. The afterimage glowed as a memory of an Indian dancer dressed only in a long loincloth, swinging his arms in front of him, with his head tilted back and his face turned sideways. Corn husks in his hair flared outward from the force of his spin. The piece called to me until I finally went back to Santa Fe and bought it from Jean Seth. She insisted I speak with the artist, and she placed the call herself. A man's disembodied, light voice, so soft I could hardly hear it, explained that* Spirit *represents a member of Taos Pueblo's clown clan—the Chifonetti—who paint their bodies in black and white stripes. Their ceremonial antics, both funny and*

serious, enliven the celebrations of San Geronimo Day in September and again at Christmas. I thanked him for telling me about Spirit. *"I love your piece," I said, and told him good-bye. As we were leaving the gallery, Jean Seth mentioned that the artist Michael Naranjo had become a sculptor four years before, after being totally blinded in the Vietnam War. Only then did I notice that* Spirit *has no eyes.*

I WAS AMAZED and deeply touched by hearing of Naranjo's blindness. My husband Ed's last tour of duty, 1969-1970, was in Vietnam, in a war that was still going on. While Ed was serving in Vietnam, I was torn between supporting his duty and disapproving of the war—an internal conflict I have never entirely resolved. Under these circumstances, the lyrical beauty in a work of such peacefulness created by a man so harmed by the war seemed especially poignant to me; and it made Spirit even more precious. At the time, I had no expectation of meeting Michael Naranjo.

During the early 1970s I wrote four biographies for the series The Story of an American Indian for young readers, published by Dillon Press. Michael Naranjo's extraordinary story struck me as a most appropriate addition to the biography series. Both Michael and the publisher agreed with the idea, and we began working together in 1973 by talking at length while I took endless notes. To gain his approval of the text I wrote, I read it to him and his tape recorder. He made a few minor corrections after a single hearing, revealing how sharply honed his aural memory had become. Later he listened to the tape again and made more subtle suggestions. From beginning the book until publication in 1975 took two years. By that time, Michael Naranjo was a friend who has my lasting affection.

Whenever I have succumbed to self-pity over these years, I have thought of Michael Naranjo. He reminds me that one can accept the most difficult fate without bitterness. From our first conversation I sensed his innately spiritual awareness. He described the little being who was his guardian, a tiny Indian with a pot belly and skinny legs, wearing a long loincloth and moccasins, who behaved with mischievous, jolly trickery. Like an imp, he led Michael to the edge of disaster in Vietnam but then pulled him back to life and helped him recover his talent for sculpture. This spirit taught him that good and bad, happy and sad, go together. In his biography I wrote, "He believes the spirit goes from one life to another. Michael thinks the spirit is somehow part of him." Recently, Michael told me that he has revised his opinion and now believes he invented the spirit because he needed help to make sense of what had happened to him. He invented him so well that his guardian exists for me whenever I see him in Michael's Spirit.

MICHAEL NARANJO: SEEING THE ENERGY

Michael Naranjo's sculpture continues to evolve, both creatively and as a challenge to his bottomless courage. In 1989 I suggested his participation in the New Mexico Art History conference in Taos where he gave a slide talk about his life and art that was later published in edited form by S*outhwest Art.* His joyful disposition and his benign manner of telling his life story, including the loss of his eyes in the Vietnam War, disarmed his audience. You could feel their emotions rippling through the auditorium. That was the first time I had seen Michael in over a decade. He introduced me to his wife Laurie, and we exchanged a warm hello.

Few artists have shared with me so simply and so honestly their spiritual imagination as Michael Naranjo has done. He thinks of God as a universal creative force or energy. Every aspect of nature has its own spiritual energy: the wind, the canyon, every tree, flower, animal or person. The soul experiences the nature of all these spirits in its evolution. Despite everything that he has experienced, he finds more of goodness in life than evil.

After reviewing his childhood and youth, Michael told me in stark detail the story of the encounter with a Viet Cong that cost him his sight. I can easily retrieve the movie of the scene I created in my head as he spoke. On January 8, 1968, he was with his Infantry squad led by a sergeant named Yazir. They had been ferried by helicopter into a combat zone in the Mekong Delta and had then formed lines to cross a dry rice paddy. Naranjo rolled over a dike to gain some protection between himself and a machine gun firing from a grove of nipa palm. Two men from his squad remained on the opposite, exposed side of the dike. They and Naranjo crawled closer to the palm grove in tandem, but as each of them stood up he was shot. A medic appeared who tried to help them. Naranjo told the man it was useless. The men were dead. Yazir crawled near to Naranjo and they moved forward together to the end of the dike. Ahead was open ground for fifteen yards. The Viet Cong were in the palms. Naranjo had already lost his helmet. He took off his pack as well and put two grenades in his pocket while Yazir threw a grenade at the Viet Cong. Then across the open space he spotted a Viet Cong soldier in a spider hole dug into the earth.

"The very last thing that I remember seeing was in a rice field in Vietnam. I looked over and saw this Viet Cong. Our eyes met. We looked at each other. We knew what was going to happen. And, in all of two seconds, we understood each other and I shot. And I can still see him looking. Our eyes locked as I shot. It's the last thing I remember seeing." (CBS, "Bodywatching," 1987)

Sgt. Yazir yelled that another VC had thrown a grenade, but Naranjo could not hear him. The VC grenade rolled into his right hand. Just as he tried to throw it back it exploded. Shrapnel destroyed his eyes and imbedded itself into him, especially in his right arm and hand.

There followed harrowing hours waiting to be airlifted by helicopter to a field hospital. After a few days, he was stabilized enough to be sent to an army hospital in Japan where he remained for two months. He recuperated sufficiently to begin walking and to restore some of his creative energy. Before entering the service, Michael had completed several ambitious clay figures, including a shiny black bear about 15 inches in length and a graceful horse of a similar size on display in his home. Memories of these pieces may have inspired him to ask the Gray Lady volunteer, a general's wife, for some clay from which he modeled a small bear. To the wonder of the medical staff and his fellow patients, he worked only with his good left hand, using his weakened right hand just for support. He relied on his instinct and memory to create the form. While still in Japan he had a glimmer of the inner sight that he depends upon today.

He was flown home and underwent further treatment, physical therapy and training in a school for the blind run by the Veterans Administration. Michael told writer Kathleen Raphael, "Making adjustments to being blind was hard. It was like being born again. You must learn to read [Braille], to walk, to do everything." At last he came home to his large and loving family.

The Naranjo family is distinguished in both the Santa Clara and Taos Pueblos. Michael's mother Rose Naranjo is a respected traditional potter. Of her ten grown children, eight are artists. Michael Naranjo, Sr., is the first Pueblo Indian to become a Baptist missionary, and he built the first Baptist church on reservation land. He was already the father of a big family when he and Rose, with their baby Dollie, left the rest of the children in the care of relatives and spent over two years at a seminary in California. Young Michael, born in 1944, was only four when they left. He wandered unfettered by rules along the banks of the Rio Grande River that runs beside his pueblo north of Santa Fe, or into Santa Clara Canyon to go fishing with his big, idolized brother Tito, or out for a climb to the top of Black Mesa where he could watch the whole valley below. Tito often took him camping in the mountains, and Michael remembers fondly that his brother always wanted to know "what was over the next hill." He has mentioned this several times in public interviews, and one realizes that pushing over the next hill could be a metaphor for Michael's own life.

His father was ordained in 1950, and his parents returned to Santa Clara Pueblo. The elder Michael then built his church. Rose and his sisters worked as potters, and young Michael sometimes sat with them playing with the clay and modeling figures on his own. He went hunting and fishing with his father and Tito for food, not sport. Skinning and butchering animals and fish gave him a visceral understanding of their anatomy. Michael was a visually acute person, and he stored pictorial memories of Pueblo village life.

In 1953, his father received an appointment from the missionary board to take over the Baptist church in the town of Taos. The family left Santa Clara, a Tewa-speaking pueblo, to live near the Tiwa-speaking Taos Pueblo Indians who joined his father's congregation. Taos Pueblo is one of the most picturesque of all Native American villages. Its multistoried buildings comprised of numerous family apartments built adjacent to and on top of each other are known to thousands of people from visits and through widely reproduced paintings and photographs.

From the age of nine until he left for the army, Michael Naranjo lived in the two-story white manse beside the church just outside the reservation. He returned to his native Santa

Clara Pueblo for ceremonials, but his rich visual memories also include scenes of Taos Pueblo feast days, foot races and many hikes into the beautiful forests of the Taos Mountains. Michael had a foot in two camps, the Indian and the Anglo. He went to school in town, lived in town, yet he had many Pueblo friends. He had a happy youth. He also lived part-time with an Anglo family named Verner in Texas. The Verners invited him to stay with them on their farm one summer and treated him like one of their family on his frequent return visits.

One by one his two brothers and seven sisters entered college, graduated, and five went on for higher degrees. His brother Tito was Director of Social Services for Taos County and then became a professor at Highlands University, in Las Vegas, New Mexico. He recently retired from that position, and once again he is free to take Michael fishing.

Michael first enrolled at Wayland Baptist College in Plainview, Texas, where he took an art course, but he stayed only one term. He then attended the Institute of American Indian Art in Santa Fe where he defied the residence requirement by hitchhiking home to Taos every weekend. This lasted for a few weeks, and then he left the institute. For the next two years, he was an art major at Highlands University, but again he was restless and unmotivated. He cavorted around with his fraternity brothers and ditched class. Inevitably, he dropped out and, just as inevitably, was drafted into the army to meet his fate in Vietnam.

The Naranjo family cares about and protects each other. When Michael Naranjo returned from the hospital, family members anxiously encircled him with their love and tried to help him. Friends who saw them leading him along the streets of Taos could not help but express their grief at his blindness. He spent some time in confusion, slowly living through the days as he pondered his future, but not for long. By January 1969 he had convinced his sister Rina that he needed to live alone, and she found him an apartment in Santa Fe. With occasional help from a driver and someone to read the mail, he set about becoming an independent, professional sculptor. When I met him, he lived in a trailer home with a Mercedes sports car sitting outside it, one of the first signs of his success. He had come a long way from his boyhood in Santa Clara Pueblo.

Naranjo taught himself to model figures with wax over a metal armature. He makes preliminary sketches in wax to work out ideas and then he executes them in larger scale. The final wax figure is taken to a foundry where a mold of it is made. An edition limited to a range of between 3 and 50 bronze sculptures is cast by means of the mold and the lost wax casting process. Even Naranjo's first efforts were convincingly sculptural, and sales of the early ones paid the costs of subsequent editions.

By 1972, when he created *Spirit*, he was already working at a scale of 20 inches. Within the first five years of his career, he was given a show in the headquarters of the Veterans Administration in Washington, D.C. He entered his *Hoop Dancer* in the all-Indian open juried show held at the Heard Museum in Phoenix, Arizona, where it won a second prize. It was important to him that his work was valued for its merit.

Such attention to the work brought Naranjo the confirmation he needed to keep going. In 1972 he was given a one-artist show by the Heard Museum. In 1974, *Flight to Freedom,* depicting an eagle dancer swooping on one leg with winged arms outstretched, took the Grand Award and top prize at the Scottsdale (Arizona) Indian Arts Exhibition. In addition to these career milestones, Naranjo has had a fairly steady level of publicity. In a few years marked by constant work he could support himself and his art with his veteran's pension and his sales.

From the beginning, Naranjo has modeled a variety of figures. He is best known for his Indian dancers whose costumes are faithful in detail to the ceremonies they represent. He has also done a consistent body of work devoted to softly modeled females, woodland animals, the Buddha, Greek mythological figures, Biblical figures and children.

His rapid success was not matched with an ease of heart. A series of aborted love affairs with women who were sentimentally attracted to a dramatically handsome, famous, blind artist ended in desertion until 1978 when he met a petite, pretty Anglo brunette named Laurie Engel. Laurie, who is wise and loyal, gives him the wholesome, loving and trustful relationship that underscores his creativity today. He and Laurie have two daughters, Jenna and Bryn. He designed their home on the outskirts of Española, New Mexico, with Laurie's help, based on his wax model. The modern adobe home is comfortable and filled with a loving energy.

Michael has two studios in the house. Off the den is his small modeling room, equipped with a bench and stool, a built-in shelf and almost nothing else. Unless someone is with him, he does not need light, so there are no windows, and the place feels like a private hideaway. Beyond the first studio is a circular, high-ceilinged room for stone carving. Its floor is thick with marble dust. In the center of it is a block of pinkish marble that Michael has been working on for over a year, bringing forth a kneeling figure of a woman.

During his years of work, Naranjo has exerted his ambition to do more complex sculpture, more demanding of him physically and aesthetically. In the mid-1970s, he created a twelve-foot version of his *Taos War Dancer.* The figure wears a "button" of eagle feathers over his buttocks and carries a shield. For years, Naranjo worked on a high scaffold, modeling the heroic figure in plaster over a metal framework. Parts of it were cast, but the whole piece has never been completed in bronze, due in large part to his dissatisfaction with the project. The white plaster original figure occupies a dominant spot outside his front yard now, making a powerful emblem of the work that goes on inside.

Within the first years of his career as a sculptor, Michael Naranjo refined his sense of touch as a replacement for his lost sight. His dream was to someday "see" a sculpture by Michelangelo with his fingers, a dream he never expected to happen. When he and Laurie went to Italy in 1983 for an audience with Pope John Paul II, he was given an opportunity to touch several masterworks of sculpture. Arrangements were made for him to touch

Michelangelo's *Moses* and an exact replica of the *Pietá*, as well as works by Donatello, Canova and Bernini.

Afterwards, walking down the streets of Rome, he says he had recurrent flashes of sensation from the sculpture he had just felt. The feelings in his fingertips translated into a ghost image in his mind of what he had "seen," and he strongly wished he could have touched more for a longer time.

In 1987 a crew from the CBS program "Bodywatching" did an extensive interview with Michael Naranjo. They filmed scenes of him walking outside in the mountains and inside his house where one of the crew noticed a photograph of Michael and Laurie taken in Rome with the Pope. The man asked them questions about their trip. Michael spoke about partially realizing his dream of touching Renaissance sculptures and the profound effect they had had on his inner vision. With spontaneous fervor, the crew asked if he would like to return to Italy and "see" more of Michelangelo's work. It was speedily arranged in only two months.

The program "Bodywatching" which shows Michael Naranjo atop an 18-foot, three-tiered scaffold in the Academy in Florence, Italy, is one of the most moving films I have ever watched. For three hours, Michael ran his fingers gently over the *David*, from each level of the scaffold. At first, he said, "I had to cry a little bit." Soon he gained control and described what his fingertips were showing him, saying such things as "His face is extremely expressive. His eyelids are beautifully formed. In the corners are the tear ducts. The pupils of the eye feel like hearts. The eyes are looking off into the distance and he's questioning something. The mouth has this calmness about it. The curl of his lips is really beautiful. The stone feels soft. It's fleshy. You know there's life inside this piece of stone."

New Mexico's PBS station KNME-TV included other footage from CBS in their interview, conducted by Michael Kamins for the program "Colores." Naranjo continued his description of *David*. "His lips are so soft that you feel the heart beating, pumping—pushing blood . . . They look like they are going to open any second and he's going to start talking. The veins in his neck are bulging from the adrenaline that he's feeling from looking at Goliath standing in the distance."

As a Father's Day gift, Laurie bought Michael a stone, tools, a chisel and a hammer to try stone carving. His first stone sculpture is a male Indian figure, crouching under a pelt. Michael is critical of it, pointing out the surface pits where his chisel slipped, yet the piece has a satisfyingly sculptural mass and clarity of form and the pits seem to make the surface more furlike. Naranjo's intimate contact with Michelangelo's work gave him a kinesthetic connection to stone which has fueled his enthusiasm for stone carving.

On "Colores," he discussed his habitual creative process:

"When I'm starting a sculpture, I get a picture in my mind . . . Where I see this gray form, gray shadow, that's a body, a human body . . . Then the excitement, the energy is building . . . My hands are working very quickly, molding, shaping, forming from this picture that my mind sees in my mind's eye and it sends messages down to my fingertips . . .

"I'm working in darkness in that I don't see anything, but there is this energy, this kind of electrical force of sorts that's flowing through my fingers and through my mind. This energy is like . . . lightning coming down from the sky . . . I have the sense . . . that the visual imagery is something that my mind receives from my fingertips, which is a world of touch, so it's not sight anymore and sound is nonexistent . . . It's a channel of touch and feeling and emotion that has taken place."

Michael Naranjo and I had several conversations in mid-1975 in preparation for an article that I wrote for *New Mexico* magazine. He said:

"The longer I work on a sculpture the more the spirit is in me—it's the creative spirit. He's always inside. He may not be alive and jumping but the moment that one thing appeals to him he starts stirring and won't stop until he's satisfied we've done something about it.

"You take energy in and you give energy out. There are lots of areas that need movement or texture—areas that are empty—that need movement of the eye. I use the outermost extensions to set up rhythm around the whole piece. You have to be careful with all this. These extensions can shoot energy out into space and it leaves the figure. Your eye would follow the direction of, say, a pointing finger. You need some other line close by to contain the energy and bring it back. You must lead the eye back."

In the spring of 1990 two of Naranjo's sculptures were on exhibit in Albuquerque at the South Broadway Cultural Center. Ed and I attended the opening hoping to see him, but he was not there. Instead, we spent a long time admiring *The Secret,* a bronze figure of a thin, old man wearing a blanket, leaning on a cane in reverie as a crow whispers in his ear. The very dark patina enhances a feeling of mystery, an emanation of something other than the visual, perhaps a message of impending death to the old one who is not reluctant to hear it. Michael's sculpture again became a vivid image that haunted my mind. It seemed to do the same for Ed who suddenly suggested we celebrate an upcoming anniversary and future birthdays by buying it. At 29 inches high, it looms above his *Spirit* and his five inch *Buffalo,* both of which we bought years ago. The gentle spirit of Michael Naranjo fills a part of our house and touches something deep in my heart, suggesting ultimate peace.

During his "Colores" interview, Naranjo spoke of *The Secret*. "When I originally made this sculpture I was going to call it *When Age Is No More,* but then once I put the crow on his shoulder I had to call it *The Secret*, because the crow is his friend. When he takes his walks in the late afternoon the crow comes and sits on his shoulder and tells him the secrets of things that he saw during the day . . . ." The crow is possibly an alternate form of Naranjo's earlier spirit guide, providing him with constant secrets, inspiring him to ever greater self-created challenges.

Long before I formulated the ideas underlying this book, I had accepted Michael Naranjo as a person of prophetic wisdom, not only for the world generally but for me specifically. Seeing him on television and in a public meeting was thrilling, but I needed to talk with him again. On a visit to his home in Española, I shared a conversation with him while we ate Laurie's homemade cookies. He made clear to me that he knew he was an artist well before the Vietnam war. Though he made sketches and painted watercolors, three-dimensional art attracted him most; and he decided to be a sculptor.

Michael spoke of his thoughts and dreams, and the inner world of his visions since he became blind:

"I don't know where the gift came from, but it's there. Once when I was still living in the trailer I was doing a *Medicine Man* and it wasn't working out, so I went into the living room for a few minutes to rest. A little dot formed on my left field of vision. The dot moved to the right side and changed form. I saw the form, not in great detail, but definite, and it was the *Eagle Dancer* who became *Flight to Freedom*. When I focused on him for two or three seconds, he disappeared, but then as I focused on him in my mind's eye I could bring him back. I could change him. I could bring him back and look at him. I let him go and went to the studio and two weeks later, after 18 hours a day in the studio, he was done. It was a total obsession.

"When I was working on the *Taos War Dancer*, I would go out to the cliff where the scaffold was in the middle of the night and work until I heard the birds singing. Once during the time I was working on him I went to sleep and had this dream of being on the scaffold under his face. And in the dream I am trying to reach under his left armpit, but I can't reach it. I thought, I may have to move the scaffold. Then suddenly, I'm looking at it from his eyes, seeing Michael. I *am* the sculpture. I can feel the steel move and I help Michael reach it. I woke up and I was scared. That was the first and last time I was ever inside one of my pieces.

"I used to have a dream of a beautiful face of a woman. I would dream of falling through a hole or off a mountain, floating through space, falling, sometimes frightening or maybe peaceful. In the last such dream I was sliding down a mountain on a road skiing, but I have never skied in my life. I ended up in this valley beside a lake. It was peaceful there beside the clear water, with high grass and trees. And I saw this woman approaching, slender, with brown hair, gentle and calm. I came up to her in my dream and it was total peace. It had to be Laurie because after that we met and I've never had that dream again.

"Another dream came when we were living in the house prior to this one. I woke up but wasn't quite awake, in that gradual drift from sleep to awareness—I love to sleep. I could hear Laurie's voice in the distance, talking to a woman who had come to teach her to weave. This cloud comes and in it there's an eagle, with his wing hanging down on a pedestal and his head looking under his folded wing. What I generally see in front of me is gunmetal gray, but this eagle was golden in color. I looked at it and realized what it was. Two or three seconds later, it's gone, then I saw it in greater detail. I got out of bed and made a model of it. Six months later, I made the sculpture of it. Where did it come from? I have no idea.

"There is some sort of magic, if we are open to it. A piece may not sell, and then two or three pieces of an edition will sell at once. Or, all of a sudden, two or three people will call us from the same state in one evening, people who don't know each other. Some energy is floating through, catching people and pulling them in. I don't work at this. I don't think I'm a good enough person to work at it. I'm too much into living this life to be a Spiritual Being. I am too involved in making my sculptures, in making my family happy. If I do my work, everything functions. When I don't take care of it, I'm not happy. Sometimes it does not come freely and I have to work at it, but if I had eyes, I wouldn't do anything else than what I am doing.

"It's okay to love your work. At first it was hard to part with my pieces, but I sell them to help give birth to new ones. I can't sell my stone pieces yet. I'm selfish for them. I'm just having a great time carving them and sensing the chisel moving in them. Stone is not as forgiving as modeling in wax. At the moment I am totally taken by stone. I always love the new piece. When it's finished, the love affair is over. When it is over, you can be the loneliest person on earth.

"I once had a dream of this incredible Spiritual Being who came to embrace me and said, 'Don't worry, everything will be okay.' I got this definite impression he was talking about my work.

"I would like to think there is some sort of energy inside each of my pieces and that it's good, even if it just makes people smile or be happy. I can't make it happen, but I would like for my pieces to give others the same happiness they give me. I have my castle now, my queen and my two princesses. I want to keep everything simple. Some people can do many things well. I can do my thing and I can do it well, and I can get better at it. All I can do is what I am doing and do the best I can. I don't have any religion, but I have this belief that I am part of a whole."

I believe Michael Naranjo's religion is his art, and his whole life is an act of faith. He is like the wounded healer who accepts his dreadful confrontation with death and blindness as purposeful and basically necessary for him. He exemplifies that a way is always provided for us to express our gifts. "The two greatest forces within me are my soul and my work," he once said to me. "Vietnam is past. The more conscious effort I make at not becoming violent, the better. My sculpture is my way of giving universal energy a shape that will last."

Each of us spends so much time mentally criticizing our imperfections, wishing we were different, that we behaved better or were somehow more ideal; and this constant negativity harms our spirit. Michael Naranjo does not do this. He has come to terms with his disability by disavowing that he has one. Michael said (in his interview for "Colores"):

"In the normal sense of being disabled, I don't think I have a disability. I'm working too hard and I'm having too much fun to think 'blind.' I forget that I'm blind. Disability is a strange thing. I think it can be worked around, gotten rid of. If we find something that we're excited about with life, then disability is destroyed. It's a challenge. It's a game. Accept this challenge. Enjoy it in the sense that it's a gift. Live. Cry and live."

*H*e Who Sleeps at the Foot of the Horse is a practicing shaman who prefers that his birth name not be published. I went to him in early fall of 1987 just before taking the first workshop in Huna with Serge King. How better to open one's mind to shamanism than by visiting a shaman?

HE WHO SLEEPS is an exceptionally tall man, fair complex-ioned with light-brown hair and blue eyes. We had spoken only briefly several weeks before my appointment; but I was confident that I would benefit from the efforts the shaman was to make, even though I had no idea what they might be. He began the session by asking me to take off my jewelry and shoes and to stand on a smooth panel. My legs tingled. Then I lay on an upholstered healing table beneath which was a treasure house of beautiful stones, religious objects and native artifacts. The shaman covered me with a blanket. With my eyes closed I felt him put beads, stones and perhaps a rosary under the blanket next to my ribs and across my chest. His apprentice Felipe drummed a subtly varied pattern while the shaman kept a steady pressure on my sternum with his hands as he breathed deeply in and out in a flawlessly maintained rhythm. When the drumming stopped, a tape of "Koyaanisqatsi" began. The shaman moved around to the end of the table and pressed his hands with firm, even pressure on both sides of my head.

Throughout the session I "saw" one picture after another with my inner eye. In the most vivid of these images a dark tribal shaman conducted a ritual within a firelit cave whose walls were painted in symbols. The figure wore a white headdress and skirt with an elaborate collar on his shoulders. Musicians and dancers moved around him. Subsequent images were of wild animals. I was focused so completely on these spectacles it took a moment to return to the reality of the shaman's table at the end of the session. A penetrating feeling of expanded awareness has never left me since that visit. Something clearly had happened within my own mind, and the ensuing training in shamanism "took" easily without the barrier of skepticism.

Three years later, again in October, I had another session, a totally different experience. Before he began his treatment I gave the shaman a list of my concerns, as diverse as anxiety about our son in the Gulf War and an outbreak of allergies. He used a variety of techniques in this session. He gave me an energy-balancing device to hold. In his trance state he applied hand pressure, massaged my feet, feathered my body, and rang a deep-toned bowl. I was not so lost in visualizations this time. Instead, I made an effort to remain in the moment and be as aware of my experience as possible.

When we spoke afterward, he told me that he could see into the systems of the body while he was performing a healing, and he shared his insight into digestion problems I had not mentioned. The result this time was a physical improvement. Before I left he recommended I read The Invisible Partners by John Sanford and Animus and Anima by Emma Jung. He explained that the source of allergies is an imbalance in our understanding of these essences within ourselves.

Several weeks thereafter, the shaman told me his pain-wracked life story. He Who Sleeps was born in Minnesota in 1940 to a family of German ancestry. He had older twin sisters and a younger brother. For a few years the family lived on his maternal grandfather's farm. Though his mother was raised as a Catholic and his father as a Methodist, his childhood religious background was minimal. As his story reveals, however, he had an innate sense of God.

HE WHO SLEEPS AT THE FOOT OF THE HORSE: SHAMAN/WOUNDED HEALER

He Who Sleeps began his story with a dramatic statement:

"My mother was a satanic high priestess who belonged to a cult. For her to either maintain or elevate her position with the cult, I was, as the first born son, to be a living sacrifice. Many years later when I was 40, my doctor was checking for a source of internal bleeding. He decided to fluoroscope my whole body with upwards of 75 X-rays. Later when I was in his consulting room he said, 'You must have been in a terrible accident.' I said, 'Why?' He said, 'Because most of the bones in your body have been broken.'

"At the age of 5 I was very tired of my life and I had a deep knowingness of what it was going to be like, so I wanted to end it. My mother's father was the abuser of that family. He was just a mean, mean being. He abused his six huge workhorses on the farm, and they were very skittish around people. No one could be near them. I remember curling around the front hoof of one of these horses. I meant to terminate my life by having a horse step on me, but when it happened I didn't want to know about it. I had trouble getting to sleep because of the lumps of dirt under my rib, and I said a little prayer saying that I had had enough pain in my life, I wasn't going to take anymore, and I fell asleep. My aunt noticed I was missing. She was always watching out for me if she could. People were hunting for me and someone saw this horse with me curled around the right front hoof. My aunt got everyone to go back in the house for fear of what these animals did when people were around. I slept for close to two hours. The horse remained totally still. I remember waking up and being surprised to be alive. I noticed that I felt better, although nothing had changed in my life.

"As I walked away from the horse, I prayed again, 'God, if you will just help me until I grow up and get away from this sick family, I will be a doctor for you.' That was my first bribe with God. The sky seemed to open up; and I heard a deep, caring fatherly voice say, 'You will have two children, the first will be a girl and the second will be a boy,' and the sky closed. I walked further toward the fence and said to myself, 'Gee, he didn't even answer my prayer about keeping me alive.' I didn't make sense of it really as a five-year-old, but years later a Jungian analyst said that horse had been possessed of the Mother archetype and was guarding me.

"Several years ago in California at the Ojai Foundation, I attended the Sacred Talking Tree Ceremony and met Swift Deer, a shaman of mixed blood, a metis medicine man of the Cherokee Nation who holds doctorates in psychology and theology. I told him my story. Swift Deer recognized me as carrying the Christ consciousness, and he gave me the name He Who Sleeps at the Foot of the Horse. He told me that every animal carries wisdom, and in times of intense experiences like mine the animal will transfer his wisdom to the person. He said the horse has the wisdom of how man thinks. He transferred it to me, and it was a permanent gift. From then on I have been able to look in people's minds and know exactly what they were thinking.

"When I was around five years old, my family moved to South Dakota. Our apartment was built in the haymow on the second floor of a chicken hatchery where my parents both worked. My mom evicted me from that house, saying I did not deserve to have food or shelter, so I found a job setting up pins in a bowling alley at night. My father built a separate room in the haymow that was not connected with the house. After the first winter, he put in a wood stove. So beginning at age five, I earned my own money, and I bought my own clothing and food. I ate in hamburger shops. I'm a real survivor."

He Who Sleeps was 13 when his mother threatened him with a knife. He warned her not to touch him again. From then on she had nothing to do with him, beginning a psychological abandonment he believes set the stage for the acute hyperthyroidism that plagued him for years in later life.

Even as a young child he knew he had a certain magic power, especially with animals. He once had an owl for a pet, and he raised pigeons for a time. "I was always taking care of wounded animals and birds that had fallen out of their nests. One of my aunts told me I should be a doctor, particularly a surgeon because I have long fingers."

Despite his strained home life, He Who Sleeps attended school in an outwardly normal manner. When the family moved into town his exile ended, and he shared a room with his brother. He graduated from high school determined to go to medical school. With scholarship assistance he earned a bachelor's degree from the state university in 1962 with a major in zoology and minors in chemistry, mathematics and foreign languages. Following graduation he married, worked in a campus laboratory and pursued both a two-year medical program and a master's degree in biochemistry. After six years at the state university, he transferred to a four-year medical school in another state. He and his wife had a daughter and son, just as predicted.

Though doctors could find no cause for it, his physical condition rapidly degenerated as his weight dropped to 93 pounds, skeletal for a man just under six feet four inches tall. His greatest fear was that he was a hypochondriac and not really sick at all; but he became so weak he was forced to leave medical school for four years. Somehow, he was able to work in nuclear medical laboratories to support his family. His intention to return to school never wavered.

He Who Sleeps went into heart failure. A cardiologist said his problem was idiopathic cardiomyopathy, but there was nothing the doctor could treat and heal. Luckily, an observant nuclear lab technician said, "You're always climbing the walls. I know you have hyperthyroidism." When tests were done, the technician's diagnosis was proved to be right. Treatment with an "atomic cocktail" reduced He Who Sleeps' thyroid function, but the most healing aspect of this experience for him was the confirmation that he did indeed have a real physical ailment. As his hyperthyroidism came under control, he set about trying to gain weight and recover his strength.

He Who Sleeps reentered medical school. During his senior year he received a grant to conduct a two-month investigation of alcoholism in Yugoslavia. He graduated cum laude at age 32 and then completed a year of internship in general practice. Afterwards he was highly recommended by his hospital.

On the basis of his references he established himself as a general practitioner in the Northwest. He was financially successful and effective in helping many patients, but he was shunned by the closed medical community of the town. Ostracism revived the depression that had haunted him since his abusive childhood. His fragile health again declined.

"In 1975, two years into my practice, I took my family on a trip to Mexico. I fell very ill with diarrhea and had severe difficulty breathing. Shortly after returning home I had an ache in my cecum, and just moments later I had massive internal bleeding and excreted blood." He Who Sleeps feared that his disease was psychosomatic yet he continued bleeding. For years he neither slept nor dreamed. Sleep deprivation led to mental confusion, difficulty in reading and exhaustion.

In 1979 a former patient died. He Who Sleeps brooded about her death although she was not under his care when she died. "I went downhill until I sat in the office one night and attempted suicide with pills. I ended up in a psych hospital for a couple of months, and I came under the care of a psychiatrist. By this time I had not slept in four or five years, and I experienced five or six psychotic breaks. I faced my own history and finally confessed to myself that I was emotionally troubled."

The psychiatrist had the prescience to notice that each time He Who Sleeps entered a psychosis, his bleeding healed. The doctor saw him through each of these episodes without administering any drugs. "That level of chaos is very, very healing and transforming," the shaman told me. "I didn't get trapped by someone frame-freezing my mind energies at one point. If you fix a person with drugs and they don't go through their madness, they stay stuck and cannot get to the place of healing." Looking back, He Who Sleeps believes he had to undergo apparent derangement to familiarize himself with the experience of others whom he now treats. The psychiatrist thought there was no help for He Who Sleeps' physical deterioration. He advised him to close his practice and just rest. The shaman said, "I expected to die."

Taking his doctor's advice, He Who Sleeps began closing his office.

"My nurse and I were in the office boxing up stuff, and again—this had happened hundreds of times by then—I had an ache in my cecum and excreted blood. This time I didn't flush it. I pulled up my pants and I yelled to her to come in the bathroom. I asked her what she saw in the stool. She said, 'That's blood, doctor.' I thanked her and asked her to get the gastroenterologist on the phone. 'Would you stay on the line and listen?' I asked her. She told my doctor she saw blood. For months this doctor had been telling me I was a hypochondriac; but he came right over, saw the blood and went into action. He contacted a radiologist who thought he saw a polyp in the area of the cecum. A surgeon and his assistant made a little buttonhole incision to take out the polyp, but they kept opening me wider because they couldn't find anything. Then three vessels ruptured, and I almost exsanguinated on the operating table. Later they decided I probably had Osler-Weber-Rondu syndrome, which is a genetic condition that leads to poorly constructed veins that are not well-located, which explained why I bled into my eye, my veins, my gut, into everything.

"Before the surgery, I had visited the Sleep Disorder Clinic in Palo Alto to find out why I hadn't slept in five years. The tests done on me showed that my brain would not induce REM sleep. They couldn't help me. Some strange things were happening to me. It was as though I de-spirited myself. My body was in so much pain that my spirit couldn't stand to be in my body. So it left. Then my spirit would come back in my body and I'd be sitting in my car or a restaurant saying, 'God, how did I get here?'"

In late January 1980, He Who Sleeps had been working late one night typing letters telling his patients to find other doctors. An hour after he had started typing, he found himself driving on a road he knew from making house calls in the past, but it was not the right way to his home. He lost all sense of movement, although the car speedometer read 35 mph. The road, which he knew to be straight, divided into a Y. He believed that he was creating one of the forks in his own mind.

"I remembered that when Christ was dying on the cross the man on his right side got to go to heaven and the one on the left went to hell. I decided to take the right fork, but the right fork did not exist. Suddenly, as my spirit came back in my body, I felt movement through space. My car hit a huge ditch, 15 feet deep and filled with water from an overflowing cesspool. I'd only been out of surgery a couple of weeks and had a huge incision. I just sat there while the car was sinking, then I squeezed my legs up around to push against the door and I got out. When I managed to finally get up on the road, I saw a long gravel driveway with a mobile home at the end. I walked there and an elderly lady answered my knock."

Details of the home are etched in the shaman's mind. He used the couple's phone to call his family; his wife and his daughter answered on different phones. The woman gave them directions for reaching the area. He Who Sleeps returned to wait at the side of the ditch for his family to come for him.

"They would never talk to me about the accident. It wasn't until 1985 while visiting my daughter that I asked her to take me to the scene of the accident. She reluctantly agreed. We got there and as soon as we stopped she blurted out, 'Dad, I want to tell you this.' Her face was afraid. 'I know you were on the phone because I was listening to you. I was talking to you. But when we got there, you hadn't gotten out of the car yet.' She has refused to talk to me about it since. There was no trailer house or driveway there. This was bizarre."

In March 1980 He Who Sleeps took his family to Hawaii for spring vacation. He was still depressed, and he told his wife he was going for a walk on Waikiki Beach. He had $2500 inside each of his socks. He wore an inexpensive wedding ring, a gold Rolex watch, and his medical school honorary fraternity ring. Around his neck on a gold chain was a ring that held a diamond valued at $100,000.

"I left for my walk at a quarter to seven. Around midnight, my wife got a call from Queen's Hospital asking her to come and identify my body. I was fished out of Pearl Harbor by the Naval Patrol. The paramedics were called. I was taken to the emergency room, pronounced dead and put in the morgue. Early the following morning, a resident took a shortcut through the morgue. Three times, he heard an inner voice that said, 'Put your stethoscope on that body.' When he listened to my chest he heard a heartbeat. I ended up in intensive care in a coma.
"The money from my socks was gone. Seven hundred bucks in my billfold was present. The wedding ring was gone, the watch was gone, the diamond and the medical school ring were still there. I got out of that hospital some days later, and I said to my family, 'You've got to look at what's going on.'"

Although he did not understand what was happening to him, He Who Sleeps sensed that his life as he had known it was over. He believed his marriage, which had never been close, was finished.

"The robbery meant that I had no more time in a way I didn't even under-stand. The doctor in Hawaii figured someone might be actually out to kill me, and he suggested I go home first and let my family follow in a day or two. At home I picked up my mail before going into my house and there was a letter from W. J., a former patient, who wrote that while I was on the operating table, she had floated above my body watching the operation. W. J. described details that the doctor had told me and I had not discussed with anybody.

"In April 1980 I separated myself from my family and moved to a nearby city. My apartment was on the eighth floor of a thirteen-story building. Since I wasn't dying yet and I wasn't practicing medicine, I needed an income. I started investing money in stocks. From 6:30 in the morning until it closed at 1:00 p.m., I studied the stock market. Then I would rest.

"In May or June I was lying on the sofa looking upward when an eagle came in right through the ceiling. She flew to me and thrust her talons into me, and I felt the pain as though someone were driving nails into my chest. Blood spurted from two of the holes where her talons were. She lifted me up, gripping me with these talons in my chest wall. The pain was excruciating. We went right through the ceiling as though it were a vapor. My mind couldn't even take it in. Way off we went to a cliff side, a place of rocks and mountains where she secured me. Then with her beak she started ripping off my flesh. She'd grab a hunk and just tear it off. I felt the pain every time she did it. Because of all the child abuse I had had, this aroused my bodily insecurity; it was such a terrorizing experience that I was lost in the horror of it. She ripped and ate my flesh until I was just a skeleton. Then she went into my head with her beak, right into the side of my skull. From that moment I realized I was watching her do this, yet I was still alive. I was so relieved to be alive that it turned into a kind of comedy. That was my formal calling into shamanism—the signal event—but I didn't have any words to explain that."

He Who Sleeps was thrust onto the shamanic path in isolation. Unlike the shaman neophyte in a tribal culture who is initiated into service within a community, he faced his initiatory vision in the midst of an indifferent, sophisticated urban society that offered no support. Yet, his transformation into the Wounded Healer is a route well-trodden by millennia of shamans before him.

Mircea Eliade mentions the frequency of psychopathic illness in the candidate for shamanism. "But the primitive magician, the medicine man or the shaman is not only a sick man; he is, above all, a sick man who has been cured, who has succeeded in curing himself." (*Shamanism: Archaic Techniques of Ecstasy*, p. 27.) Eliade points out that the shaman is chosen, set apart by his peculiarity and afterwards has "direct relations with the sacred."

In her book *Shaman: The Wounded Healer*, Joan Halifax includes illustrations of an eagle abducting a man. She writes, "The steps of the journey of shamanic initiation seem to have a patterned course." (p. 6.) The initiate undergoes a ritualistic death, a leave-taking of the former life. He or she answers the call with a necessary obedience and a willing submission to an inner discipline. The violence of the initiatory event with its attendant fears creates a psychic opening "towards the unknown, the *mysterium*." (p. 6.) Two statements by Halifax are particularly relevant to He Who Sleeps. "The seemingly irrational is found to be ordered though paradoxical." Throughout his journey, He Who Sleeps has found interrelationships of events that seem to form a pattern leading him into further transformation. Secondly, "Dismemberment by ravenous spirits allows for the reconstitution of the candidate to a new and higher order of being." (p. 19.) At the time of his vision, He Who Sleeps had no context in which to explain the extraordinary vision he had experienced. Half-expecting to return to medical practice, he feared that if anyone heard of this event he would be judged insane and unfit to practice. "I held this very, very secretively to myself." More was to come.

"As soon as this experience happened to me, I had direct visual and audio communication with the Christ.

"The only mystical connection I had was with W. J. She is a married woman with two children, not a nun, but she worked at a healing center in a Catholic monastery. I started going out there to their healing sessions because I thought they might be able to do something for my sleep and bleeding problems, but every time I went there they assigned me to heal other people. No one worked on me. Two or three years later, W. J. revealed to me that the nuns had meditated and talked to the Christ about me and were told no one was to touch me. I was under his care and his alone. He said I was a gifted healer and I was to be put to work.

"The monastery introduced me to healing by laying on hands and saying Catholic prayers. That's all I knew how to do. A Catholic priest, who was known there as The Father of Inner Healing, had an abnormal heart rhythm which was documented on an EKG. I healed him of this very serious heart disturbance. Afterward, his maintenance of a normal rhythm was also documented on EKG. I found this strange. I was trained in the allopathic field; and I felt this spiritual type of healing was a placebo thing, a response to a need for tender loving care.

"One day during intermission of a conference at the monastery, I overheard a woman say the words 'Mother Bird of Prey Experience' and 'calling into shamanism.' I'd never heard of that before and it went to the very core of my being."

These few words were quoted from *Dreams: God's Forgotten Language* by John Sanford. He Who Sleeps tracked the quote and found that Sanford, a Jungian psychologist, practiced in Southern California. In time, he went into analysis with Sanford. "I needed some kind of teaching and far beyond that, I needed some help with my disordered state, my painwracked body and my painwracked mind," he recalled, but before he could act on this first glimpse of the truth about what had happened to him, the inner voice of the Christ became insistent that he go to Brazil and help a young man. Where in Brazil or who he was to help, the voice would not say.

"Then, the Christ disappeared from my inner view and did not return for days and days. Nonetheless, I felt I was under his guidance to go to Brazil."

He Who Sleeps left for Brazil in September 1980, as planned. Synchronicities provided him with a destination in Sao Paolo suggested by his broker. On arrival he bought a small English/Portuguese dictionary and walked down the busy street near the Hilton Hotel. He felt guided to a church where he saw a man with his head in his hands.

"Christ then reappeared—I saw him visually and heard his voice—and he told me this was the young man I was there to help. His name was Jair. We ended up going to his hometown of A Rancheria in the interior, a few miles from Paraguay. Jair's father was an alcoholic and very abusive.

"I knew I was supposed to be involved in this situation. My fellowship in Yugoslavia, given by the World Health Organization, established with high statistical accuracy and double-blind studies that alcoholism is set in motion before the age of five, when no one has begun drinking."

During his two weeks in Brazil, He Who Sleeps continued the research he had begun as a student of allopathic medicine by studying family trees of alcoholics.

"I learned that alcoholism also has a spiritual side. The shamanic or mystical side is an additional component to alcoholism. It is a psycho-spiritual disease. There isn't an alcoholic in the world who isn't a gifted healer. One part of their problem is they have abdicated their destiny. People who abdicate their spiritual calling have hell to pay. They can't get through their addiction, their alcoholism, until they heal others. That in itself is essential, and also they must have absolute clarity about what their life has been about. The healing gift in the male is through the anima. In the female it is through the animus. Alcoholism roots in the male's oppressive, destructive, hostile relationship to the feminine. The man cannot get his healing together as long as he maintains his hostile relationship to his anima. He has to go back and renegotiate this relationship with the inner feminine.

"My two weeks in Brazil were the beginning of my introduction into shamanic healing. Lines and lines of people came to me to be healed. Jair was my assistant. He talked to me in Portuguese, and I got so I could understand some of it. With his help, I healed several hundred people.

"My physical situation had not improved. I was still bleeding from my rear end, had not slept in years, and while in Brazil I developed pneumonia in both lungs. I ran high fevers to chills, and I coughed up blood. The pneumonia improved somewhat, and I did not want it to interfere with the healing.

"We were doing wonderful work in Brazil on that first trip. There were long lines of people waiting, and one of them was a woman who brought me her ten-year-old severely retarded daughter. I was totally wiped out, still coughing up blood, with a very high fever; but I put my hands on her head for ten minutes and said my Catholic prayers. In 1984, on my fifth trip into Brazil, when I returned to that community, a 14 year old girl came up and introduced herself. She told me a story I couldn't believe. She was the mentally retarded girl. She had been a straight-A student since I worked with her. The school had not seen such an artistically talented student before.

"I have had Christ as my guide since 1980 when I had my Mother Bird of Prey Experience. He has taken me on thousands of journeys to look at people's bodies and into the way they think and at their mental aberrations. He tells me why the person's life has come to this certain point. He says, 'Here is where you place your hands.' At first, I didn't know anything about healing. Someone would come to me and Christ would tell me to put my hands in this particular position on this body. If I said, 'What's going to go on tomorrow?' he would say, 'You're going to see 11 people. The first one is 12 years old with this problem. You will put your hands here.'"

At the end of the day the apprentices would be astounded that it had worked out exactly as predicted.

Under the inner guidance of Christ, who is the outstanding model of the Wounded Healer, He Who Sleeps has been instrumental in the healing of a paralyzed man and of a deaf-mute who lost his ability to hear and speak at 13 months of age from encephalitis. He has brought a 95-year-old man with Parkinson's disease back to self-control and energetic life. At great risk to himself—under the guidance of his inner voice and under the fear of a vision that his daughter's life was in danger if he refused—he adopted into his home a severely demented Brazilian youth of Italian extraction named Ricardo. To cure him he undertook a four-day exorcism, a rite he had only read about in a Catholic church pamphlet. After the ordeal, He Who Sleeps took his ward to the monastery, and the priest pronounced that Ricardo was free of possession.

The task of healing was not yet complete, however, so when He Who Sleeps moved to San Diego to go into analysis, he took Ricardo with him and continued his focused healing effort. Ricardo returned to Brazil healthy in mind after two and a half years, and he became a successful business man.

After Ricardo left, He Who Sleeps moved to a beach in Baja California where he withdrew to confront the deepest wound in his nature. His mother's abusive treatment of him for thirteen years had caused a deep conflict with his own anima. Through meditation and prayer, he hoped to heal this wound in himself. As a shaman, his way to accomplish this was, in part, to heal others. Word got around that he was a healer and many people came to him.

He still could not sleep. Rather than waste these hours he had the habit of saying Catholic prayers, particularly the Hail Mary, for other people. In Mexico he walked the beach through the night, saying the rosary and invoking the power of hundreds of thousands of prayers.

"A prayer," he said, "has its own consciousness. Prayers are like a living entity, a living form. If you engage it, it will teach you. Prayers heal whoever is saying them and they unfold us. To the extent that we invest in prayer, we can facilitate the unfolding process." He compares the investment in prayer to a bank account. The more investment there is, the more power to draw upon in need. "In Mexico droves of kids waited for me to come outside because when they touched my rosary they would see auras. They noticed that their bodies vibrated." Other sensitive people sometimes see angels hovering near He Who Sleeps. He sees them himself, and he believes that the power of continuous prayer congregates the angels.

The shaman had a crisis in his prayer life when the Divine Mother came to him in a vision and said it was time to let go of Catholic prayers. "I had no other prayers for my meditation and healing work. So I was suddenly gutted. I came to understand that I was being asked to let go of that which is separating and dividing."

Through experience he found Catholic prayers are best said for healing those parts of himself still in opposition and conflict. When healing others with similar conflicts, he continues to say the Hail Mary, which is a prayer based on the concept of an "I" and a "Thou," a Self and Non-self.

For those areas of himself and others that are integrated and in balance, a unifying prayer seems to be most effective. He knows clairvoyantly and clairaudiently, with the gift of the horse he received so long ago, which prayers he should say silently for any person he is healing. He particularly favors this Buddhist prayer that sits on his desk:

The Four Great Vows
All Beings without number, I vow to liberate.
Endless blind passions, I vow to uproot.
Dharma gates beyond measure, I vow to penetrate.
The Great Way of Buddha, I vow to attain.

In 1984 the shaman drove from Mexico to Ojai, California, to attend an international gathering of shamans, Awakening the Dream, the Way of the Warrior. During the month he was there, he received his name from the medicine man Swift Deer. On the night of a full moon, he was called to help control a well-known man who was in an alcoholic rage, spewing venom and attacking another man. He Who Sleeps conducted a four-hour exorcism on this deranged person. He lay down beside him and focused his energy completely as witnesses observed with their own shamanic vision a continuous long, black snake emerging from the man's mouth. The man was cured of the root cause of his alcoholism.

A few days later the shaman was meditating within a Medicine Wheel laid out facing magnetic west, when he had a vision of an ancient Native American woman. She brought him a message, saying that the Christ was assigning him to the guidance of the Great Mother. Symbolically, this meant to him that he had balanced his anima and animus and was no longer in conflict with his inner feminine spirit.

The Great Mother made two immediate demands upon him. He was to return as soon as possible to Brazil where he was to confront the darkness of voodoo. She could not guarantee he would live through the test. "I realized that it did not matter if I lived or died. What mattered was that I engaged the process." He survived an attempt on his life in Brazil and stayed on many days longer to heal those who came to him, having numerous miraculous results. It was his last trip to Brazil.

Then the Great Mother said, "My son, be the Christ." This second demand was far harder for him to accept because it aroused his unassuaged doubts about the nature of spiritual healing, and it caused him to again question his own sanity. He had seen deranged people in mental institutions who believed they are the incarnation of Christ, and he rejected the thought of embodying the Son of God.

Months later a plebeian episode resolved the injunction to "Be the Christ." Someone he knew bought a healing crystal he craved but could not afford. He became outraged, furious and jealous.

"I was at the highest level of ego inflation, which hid the deepest ego devaluation I still had underneath. This whole incident had been an invitation to that area of my woundedness. I came upon a wonderful teaching:

"Christ's life is a give-away. If you are the Christ, you give that (life) away. And, then, you aren't (the Christ). If you have to hold on (as in attachment) you can't be the Christ anyway."

He Who Sleeps has shared this teaching with others in his lectures and individual counseling, and it has helped them to integrate their misunderstood ego inflation as it did his. To be the Christ is to surmount ego. This is not only the shaman's task: it applies to everyone.

In 1985, after the Great Mother took over as his inner guide, she in turn assigned the shaman to the Father God. "That was one of the most painful experiences I have had, because I had no basis to connect with him. Then I remembered a prayer a Jewish mystic taught me to call Father God to council. I experienced the Father God as formlessness, but with enormous love and understanding, the depths of which I couldn't even begin to describe."

Wherever he goes, He Who Sleeps is sensitive to the embodiment of the God-consciousness in that culture. In India and Bali he recognized the spirit of Vishnu and Shiva. His guides, he says, are "like stepping stones." He thinks everyone has them. The Christ represents the Wounded Healer. The Great Mother presides over magic and manifest reality. "When a certain critical threshold has been reached, she sends the person on to the Father God." At that point, the individual has integrated the unconsciousness with consciousness. He Who Sleeps said this happened to him when he came into relationship "with my essential beingness." The goal is to know and confront the mind, allowing it to yield its pain.

He Who Sleeps is a shaman in process. Revelations are coming to him with increasing frequency. Over and over in the course of his journey, he has been denied help from those who, it appeared, could explain his path to him. Finally, he says he accepts that "I am a wounded healer who is supposed to heal himself."

I asked He Who Sleeps, "What are the conditions for healing?"
He replied:

"Everybody here is magical. Everybody here is a soul essence who comes into the earth plane for a variety of experiences to age the soul. The connection with the spiritual aspect of ourselves is often through pain that occurs in the early stages of our life when we are working on our ego structures and are ill-equipped to deal with it in any kind of meaningful or transforming way.

"We avoid our pain by moving more and more into the physical, tangible world. At some point we need to reconnect with the spiritual aspect of ourselves. We do that through our wounds. There is only one gateway into eternity and the light—this is through our woundedness, into our deepest humanity. When wounds are so painful, people are extremely reluctant to ever engage them again. Through disconnection, they manifest things like diseases, hate systems, destructive behavior and disordered minds.

"When they decide to reconnect with their essential beingness, their true nature, they will open the door to the old wound, explore it and heal it, which releases the spiritual essence, reconnects it to the normal side of beingness and opens the doorway to transformation, including healing and wholeness."

I then asked, "What is the role of the healer in this process?" He Who Sleeps differentiated the healer's role depending upon the state of the person who needs healing. "If the person is in a space where it's not their function in this particular lifetime to unfold themselves and transform the wound—which is the beast in its untransformed state—to its magical beauty in its fully transformed state, the healer functions by simply laying on his hands; and the disease disappears."

In the opposite case, when the person's destiny is to realign with his or her essence, the shaman aligns with that essence, assuming its vibrational level, and deposits within the client's mind the needs of that essence. "Then miracles occur in a moment. It is said, all disease is alienation from God. All healing takes place when this alienation is corrected."

Albuquerque artist Cynthia Ploski, after two healing sessions with He Who Sleeps, had an insight while reading *Guilt Is the Teacher, Love Is the Lesson* by Joan Borysenko. The author reminds her reader that the word compassion means "to suffer with" (p. 95-96) and says that compassion builds an interpersonal bridge between the temporal and spiritual planes. Ploski believes that He Who Sleeps effectively lowers the barriers in the client's consciousness and opens a channel of divinity. My healing sessions with him have given me an uplift of spiritual energy, so I think Ploski's intuition is correct.

The shaman-healer makes a gift of his own spiritual strength to empower the client's efforts to realign with God and to heal. The shaman begins a transformational process for the client through his gifts of clairaudience and clairvoyance. The client receives the insight needed to bring into consciousness formerly hidden wounds and to continue the process of self-transformation.

He Who Sleeps finds that people in Third World countries "function largely under the base sacral chakra, which has to do with relationships and sexuality." In the United States, family structure is usually less binding; and a person is expected to individuate.

"If I want to see a miracle in Brazil, I work with one patient. But up here in the United States, I have to grind out a miracle. Why is that? We've sold all the true spirituality off. When a child is little, churches don't go into all the things that are gray; they say this is right, this is wrong. This is black. This is white. They polarize. Polarization is created out of conflict. That is a vital part of one's unfolding, but it is for kindergartners. I don't mean to be pejorative, but the truth is churches carry duality.

"It is time for the people in this country to come from the heart chakra. [To help people come from the heart chakra] . . . the shaman has to see their uniqueness, the special fabric which is theirs. Where that uniqueness is not being honored or they are out of alignment with that uniqueness, the shaman can hone in on it and dialog with the person in such a way that she or he can realign with it. Then you can find a miracle as often as you can find them in Brazil. In Brazil the people's sacral chakra is organized. It's so powerful, it aligns all their other chakras. Disease just goes away. The sacral is the second chakra, about the third lumbar vertebra. In this country, we have to come from the fourth chakra, the heart chakra."

He Who Sleeps said he had felt the opening of his heart chakra only a few months before. I asked how he knew it was open, and he said when it happens you feel it. The heart chakra, I had thought, represents compassion and unconditional love. The shaman said, "You can have love that is emptied of all conditions, but you will not have unconditional love. Unconditional love is a phenomenon that happens out of the divine energies. A gateway opens and you experience what unconditional love is; and it has absolutely nothing to do with conditional love emptied of all conditions." All of a sudden, he said, a vertical something happens upon that structure. And that is the mysterious opening of the heart chakra, which is the challenge Americans now face.

Step by step He Who Sleeps has followed his shamanic path and deepened his ability to heal. While living in Baja California, he underwent for the first time autonomous movement of his hands, which assumed contorted positions beyond his will in their placement on a client's head. He regretted that he had not been able to photograph these extraordinary positions until it came to him that he does not "own" what he does during a healing process. No two healings are alike. He is required to let go of all understanding and simply trust that he will be led to the best actions for his purpose.

He Who Sleeps makes an effort to be completely open to the suggestions that he still receives through his inner guidance. An extreme result of this effort happened in 1990. He had been working with a woman who was severely deformed by arthritis. He then left for a long anticipated trip to Bali. After arriving and while in his hotel room, he was unable to control his body for seven hours as it went into contorted actions, totally autonomously.

"In a shamanic trance state, I went back in her beingness to the Age of the Reptiles and found the disease rooted there." He became reptilian—a lizard living during the primordial Age of the Reptiles. Psychologically it terrified him, but he found in the distant reptilian age the origin of a deposit in the genetic lineage of his client that manifested as arthritis. In his lizard state, he ate the flesh of his patient. In ordinary reality, the memory of it made him sick. The experience was so devastating he could not sight-see or visit the shrines on the island as planned. In fact, he stayed in his hotel room until it was time to leave.

"I arrived back here and a few days later she came for her appointment. She got on the table, and I ran my hand up and down her spine. It was straight. She said it didn't feel so twisted anymore. Her Feldenkreis therapist, at my request, looked at and commented on her spine. The therapist said there had been 'remarkable reduction in the curvature of the spine. The scoliosis was gone.'"

In ensuing weeks, the curvature of his client's spine continued improving. The shaman said it took a long time for her to get rid of her frozen fear. "She had suffered from so much emotional pain that she froze up her whole being." She had idealized her family as loving, but, in truth, her parents were not supportive. He says that often emotional pain helps create physical disease.

In his trance state He Who Sleeps has become reptilian in other instances. In this condition he actually sees his own limbs as if they were those of a lizard. "It is in the reptilian aspect of our beingness that we have the greatest level of magic for transformation of our vehicles at all levels," he said cryptically.

One of the last cases He Who Sleeps shared with me dealt with a psychotic woman who has had bouts of anorexia, bulimia and nervous breakdowns. By letting go of all understanding and simply accepting whatever his inner voice told him to do during a session with her, he found that he began taking on the behavior he remembered from his own psychotic episodes.

"If you present something to someone who is at risk for a psychotic break, something that will make the person become conscious, you can almost see the person fold in like a flower. These people will suck themselves right back into the collective unconscious. They implode. It is a tangible, palpable thing. When this woman was here for a session, all of a sudden I experienced that I was folding back in, as though I were undergoing a precipitation to psychosis. I watched her, seeing that she was now free to allow the new material into her consciousness without regression into the psychotic state. She was dealing with the content that was surfacing. I kept saying to myself—over and over—surrender, surrender for protection. She accessed data from her early childhood that had resisted all other kinds of therapy. She said it was the most transforming event in her life. That was a turnaround for me. I understood the reason I went through psychotic episodes myself, so as I walk through that space in someone else and carry a part for them, they are free to lift forward into consciousness, to heal and grow. She was able to get into the pain of incest when she was three years old and to deal with it. That's the magic of my taking this on."

His own experience with psychosis has also made He Who Sleeps sensitive to the plight of the schizophrenic. He believes if schizophrenics are assisted through their initial psychotic break without drugs, it will allow their chaos to heal them. Some of them will be our most gifted mystics, artists and inventors, because they have this potential. Once the psychotic is drugged, however, he is locked into that portion of his dislocation and it becomes harder for him to recover. In the shaman's understanding, the schizophrenic break is of a spiritual nature; it is a searching for God.

As a prophet He Who Sleeps says:

"We are moving like an aggregate psyche from the solar-plexus chakra issues to heart issues. One of the difficulties in our particular culture is that we are front-runners or explorers in this movement. Heart issues speak of balance and the uniqueness of soul in each individual. The heart chakra has been terribly damaged by the patriarchy that has oppressed women for at least 2500 years. It is the space of the Christ, the wounded healer."

He believes we are already prepared for this transition.

"We all carry the totality of all vibrations from the densest or lowest frequency to the highest and all in between. Each particular vibration has within it a facility, a readiness, a capacity to understand that which cannot be understood at another level.

"You've signed up for an inner university. That university may include severely abusive parents or reasonably healthy parents; either way, there is a beauty and a beast side to everything. The impaction or imposition upon your life of a negative experience has as its primary contention to allow a beauty to come forth. Your challenge is to take the beast and transform it, releasing the treasure. You can put a seed on the finest Italian marble, leave it sitting for centuries; and it will never flower. It flowers if you put it in horse shit. The goal is in the dung. I've never seen a life experience so devastatingly destructive that the person could not reframe it; that is, extract its beauty.

"This whole transit we call a life is actually a delivery from a birth canal. Everything around us creates the birth canal which we are transiting from the time we leave the mortal womb, which is our entry into life's birth canal. Imposing, modifying, constricting or opening, everything helps to color the kinds of experiences that will unfold for the soul's requirements."

We spoke for a while about the role of darkness in our transit through this life. The area of New Mexico in which I live is a natural attraction to New Agers who move to the state in their search for "light." He Who Sleeps made an astute observation when he pointed out that the state's crime rates have risen and the crimes reported are now more violent than ever. What is true locally is also true on the national level. Crimes are more outrageous; films and television are more violent. New Age seekers, He Who Sleeps explained to me, have reached high levels of light vibration but they are refusing to deal with their own darkness. Reaching unbalanced lightness through all manner of meditative rituals and spiritual practice without recognition of our own dark shadow creates a vacuum. Nature compensates always for anything that is out of balance, hence the highly visible increase in dark forces. He Who Sleeps suggests that it is our own judgment that labels something "dark" and we will solve many of our problems of balance when we claim all of ourselves without judgment.

The call to shamanism and subsequent journeys have healed aspects of his own woundedness, opening him to higher vibrations of understanding. In the decade of service and self-discovery since his initiation, He Who Sleeps has discovered new shamanic teachings, the beauty he calls Golden Nuggets. Here are some of them:

Let go of all teachings when they are no longer appropriate.
Be flexible.
Honor what you believe to be true.
Be who you are.

"I think one of the functions I serve here in terms of shamanic hope is to help people find the courage within themselves to progressively become more of whoever it is they are at any given moment. They will come more and more into their essential beingness."

In these last years He Who Sleeps has done thousands of healing sessions long distance. By word of mouth, people from 25 states and 23 foreign countries have found him and come to him for healing sessions. He is healthier and now sleeps several hours a night, which is enough to give him rest. He is no longer thin. He lives in solitude, but not loneliness, accompanied by his cats. His own pains of psyche and body have lessened, and they have never interfered with his shamanic vocation. On the contrary, his woundedness and his vocation are as one. As he heals others, he furthers his own healing.

An air of sweetness surrounds this man as he focuses his trance-state totally on behalf of the person in his care. Nothing threatening occurs under his protection. Instead, he affects a vital transformation in his client. A woman who is a therapist in her own right told him she had found no "fatiguing of her unfolding" since her sessions with him several years ago. The same is true for me.

He Who Sleeps believes he has been called to be a "Healer of Healers." The vast majority of people who are drawn to him, he finds, have the gift of healing in themselves. Each person who benefits from the shaman's gift for healing, in turn, receives not only the strength to pursue self-healing but also a shamanic ability to serve others.

"Shamans are different from medicine men and analysts. Analysts help bring the eruption into consciousness of symbols in the person being analyzed. Medicine men help bring a new order into a person's beingness by using symbols given to their tribe years before. The shaman contains and is a living symbol. My symbol was given to me by the Great Mother. The image is an extended ankh above a symbol of infinity. It means: To Bring the Will of God to Man to Make Men Whole."

*S*everal people mentioned

Mary-Margaret Moore to me, describing her as a channel

for an entity called Bartholomew, or Bart. Each month she drove from Taos to

Albuquerque to speak to people gathered in a high school auditorium, eager to hear her.

I attended for the first time on November 24, 1985. I had heard a spiritual message

without internal arguments, not a single one. I had found a voice to speak to my inner

voice. Bart's words felt like water on a parched desert, a balm, soothing and encouraging.

They seemed to be coming from a source of truth that felt convincing and harmonious

with my own thinking. The auditorium was filled with people of all ages, some I

recognized. I felt these were people with whom I had a common interest.

I HAVE NOW HEARD Mary-Margaret channel Bart many times *and, in the event I miss her "Sharing" in Albuquerque, I order a tape instead. Mary-Margaret provides a spiritual overview of current events and gives practical advice to those who hear her speak, go on tours with her, attend her workshops and seek her counsel. I feel a compassionate friendship for her, and I respect the dignity and courage she displays as an intellectual, creative and committed person. She has been the source of four books of Bart's messages that digest practical wisdom in pithy selections:* I Come as a Brother, From the Heart of a Gentle Brother, Reflections of an Elder Brother *and* Planetary Brother. *These well-designed, useful books are the work of Mary-Margaret's friend, artist and editor Joy Franklin, of High Mesa Press in Taos.*

Mary-Margaret's most lasting impression on my spiritual growth has come from watching her Bart energy undergo its own transformation into an ever wider field of vision. The emphasis of their message has changed from helping others reach their inner light to challenging people to encounter their fears, look into their shadows and find God in everything, not just in the light but also in the deepest unknown terror. In her own process of change, Mary-Margaret has undertaken an increasingly shamanic role as a giver of wisdom, a teacher whose words can lead to a balancing of polarities and to self-healing.

MARY-MARGARET MOORE: WELCOMING BARTHOLOMEW

Mary-Margaret Moore is a Goddess-woman: female, maternal, tall and full-bodied, with blonde-brown luxuriant hair and fair skin. Her voice has pleasant vibrations. Her humor and laughter bubble up easily, lighting her pretty face. Wearing soft clothes that drape around her, she sits comfortably on a cushion between her husband Justin Moore at her left and her colleague Joy Franklin who is manning the tape machines on her right.

Over time, as the energy fields of the entity Bartholomew and Mary-Margaret have melded, she has gained in authority and confidence. Bart cautions the audience to be responsible listeners, not to consider the information one hundred percent correct, but to determine their own truth. Over the years I have gathered these quotes of Bart's:

"There is only one message. Be masters of your own destiny. No one can do it for you. Be serious. Unbury the true self. Ask yourself, what skills are yours. Each of you is wondrously, beautifully unique. Over lifetimes, you have accumulated skills and knowledge, but you've forgotten them. When you've found what you need, quit coming."

Someone asked, "What are the rules or standards to live by?" The answer was, there are none.

"From the time the Self came first to Earth, the Deep Self began recording, assessing, eliminating, cherishing. The only things retained are what your soul knows are in line with Divine love and natural law. No exterior rule is needed. Pay attention. You are running so fast you can't hear God when he yells at you. Have the courage to do strange and wonderful things. Adopt the warrior stance. Trust that your inspiration and strength come from inside.

"People are energy vortexes, undulating energy fields of color and power. You don't need an outside source for information about yourself. Take six hours and listen to your thoughts. Your job is simple, go within and when you feel the total integrity of your being, stay there as long and as often as you can. Move from that point of grounded power. You can deal with anything if you are grounded."

In the spring of 1986, I was responsible for the care of my mother, whose mind had been failing in a seemingly healthy body since my father's death in 1982. I was coping with despair when I went to Taos to interview Mary-Margaret.

Mary-Margaret's own mother was ill, and we both were questioning life and reviewing old memories. Some of her answers were as melancholy as I felt; but time passed, anxieties ended, and neither of us remained locked in our worries. Mary-Margaret, like Bart's listeners, is on a quest for spiritual certitude. Paradoxically, she, the channel, is also the student. Watching her unfoldment as Mary-Margaret confirms Bart the teacher.

Soon after Bart's arrival in her consciousness, he directed Mary-Margaret and her husband to live in Taos and open either a school or a press. They started Vista Grande, a private preparatory school. Justin was the principal and Mary-Margaret taught for a number of years. Their colleague Joy Franklin founded High Mesa Press eight years later. Due to the pressures of Mary-Margaret's work with the Bart energy, the Moores have turned the operation of the school over to others.

In every aspect of her life that I have witnessed, Mary-Margaret is creative. She writes frequently and is a striving painter. As we talked, I felt the same stirrings of curiosity about her breakthrough to channeling that I feel when I interview artists. I wanted to know where she came from, how she was educated and how she expanded her spiritual knowledge.

Mary-Margaret Moore was born in San Francisco and raised in a family of comfortable means on the island of Lanai in Hawaii. Her father managed the whole island for the Dole Pineapple Company. He evenhandedly respected all the religions of those Islanders in his charge. Mary-Margaret went with him to each of the island's churches, including the Roman Catholic, Buddhist, Four Square Gospel and Hawaiian Congregationalist. She also learned something about the ancient Kahuna tradition of wisdom from the native people. This brief exposure to religions did not answer Mary-Margaret's many questions about mortality. Mary-Margaret was faced with the finality of death when several siblings died at birth and her brother died in childhood. Her parents did not talk about these deaths.

Walking along the lanes among the pineapple fields, the child Mary-Margaret yearned to experience God and she began searching for him. At age 13 she was sent to a boarding school on Oahu where she was required to attend religious services of her choice. She picked the nearest church, which happened to be Congregational. "I decided to take this God-offering seriously and to be confirmed. The minister said that the day I became a member would be my special day. I remember feeling that God was going to present Himself to me in some way, and I was excited by the proposition. I thought there would be something magical. But nothing happened."

After she had earned bachelor's and master's degrees from Stanford, was married and had two children, she lived in San Bruno, California. John Powell, an Episcopal priest, became for a time her spiritual teacher. He brought her books and answered her questions every week, but knowing her history he advised her not to attend church. She did so anyway and once again was disappointed. "I kept thinking there had to be more to God than Jesus, as beautiful as He was. Because, you see, I had been raised with the Buddha, the spirit of the Kahunas and the openness of the vast Pacific. To me, God could clearly not be limited to Christianity."

The family moved to Southern California where Mary-Margaret discovered the writing and the shrine of the late Yogananda. While practicing meditation in keeping with his teaching, she sometimes had a spiritual vision of a gold and white Being—the room would fill with the odor of roses—but this wondrous presence was not always available to her. Instinctively, she knew that she still had to search for a dependable access to God. "I had the idea that if I wanted God and He wanted me, it couldn't be this hard. If God wants us, it should not require special postures and exercises!" She began investigating Zen Buddhism with a Roshi in Gardena and found an affinity with this intellectual, nondemanding path.

In the midst of her on-going internal quandary, Mary-Margaret's marriage collapsed. She had to decide how and where to raise her three children, and she had to cope with her disappointment, grief and confusion. She moved to Santa Barbara with her children and slowly recovered from the trauma of divorce by practicing Zen meditation on a little stool in her garden. To her deep solace, she again envisioned the Golden Being. In the writing of Zen patriarchs she read, "If you will still yourself sufficiently, you will experience True Mind." Mary-Margaret explained, "Something now had shifted in my life. As the masters put it, 'There is a blind Buddha in your hara (abdomen). Make him see.' Now that, for some reason, I could understand."

The shadow on her life lifted. In 1969, she married Justin Moore—also a spiritual seeker—and the family moved to Greece where they lived for a year. Just after their daughter Justine was born, they moved to Santa Fe, New Mexico. A few years later, Mary-

Margaret, at 46, sought help for her painful back problems and depression from two retired physicians, her longtime friends Drs. John and Louisa Aiken. John Aiken was a spiritual explorer who had guided Mary-Margaret to *The Course in Miracles* and the books by Jane Roberts, who channeled Seth. She trusted him completely and she asked him to hypnotize her in hopes he could find a cause for her troubles.

The day was December 3, 1977. Mary-Margaret has described what occurred: "[John] started with a mental suggestion: Go down the hallway and open a door. So I did, and I opened the door and started into this past life, and Bong! there's a total other feeling that comes over me. And what we've come to call Bartholomew started talking to John."

In 1985, Mary-Margaret wrote:

"Apparently, something unusual happened, about which I heard when I returned to my usual consciousness . . . The voice speaking was mine, but the 'energy' seemed much more than mine. Speaking to the doctor, it (?), he (?), said, 'We have been working with this woman for a long time, and we are glad to have this opportunity to speak to her more directly, through you. With regard to her (back) problems, will you please tell her . . . ' and some very helpful suggestions were made. Then this Energy asked the doctor if he had any questions, which he did, and they were well answered."

Aiken had conducted research in metaphysics for over 60 years. He did not channel, but his intuition was of the highest order and he was respectful of many gifted psychics. He knew the late medium Arthur Ford and the contemporary sensitives Brenda Crenshaw, Ruth Montgomery and Jeanne Dixon. He told me that these were all sincere people and that he never found charlatanism among them, although he thought they had varied levels of talent. On the basis of his experience, he was astounded at the quality of information Mary-Margaret brought through.

Aiken helped Mary-Margaret understand the importance of her breakthrough in consciousness. Despite her misgivings, he encouraged her to continue contacting the Bartholomew energy. In 1985, he taped an interview with her, in which he said he had pushed her. Mary-Margaret verified, "Yes, absolutely. A few weeks later you came to Santa Fe and asked to do another session . . . I recall that you had asked Bartholomew whether we would be able to contact him again, and he had said yes."

Mary-Margaret said that her opening to channeling was a torment to her. "I went through Hell trying to decide whether or not to continue working with this energy. What I thought about was Zen. The highest I had known in my spiritual search was Zen, and I wanted to be as Zen-like as I could. This was not Zen-like . . . The reason that I proceeded with it was the feeling of rightness. It just felt wise, large, safe, deep, clear."

Followers of Bart are curious about who or what he or it is. In *I Come as a Brother*,

Mary-Margaret said: "It is a part of me, but greater than me, or who I now believe myself to be. It is energy—this I absolutely know . . . This energy has a vast range of perception. Past and future are bridged with ease, and grace, and accuracy . . . The energy has a spiritual flavor, rather than a karmic one."

In 1978, Mary-Margaret wrote: "I had come to a crucial point in the life of the Spirit. Bartholomew's coming into my life has produced great turmoil and difficulty at times, alternating with feelings of great gratitude for what he has done for me, for my family, and for others . . . I knew within my own Being that he was a true Spirit of the One God."

Bart's energy manifests for Mary-Margaret as a field of dancing light. She said:

"I have seen . . . that what is said is not important; it is not the words that they [the listeners] are absorbing. The changes are taking place because of their own energies, plus what Bart brings in, which brings a new vibration to their bodies, a whole cellular reaction; the cells begin to sing a little louder, with a little more volume . . . Over the years, the words are the same, and so why do so many beautiful people keep coming back? They get a 'shot in the arm,' a new jolt. This I see as moving energy . . . "

In response to many questions, Bart made it clear that he has come to help people find out who they are and to point their way home. I believe he does a lot more than that. Hundreds of audio tapes, compiled by John Aiken, are on subjects as far-ranging as any philosopher has dealt with, among them: *The Way of the Christ, Moving From Ego to the Divine Mind, What Is It?, Meditation: Goals and Techniques, The One Mind, The Illusion, Emptiness and Grace, Seven Bodies of Man, Functions of Teachers, Western Attitudes Toward Death* and *Humor on the Path*.

Bart, through Mary-Margaret, has channeled a cosmology related to the purpose of a single soul incarnated on earth. He describes himself as an Elder Brother and he insists that there are Elder Brothers and Sisters for everyone. Each of us can call on them by simply asking them for help.

Whatever Mary-Margaret says for Bart, I always derive strength of mind and spiritual energy from it for the month that lies ahead. The dominant idea she conveys is affirmation. Bart affirms human power and worth. He says, "You are looking for a Savior, and you already have one. It is you."

The cosmos Bart pictures is one of dynamic, thoroughly connected energies. The process of coming to life, dying and being born again is integral to the cosmos. Prior to life, in this concept, a soul creates its own blueprint for the energies it will include in its next "sphere of consciousness." The soul is on an evolutionary journey. Though it animates a body, the soul's true nature is a vast energy field, connected to vibrational levels far higher than the earth's. The purpose of a person's life is to penetrate the density of the earth plane and awaken to one's Higher Self or God-consciousness. Bart helps in the awakening by reminding individuals, through Mary-Margaret and their own inner Beings, that they are already enlightened. Earth is a valuable experience because it provides a challenge to the soul. Vicariously, through his creation, God savors human emotions, particularly delight, laughter and joy. Every individual contributes to God's enjoyment. A primary aspect of this worldview is that each human being is a part of God and a responsible cocreator of this universe. The God-Self is infinitely expandable, and includes All.

I have distilled five central categories from Bart's ideas: Cosmos, You, Guilt/Fear, God, and Be Still.

The Cosmos:

"Creation is expanding and explosive. People are energy vortexes, undulating fields of color, constantly in motion, moving as a unit. They have chosen to inhabit small bodies, but they are not just bodies. A person is a spherical consciousness, not linear, and is porous to information that flows through that sphere. Each person has a number of bodies, or levels of consciousness, encircling the physical one. These are the emotional, the mental, the astral (which connects with the angels, devas and so on), the spiritual (which is far higher in awareness) and upward into the levels of cosmic consciousness or God-consciousness. Great power fields—Christ, Buddha, all Gods and Goddesses—contain knowledge of how to expand awareness. The Comforter is a pattern of energy around the world which contains the Christ energy, as well as these others."

You:

"You have an electromagnet in your cellular field that connects to the power of The Comforter. Energy follows thought. You get what you ask for, so watch your thoughts. What you dwell on will show up in your future. You have integrity. You have an inner Miracle Worker. You have the ability to raise the frequency of the planet, to know who you are, to bring Divine energy down, to be the receiver. You can make a difference. Create a vision of yourself as radiant, magnificent, expanding, alive energy arising out of the deepest part of the heart of God and moving through time and space. You are dynamic energy. The shapechanger is you. You created separation, but it doesn't work. You act as a mirror for others. You can extend your awareness to caress another. You are responsible for envisioning that which you wish to manifest for others as well as yourself. You must serve yourself to find the light. You are all artists of the soul. You are part of the Whole. It is the destiny of each of you to know. Feel your strength inside you coming to you from your God-Self. You are perfect just as you are because 'God don't make no junk.' Within you, there is a place of perfection that cannot be polluted. You are pure. Every action you perform is a blend of God and you."

Guilt/Fear:

"Nowhere is there a God such as you describe. Religious rules can make you afraid of God. More rules, more guilt. Get rid of religious beliefs that hold you back. You have believed lies about how sinful and evil you are. Churches cut you off from the physical. Guilt kills the joy of your being. Your guilt always chooses against you. Guilt is not working. Karma is not a useful idea if it's a vise around your neck to recall old errors. Jesus changed the old law of Karma instantly at his death. Depression is a low-grade spiritual experience and fear is a higher grade of spiritual experience. Fear attracts the forces of nature (floods, volcanoes, fires, etc.) and the societies that attract these things are troubled societies, wracked by fear. Fear is not permanent."

God:

"God feels good. God needs human joy and laughter. Walk as if you were in bliss. Bliss comes from remembering what gives you bliss. Nothing outside of yourself can make you happy. After this life, you will only remember what moved you, what you loved. The only gift the other side of this manifestation can give you is to keep reminding you that you have available, with little effort, the knowledge that you are light, peace, joy—a part of the whole. Love is the only healer. 'All beings are Buddha. All sounds are mantra.' The Divine within you is dynamic, helpful and listening. Christ has given us love and Buddha has given us mind as openings to the Divine. You are God meeting God. Love runs the universe and it is stronger than your blocks. When you work for God, you work for yourself. How you create your world is not God's business. God allows you to create your own world as you wish, but the Divine power has placed limits beyond which the human mind cannot go. Unless you stay in the moment, you are creating out of the shadow part of your consciousness.

Nowhere is there more God in you than now. There is no more God anywhere else than here. What you are looking for is already here."

Be still:

"Go within and stay there. 'Be still and know that you are God.' Listen as often as you can. The Messenger comes. Practice receiving, not just giving. If you do all the nurturing, you won't get any. Prayer and remembering are practicing the experience of God. Listen to music. Do yoga. You have a Listener in you. Pay attention to how you feel. Be so aware of each moment that your decisions give out a signal. Live in awareness of inner transcendent power giving you a signal. Watch for God-consciousness in as many moments of a day as possible. Be your own shaman. Spiritual Warriors release fear by opening to their feelings. Be a finder, not a seeker. Break out of your isolation."

When I heard that Bart was leading a trip to Hawaii, I joined the tour because Hawaii had two major connections with my life. My father was an army officer stationed in Hawaii on December 7, 1941. I remember in vivid detail standing under the bougainvillea vine over the entry to our quarters at Schofield Barracks, Oahu, watching a small plane less than 100 feet in the air, with a rising sun on its wing. The pilot had probably just finished bombing Wheeler Field, which we could see burning not more than two miles from our house. Wearing a close-fitting leather cap with its strap unhooked, he was headed toward the large concrete barracks at the far end of our street to use up his remaining ammunition. We were evacuated to those barracks eight hours later, long after my father had left for his artillery battalion in the field. My mother, sister, brother and I were evacuated from Hawaii in April 1942 in a convoy, leaving my father behind.

In 1970, on R & R from Vietnam, my husband Ed met me in Honolulu. We went to Kauai. After six months apart, fears subsided and we could enjoy being together for a brief few days. They ended in a sad farewell at the Honolulu Airport. Ed went back to Saigon and the war for another six months. Despite these memories, Hawaii was our Shangri-la, a time out of mind.

When friends and relatives asked why I was going to Hawaii, I said, "to recover my giggle." I had lost it somewhere in the last years of my mother's life. She had died on November 17, 1986, and I was worn out from many unresolved emotions.

A friend and I shared two weeks of beauty and discovery on four islands, Oahu, Maui, Kauai and Hawaii. Every day, Mary-Margaret channeled Bart, but most of the time she was happily revisiting her childhood home. She blossomed on that trip. I too was reconnecting with one of my many childhood homes. For me, two experiences stand out from all the rest.

Thanks to Justin Moore, we took part in a ritualistic release of old spiritual and emotional baggage at the edge of the Kilanea Crater, the live volcano on the big island of Hawaii. That night in the government hotel, I went out on the balcony under the full moon and watched the red glow of lava flashing here and there. It was an uncanny time, spectral and filled with the presence of Pelé, the Goddess of the Volcano. Justin told us to be alone and write down things to eliminate from our lives. And we were to put something personal with the list, perhaps a strand of our hair or a fingernail paring. In the dawn mist we met near the end of the hotel porch. Under some dripping trees at the crater's edge, we chanted and ceremoniously burned our lists. Justin gave us a ti leaf and a cigarette in respect for the Hawaiian's traditional use of tobacco in sacred rituals. We enclosed the cigarette and personal item in the ti leaves, and Justin anointed them with liquor before we hurled them into the crater. The ritual worked for me. I left my sorrows behind in that holy place.

Another event occurred on the Hawaiian tour with Bart that became very important for many of us. On Kauai, our tour group met Dr. Serge King, a master of Huna, the ancient wisdom of Hawaii. Later, I studied with him.

Like many other spiritual teachers, Mary-Margaret has been visiting ancient sacred places around the world. She has led groups to Peru, Egypt, Greece, England, Turkey, Bali, Japan and Australia. She is sensitive to the subtle energies in these places and appears to make a reciprocal exchange with them. Bart reveals information pertinent to the site. Mary-Margaret is part of the reactivation of areas people refer to as the earth's chakras or acupuncture points. With increasing frequency, one hears mention of the correlations between energy vortexes on the human body and sacred sites on the earth. Mary-Margaret ministers to these earth zones.

I am not immune to the attraction of specific sites. They are not all of equal interest to me. For example, I have no enthusiasm for visiting Bali, but I am compelled by Celtic Britain. These magnetic positives and negatives are related, in my mind, to the trigger words we are born with. We have definite relationships, perhaps past or future ones, with certain parts of the world.

Early in 1990, the information Mary-Margaret channeled from Bart underwent a profound change. She/He announced a forthcoming end to sharings. Bart counseled that he had been coming for twelve years. A new cycle was beginning.

As the year unfolded, the message dwelt on the concept that there is only one Source. "That Source must have the same feeling tone to it, regardless of what it is doing. Whether you are feeling anger, lust, fear, discouragement or bliss, it all comes from one Source. You are used to judging. Leave behind the idea of what God is." In a burst of enlightenment, Bart shared the idea that the basic component of DNA is love. It is an energy infusing every cell.

Rather than focus upon the light within, Bart turned his attention to our need to be fully awake and to seek the wisdom of God.

"Let energy run from the heart chakra through the mind. Visualize it. Let judgment soften. Separated judgment will destroy the planet. Try to have a non-judgmental mind, which does not mean you should give up discernment. Claim your pain. Take a stand against fear, but don't deny fear. Part of the reason the world is going mad is so you can feel your bliss. Remember, God wants what has been created. Trust and walk on. This planet and its journey are not a mistake. The beauty is here. The ugliness is also here. It is all God. There is only one Whole. THIS IS IT!"

*O*ne of my first art writing assignments was to do an article about
the artist Peter Rogers. He and his wife Carol Hurd, daughter of
famed artists Henriette Wyeth and Peter Hurd, live on the family's Sentinel
Ranch in the village of San Patricio, New Mexico. Nestled against a hilltop,
the Rogers' two-story adobe house and studio, white with cobalt trim, are
separate from the rest of the family. On the wintry day in 1974 when Ed
and I drove there for my interview, sleet and snow fell all
afternoon while Peter told me his visions. That conversation
was a preview of later ones for this book.

*ROGERS WAS BORN in London on August 24, 1933, following
two older sisters. Aesthetic sensitivity and Christian tradition marked his childhood. His
paternal grandfather was an Anglican priest, but it was his schooling that gave him familiarity
with the Bible. His maternal grandfather, Harry Marillier, was one of William Morris's circle,
and he knew the Pre-Raphaelites. Mementos from that period were in Rogers' boyhood home.
During World War II, his prep school was evacuated to an Elizabethan country house where
he lived among paintings by Rembrandt, Van Dyck and the finest British portraitists. He went
on to Sherborne, a school comparable to an American junior-senior high school plus junior
college, and there he was introduced to classical drawing by a teacher who encouraged him to
take a serious approach to painting.*

*Following graduation at 19, he did his two years of National Service, training with the
Welsh Guards, then serving in Germany as a lieutenant in the Queen's Royal Regiment. After
his discharge in 1954, he enrolled at St. Martin's School of Art in London. He entered the
professional art world in 1956, sustaining himself by painting portraits. His gallery paintings
from this period were figure groups—mostly women—painted in a contemporary version of an
archaic Greek style, reminiscent of early Picasso. Echoes of the archaic remain in his work
today. Rogers was elected to membership in The Royal Society of British Artists in 1958, a
prestigious tribute to his excellent draftsmanship and technical mastery, but he later resigned.
Sometime between school, the army and St. Martin's, when orthodox Christianity lost its hold
on him, he formed the habit of reading widely. He became especially alert to spiritual information.*

PETER ROGERS: THE QUEST

Peter Rogers is a visionary artist. He is best known for his continuously evolving
oeuvre titled *The Quest*. Works in this series form an illustrated narrative in the genre of
John Bunyan's Pilgrim's Progress, and their theme is similarly a search for truth.

Bearded and fit, with a well-bred British accent, Rogers projects a robust masculine
energy and retains the effects of his exposure to military discipline. In appearance and
manner he synthesizes polarities: dreamer and activist, romantic and academic, poetic and
practical, elusive and precise. More than most artists I have met, he has integrated his
feminine anima in himself and his work.

While still in art school, Rogers became engaged to Jenny, a professional ballerina.
He visited her in Monte Carlo where she was dancing in 1956, intending to set a date for
their wedding. Alone in his pension one evening, he had an extrasensory experience, the
first of several that have marked his life. A voice speaking clearly over his right shoulder
said, "Seek first the kingdom of heaven within, and the rest shall be added unto you." He
was unsure what "the kingdom of heaven within" might mean, but this clairaudient message

was so startling he felt he should trust it utterly and await "the rest." Rogers' spiritual quest, which he compares with the "intensely private interior journey" of the early Gnostics, was initiated that night.

Jenny and Peter married in October 1956 and lived for a time in Monaco. In that unlikely setting, he was inspired by photographs of the Shroud of Turin to paint a large *Crucifixion* with a huddled group of soldiers casting lots beneath the cross. Although he had no way of knowing it then, these figures were to become a pivotal means of revelation to him.

In 1958 Peter was living once more in London while the world was allowing Russia to brutally crush the Hungarian Revolution. He became obsessed with painting numerous versions of the three hulking bodies and grotesque faces he originally had done for his *Crucifixion*. These faces, he felt, "certainly evoked evil." He continued to paint variations of the three men, but they were so depressingly negative he asked himself, "What is the opposite of evil?" The obvious answer, an image of good, seemed inadequate. He was still wrangling with this question when he joined Jenny at the Edinburgh Festival where she was dancing.

On that trip Rogers read a book by Krishnamurti. He was drawn to the contention that men are divine beings whose goal is to overcome the illusion of separation and to regain conscious oneness with God. Standing in the corridor of the crowded night train while riding back to London, Rogers again heard a voice speaking to him, saying these Krishnamurtian phrases aloud: "The illusion of separateness" and "The understanding of oneness." A vital connection between these words and his painting was awakened in that moment.

In his studio once again, he painted the three men. This time they were huddled in fright. What had seemed to be evil about them now appeared to be *The Illusion of Separateness*. He then painted three serene women in a seated position facing outward to illustrate *The Understanding of Oneness*. Shortly afterward he read a passage pertaining to the three original Muses in Greek mythology: Meditation, Memory and Song. On reflection, it disappointed him that his painting of the three women seemed to represent the Muses more than it did Oneness.

Rogers did not paint three female seated figures again for 19 years. Nonetheless, he concentrated upon the concept of separation and oneness. In his paintings of the 1970s, Rogers portrayed a group of three males as *The Giants*. Sometimes these symbols of ignorance and fear were transparent, and at other times they were solid and all too real. Until the 1980s, his chosen symbol for oneness was a group of standing figures, usually female, enclosed by sunlight.

Meanwhile, he was inspired by another extrasensory event which he described in our first interview. This central vision has shaped his aesthetic and philosophical preoccupations for thirty years:

One evening in 1960 he attended a concert at the Albert Hall in London. Sitting with his eyes closed, listening to a symphony by Cesar Franck, he suddenly saw a dramatic night scene forming itself behind his eyelids. Coming towards him on the right side was a shining white, youthful female figure. Gazing upward on the left was an awestruck crowd of spectators. Kneeling in the center, an older woman dressed in blue held her arms aloft in supplication. A moment later a brilliant fireball with an extended tail soared in from the upper right.

Rogers said this vision, ". . . was the most powerful experience of my life." He believed he had witnessed the Ascension, although Christ himself had not appeared. He wondered: Was the fireball the Biblical "cloud that received him out of their sight?" How did the young girl fit into that event? The pictorial possibilities of the composition tantalized him and he soon made his first attempt to paint it.

This episode occurred shortly before Rogers was forced to recognize that his marriage was in jeopardy. He wrote of this period, "Partly as a result of the inevitable crisis that ensued and all the unhappiness that went along with it . . . something quite unexpected happened—I gained what was, for me, a new insight into the Christ myth."

Rogers revised a composition of a figure group and characteristically received a fresh understanding through his art. "It struck me that the painting resembled an annunciation of the birth of Christ . . ." Rogers then painted a series based on the *Life of Christ*, including another *Crucifixion*. His formal concern was to create a relationship between a single figure and a group of figures. He chose to paint episodes from Christ's life that lent themselves to such compositions. However, while washing his brushes one day after the series was shown and sold out, Rogers had the sudden realization that the series was autobiographical.

Rogers said, "My painting is always ahead of my understanding. It is a sort of teaching process for myself, a way of spiritual knowledge." He believes he was so lost in his ego's pain, he crucified the Christ in himself and then experienced the resurrection as a healing. In his remarkable book, *The Painter's Quest: Art as a Way of Revelation,* he develops the relationship between his *Life of Christ* series and his spiritual growth.

"I had begun the series when I was feeling sorry for myself. I had been totally involved with my ego, which had been hurt; and I was behaving like the apostles in the boat on the stormy sea, crying out because they thought they were sinking."

Rogers explained that the first image he painted was *Christ Walking on the Water*, followed by eight paintings, equally descriptive of specific states of consciousness that he had gone through while painting this series.

"It seems to me that the Christ myth demonstrates a choice; we can associate with the Christ of our own being and so receive our inheritance as children of God, or we can associate with our ego, or small sense of self, and suffer the consequences."

The break up of his marriage drove Rogers in 1962 to Mojacar, Spain, where he built a home overlooking the sea on land provided by the village. He spent a year there while he reimagined the vision that he still thought of as *The Ascension*. For several months he painted a large version of the scene on his bedroom wall as he contemplated its possible meaning. It was during this time that he came to understand The Christ as "one's own personal channel of awareness."

Rogers met Carol Hurd in Spain and accompanied her in 1963 to New Mexico to meet her family. After settling his affairs in England, he married Carol and adopted her two small children, Pedro and Gabriela. Their son David was born in 1964. He moved into domestic life within the enclave of Sentinel Ranch and paid the bills with commissions for land-scapes, portraits and murals. On other canvasses, he expressed the continuing evolution of his consciousness.

Since 1960 Rogers' basic inspiration has remained rooted in the vision he had at Albert Hall. Reading and concentration have ripened the vision, deepening its connotations.

For example, the fireball in his vision has been substantiated in its physical mass through Immanuel Velikovsky's *Worlds in Collision*. Rogers connected the fireball with Velikovsky's theory that a huge comet came dangerously close to Earth, causing severe devastation and loss of species before being snatched into the sun's orbit as the planet Venus. Then, the spiritual symbolism of the comet with its fiery tail was corroborated by Jung's *Flying Saucers: A Modern Myth of Things Seen in the Skies,* in which Jung said that circular forms were "not only soul symbols, but God-images."

In 1966 Rogers discovered he could place his paintings in a certain order to form a narrative of a spiritual journey that he named *The Quest*. Almost every year since, Rogers' exhibitions have been variations of *The Quest*. They reflect his versatility as an artist and his ever-deepening understanding of his original vision.

Rogers renews *The Quest* through his determined technical experimentation. He keeps the narrative fresh by varying the works in size, surface treatment, composition, color, brushwork and emotional tone. Yet he says, "The more I cut out the cerebral, conscious, thinking process, the better the painting is . . . Being clever has nothing to do with art."

Through spontaneity, Rogers achieves a dreamlike mood in his work, similar to that in the work of the mystics Ryder, Rousseau and Chagall. He also makes discoveries. He begins his paintings on prepared masonite panels or canvases that he has coated with gesso, a refined white plaster. On this ground he usually draws his image and begins to paint, but he had a breakthrough when he broke that pattern in 1972. Spontaneously, he threw black acrylic paint across the gessoed surface and created an unpremeditated abstraction. Within these black random markings, he discerned the figure of an old man on every panel. Later he was to call him "the hermit." As Rogers developed the paintings on the abstract under layer, he retained the hermit as a new symbolic figure, not just in this series but also in subsequent ones.

Rogers' symbols are all aspects of the human psyche. They include: three feminine and three masculine archetypal figures; a man (animus) and a woman (anima); the hermit; a horse and a dove; an angel; a column of light; the comet; a pool and a forest. The Holy Grail at the end of the quest is enlightenment.

When he could afford it in the 1970s, Rogers published a catalog for each show. These essays and their illustrations trace his aesthetic and his philosophical evolution. In 1971, "The Quest: The Story of Man's Fall and of His Quest to Regain Union With God," was a substantial 29-page catalog in the form of a mythic poem with a Biblical foundation. Its hero, Everyman, tells his story of leaving Paradise and entering the Wheel of Life and Death.

Everyman meets an Old Woman (the Hag) who advises him to love God (the whole) before he loves the part (other people). Other figures in the story were a Maiden, a group of men, the comet, the Christ child, a dove and Mary. Rogers concludes his commentary with the thought that Heaven is wherever there is a man who knows his oneness with God.

By 1974 Everyman had evolved into a couple who represent the conjoined male and female aspects of personhood. The hermit who appeared spontaneously in Rogers' paintings fills the roles of inner teacher similar to Jung's Wise Old Man, the conduit of spiritual understanding. The channel of awareness that the couple seeks leads to its source in the hermit whom Rogers accepts as the Father within. Was it the voice of the hermit who spoke aloud to Rogers? Perhaps so. He believes the voice is his own Higher Self, another possible name for the hermit.

In 1975 Rogers understood the Ascension to be symbolic of the individual ascension of Everyman, " . . . essential in order for his consciousness to become a channel for the Light of God to manifest in the world." More than any other of his catalogs, this one carried the seeds that became his book in 1987.

Fairmount Gallery in Dallas showed *The Quest* in 1976 and published a brief statement: "Art is a definite way of knowledge or approach to truth . . . I do not get an idea for an image and then paint it: rather, the painting reveals to me, in the same manner as dreams, imagery that usually remains buried in the subconscious. The fact that in the course of time these images formed a pattern or story is a source of wonder to me and enough to give me confidence in their validity."

Eventually, Rogers was compelled to write *The Painter's Quest: Art as a Way of Revelation*. It is one of the most revealing and idealistic documents ever written by an artist. The book is an autobiography and mythic exegesis, disarmingly fervent and inspired. He follows the spiralling order of his discoveries through his recurrent themes.

Though Rogers denies that he is an intellectual, he has a capacious mind nourished by painting, meditating and reading, and he has an active intuition by which he restructures data with creative alchemy. I believe the catalyst for his mixture of intellect and intuition is his passion. Rogers' passion for making art is matched by his desire to make sense of his visions. He looks inward and artward, checking one perspective against another. Revelation by revelation he has penetrated the symbolism of each element in his vision. One might view his vision as a symbolic organization of his own deepest interests; but at the time of his numinous encounters, Rogers explains frankly in his book, he did not readily grasp the mirror-like nature of the messages he received.

A central portion of Rogers' book is devoted to reproductions of paintings culled from the various *Quest* series which he discusses in the text. He includes *The Crusaders*, the man and woman who attack the Giants only to find they are attacking a mirage. These giants that first appeared in his paintings as the soldiers at the foot of the cross, evolved into a symbol of separateness from God, and underwent even further development after Rogers read Chogyam Trungpa's *Cutting Through Spiritual Materialism.*

Trungpa, a Tibetan Buddhist, describes the Three Lords of Materialism: Mind, Speech and Form. In a flash of insight, Rogers recognized that his three male figures were Trungpa's three lords. In the excitement of this discovery, he recalled painting in 1960 three females he had thought of as the Greek Muses: Meditation, Memory and Song (which he later changed to Music). The Lords and the Muses are matching trios. Rogers has pursued their form and meaning for a decade.

During 1983 Rogers was in England to give a talk about his art. Glen Schaefer, a mathematical physicist in the audience, told him about the current synthesis in science known as the New Paradigm. Schaefer advised him to "get the girls (Muses) and boys (Lords) together" in one holistic image.

Like a focused laser beam, Rogers has concentrated on a series of paintings he titled *New Paradigm.* These are interlocked pyramidal compositions of three males and three females. The male and female triangular groupings, interpenetrating and affecting each other, are his icon, an homage to oneness, a unification of male-mind-intellect and female-spirit-intuition, science and art, heaven and earth. Originally the two trinities were separate, but they can now be read as a six-pointed star. In India, this form which is now so identified with Israel was considered the sign of Oneness. Crucial to their unity is the transformative effect of the spiritual, feminine Muses of Meditation, Memory and Music (who might well represent the abiding Earth) on the volatile, masculine Lords of Mind, Speech and Form. Rogers explains:

"The fundamental thing about the Three Lords is that they create reality as we perceive it. From that point of view, you can say we are ruled by them because we are dominated by our perception of reality, brought about by our dualistic consciousness. This thinking is transmitted by speech. What ends up 'out there' begins in our beliefs and fears. It is a vicious circle—mind, speech, form, round and round. We cannot get away from the circle, but it can be absolutely transformed by the Three Muses. With the effect of Meditation on Mind, thoughts change."

Rogers implies that when thoughts change, reality changes also.

He writes: "No man can hope to make progress on the Quest without help from the Muse/Goddess. Symbolizing as she does the feminine, intuitive aspect of the psyche in men, she is vital for balance." This statement accords with my belief that holism begins within each of us as we bring our feminine and masculine characteristics into balance.

Rogers had a major breakthrough when he recognized that the symbolic Maiden in his vision represents the anima, but he explains, "I am much concerned that people don't jump to the conclusion that my paintings are autobiographical and illustrate my own quest . . . So the distinction must be made between my quest and The Quest and the fact that I paint the latter, not the former."

Rogers' Quest charts a path to truth that is applicable to me and to other women. In the years I have followed his evolving paintings of *The Quest*, his thinking has often provoked me to consider the role of the anima in my spiritual journey. I have found the classical psychological anima/animus dichotomy a stumbling block to self-understanding.

If a man's progress toward wholeness is in acknowledging his anima or feminine side, then logically, a woman should find wholeness by recognizing her animus, the masculine in herself. Somehow, I do not think this corollary holds true for me. The animus, the active principle, is associated with transcendence and the light. In actual practice as a woman, I find it paradoxical and unworkable to seek my unacknowledged self in the light, active animus. I don't believe it is there.

I, too, experience the unknown aspect of myself as the dark, the lunar, the feminine. Often, as a woman, I am disengaged from my feminine nature just as a man can be from his anima; and I crave the comfort of the anima, the mother in myself. I feel that our society demands, if I choose to play the game according to prevailing rules, that I express my animus through acquiring knowledge, performing in the outward roles I assume in my life, and striving toward goals in the world. These actions are necessarily of the dominant masculine pattern, based in competition rather than unity. They are controlled by the Lords of Materialism Rogers has been painting all these years, Mind, Speech and Form.

Perhaps after centuries of patriarchal dominance, the archetypes of anima/animus and yin/yang require a more elastic conceptualization than tradition provides. A single order of shared characteristics in various proportions, rather than two lists separating human attributes into the masculine or feminine, will aid the effort to become more holistic. We must claim all human aspects that belong to each of us. Such a unification is what Rogers is embodying in his painting.

I have set myself a requirement to read the current books on women's spiritual quest. The drumbeat in these books is the search for the Goddess, or the feminine aspect of God, to validate the spirituality of women's nature, to worship and to enjoy. More and more,

PLATE 2

"The Return of the Goddess"
Peter Rogers

women are saying the feminine principle is vital to wholeness—not to rule, but to balance the male principle.

Rogers shares this point of view. "We have lost a great deal by our rejection of the Goddess as Mother Earth," he writes in his 1993 catalog. "Our failure to recognize the divine, not only in ourselves, but in all of nature has resulted in our sense of separation from God, and ecological disaster." He comments that there are many positive signs of a new order of consciousness, and this is because " . . . the feminine side of the psyche in both men and women is beginning to influence the masculine side."

Rogers' painting of the *New Paradigm* has touched a chord in my mind as a symbol, like the Tree of Life in the Kabbalah, for the ultimate unity that I believe will heal the Earth. Clearly, this structure is Rogers' most important pictorial summary of *The Quest*.

In a recent catalog statement he wrote,

"As far as I know, the images of the Lords and Muses have never been juxtaposed before. The former derives from Tibet, an ancient center of Eastern religious tradition; the latter derives from Greece, the cradle of Western civilization; put together, they fulfill the requirements of the universal myth . . . It restores the female principle to its rightful place in the scheme of things. We are entering a new age, and the reemergence of the feminine principle is the hope and hallmark of that age. So, while the Quest itself is the myth for our times, the New Paradigm is a symbol for our times and the times to come."

Under the title of his 1993 series, *The Return of the Goddess,* Rogers deals deeply with the transformation brought about by combining Mind with Meditation, Speech with Memory, and Form with Music. Once these masculine/feminine archetypes fuse in the consciousness of a person, he posits, a Channel of Awareness is opened. This channel is synonymous with the Christ as a way to the truth that people are seeking in their effort to make sense of life.

In his book, Rogers cites two sources that form "parentheses" around his philosophical conclusions as an artist and seeker. He quotes Heraclitus: "The Real World consists in a balanced adjustment of opposing tendencies. Behind the strife between opposites there lies a hidden harmony or attunement which is the world." Painters who harmonize the parts of their painting into the whole, Rogers believes, "are painting the Real World." The closing parenthesis to Rogers' insight is Christ's commandments, to love God and to love one's neighbor as oneself.

Rogers contends that artists, by attending to every part of the composition as well as the whole, are engaging in a spiritual act. "This love for the composition as a whole is comparable to spiritual love, for spiritual love implies a love for God, and a love for God is a love for the Whole." He concludes, "Properly understood as a question of focus, unconditional love is the creative process."

With his prophetic voice, Rogers challenges us with his suggestion that the dual focus artists apply to creating a "whole" work of art is essential to the spiritual task all humans face. We must concentrate on loving both God-the-Whole and self/neighbor-the-part. He says, "Unless one's focus is on the Whole all the time, one will never get the parts right, however much love one lavishes on them."

Rogers stresses that the function of the artist is to give testimony to spiritual reality. His own most courageous, creative act might be the proclamation in his art and writing of his vision in which the spiritual infuses the material world. Although his life has led him to make use of Christian symbols, Rogers grows increasingly eclectic in his references to mythology. He does not conceive of the path toward spiritual enlightenment in a narrow way. He writes;

"There is much talk these days by such as Joseph Campbell that we are desperately lacking a relevant contemporary myth, a myth to help us over the difficult transition from the Age of Pisces into the Age of Aquarius. Since we are becoming more and more aware of the fact that we are all one family on this small planet, what we need is a universal myth for the whole family.

The idea of a spiritual journey, or quest, is fundamental to all the world's great religions and yet tends to be obscured by man-made dogmas and the outer trappings of religions. Nevertheless the concept of the Quest is the common denominator and needs to be stressed."

Sharing his beliefs with the world so openly in imagery and words has taken Rogers into the role of spokesperson for the spiritual in art. He is a prophet in transit. The Quest does not end.

*H*una is the ancient wisdom of Hawaii. When I toured Kaui with Mary-Margaret Moore, Dr. Serge King, psychologist and kahuna kupua *(a master of Huna)* joined us at a heliau *(sacred site)* called Poliahu. Serge King, whose ancestry is English and Italian, has penetrating brown eyes, dark hair, a mustache and a beard. Around his neck he sometimes wears a shaman's necklace of kukui nuts. It seemed appropriate to sit on our tropical grass mats under yellow-blossomed salamander trees and listen to the haunting sounds he played on his nose flute. He introduced Huna by telling us the traditional legend of the Menehunes:

These Little People brought the knowledge of Huna with them when they came from the Pleiades. (Throughout the Pacific, present-day Polynesians still call themselves "People of the Sky.") Some of their party went to another planet which was later destroyed. The Menehunes settled on Mu, the Lost Continent of the Pacific, also known as Lemuria. Mu was broken apart in a violent cataclysm brought on by the selfishness of the Menehunes who failed to go to the aid of their distant relatives on the other planet.

Remnants of Mu are found today in the Peruvian Andes, Easter Island, Samoa, Tahiti and the Hawaiian Islands. Elements of the esoteric language created by the Menehunes to transmit Huna wisdom, as well as vestiges of their "secret knowledge of all things" can be detected throughout the world. Serge assured us we did not need to accept the legend as fact in order to benefit from Huna.

HUNA HAS NO ORTHODOXY, but Serge knows people will inevitably try to set up a Huna catechism. He avoids this by continuously recreating the training. He invites former students to repeat any workshop as often as desired for refreshing and further knowledge.

Serge taught us the breathing exercise called piko piko, which is to breathe in "love" from the crown (top of the head) and breathe out "peace" through the navel. With a few inhalations, piko piko increases mana, the love-energy power of Aloha. It generates a feeling of accelerated vibration and, at the same time, a feeling of deep stillness. (When I returned home, I had a chance to test the effect of this exercise while using a device in our natural history museum that allows you to measure your own electromagnetic field. With each breathing cycle, I watched the dial move higher.)

Before he left us that day, Serge led a brief circle ritual that seemed to expand our energy. I was positioned across the circle from him, and even at that distance I could feel the force of his intense, contained power.

King is an artist-shaman. He sculpts, paints, and writes poetry, novels and expository books. Significantly for this project, he also behaves as an artist in his shaman work. Every aspect of the framework he uses to spread his teaching—the curriculum, training devices, publications, logo, schedules and the preparation of satellite teachers—is his creation. To be an effective teacher, he says he must perform almost as an actor, attuned to timing, behavior, props and anecdotes. I made arrangements to take the third level Huna workshop in Hawaii, where I interviewed King for this book.

Serge King has made it his life work to pass on knowledge that has the power to heal people and even the Earth itself. Affirmative, good-humored, noncombative and confident, he exemplifies the Huna system with health of mind and body as well as spirit. His family is strong, and he has supported them through good business management in the market place. He functions on a number of levels convincingly, without sentimentality or theatrics.

From my perspective, Serge King is a world class teacher, and the Huna system is the most useful mental discipline I have found. His lessons appear purposefully timed to be dispersed at the intersection between an age that is passing and an age that is yet to be, the one we are in the process of creating.

SERGE KAHILI KING, HUNA MASTER

Serge King is a kahuna. A kahuna is a master of Huna and a kupua shaman. He says that shamans have a worldwide telepathic network. The shaman is a *healer*—of relationships in mind and body—through telepathy and clairvoyance; a *releaser* of blocks such as anger, fear and guilt; a *manifestor* of events, relationships, possibility, and prosperity; and a *shapechanger* with the ability to move in and out of other dimensions and roles. The Huna shaman *blesses* with the loving spirit of Aloha, is a *peacemaker* and a *teacher* who shares knowledge from authority by example. Finally, in Huna, the shaman is an *adventurer*, willing to explore.

"Huna knowledge was present in the world and then lost," Serge explained. He has devoted himself to bringing it back to the world. In 1973 he founded the Order of Huna International in California, and he has been training people in this ancient wisdom ever since. Among his books are: *Kahuna Healing,* which he first wrote as his dissertation for a doctorate in psychology; *Imagineering for Health;* the *Pyramid Energy Handbook; Mastering Your Hidden Self,* which includes a comparison of Huna and major psychological systems; *Urban Shamanism*, which is an effective text for King's Huna classes; and *Earth Energies*, a handbook on geomancy.

Serge writes in *Mastering Your Hidden Self:*

"Huna . . . is religious in the sense that it inspires man to attain spiritual perfection. It is scientific because it deals with the physical . . . and its techniques produce repeatable effects . . . Huna is a philosophy of life with a strong but simple code of ethics. Some consider it occult because it works with forces that are unseen but very real . . . all embracing . . . every religion contains parts of it." (p. 4.)

Huna is "The Way of the Adventurer" in contrast to "The Warrior Path," as described by Carlos Casteneda. "'The Warrior Path' deals with good and evil," Serge said. Huna does not require conquering evil with good. It is based on Aloha, which is both "loving power and powerful love." Love is the only ethic of Huna. The adventurer's and the warrior's shamanic paths lead to the same goal of enlightenment; they are just different routes to knowing the oneness of all things.

"A person who decides to become a shaman is automatically chosen. When you give a person the power to transform, she or he becomes part of a shamanic network, part of an order. More women than men are in Huna training because men are still afraid of it. My next few books will change that. In the shamanic order, no one has power over anyone else. There is no hierarchy. Everyone has shamanic abilities."

When I first heard Serge describe the seven Huna principles and corollaries, I recognized them as the perennial wisdom of the mother culture, the core beliefs I had been searching for in every book and experience.

1. The world is what you think it is.
   All systems are arbitrary.
2. There are no limits.
   Separation is a useful illusion.
3. Energy flows where attention goes.
   Everything has energy.
4. Now is the moment of power.
   Everything is relative.
5. To love is to be happy with.
   Everything is alive, responsive and aware.
6. All power is within.
   Everything has power.
7. Effectiveness is the measure of truth.
   There is always another way to do anything.

Huna is not dogma nor is it exclusive. "If it works," Serge quipped, "it's Huna." I felt as if I had found a home.

The story of Serge King's becoming a kahuna kupua begins with his father Harry Leland Loring King. If Harry's life had been a movie, Errol Flynn might have played his part. Harry's parents were British citizens on the way to Vincennes, Indiana, when their son was born at sea, so he had dual citizenship. Harry lived on his family's farm until he was sent as a young boy to England for schooling. The family is distantly related to the royal family and an ancestor, Captain John King, was one of Catherine the Great's many lovers.

Harry's adventures began in his teens when he joined a scientific/political expedition to the Gobi Desert for the British Government. When he and his companions were caught in a violent sandstorm, he quickly walked his horse to some nearby ruins and crouched down. Suddenly, the sand in front of him gave way, and Harry saw a stairway opening at his feet. Curiosity aroused, he walked down into a temple-like room with frescos on the walls and an altar at the far end. On the altar he could see a bracelet. Just as he picked it up he heard sand filling the stairway behind him, so he raced back and climbed out. When the fierce storm abated, no sign remained of the sunken temple. He told his companions of his experience, but they ribbed him for it, so he kept the bracelet in his pocket without mentioning it.

On returning to England, he reported to his superior and showed him the bracelet. It was made of silver set with a yellow stone surrounded by nine colored stones in the design of the solar system. Pluto was not discovered until 1930, therefore nine planets was information in advance of human knowledge. The department director was visibly excited and borrowed the bracelet to show to others who must have recognized its significance. Through his superior, Harry was initiated into a group he simply called The Organization. For some months, Harry received esoteric training in this group and then, in 1912, he was sent by his government to Hawaii. His instructions were to locate a particular man on the island of Kauai named Joseph Kahili Okamoku, which means "Wanderer of the Islands." Joseph was a kahuna, a master of the ancient Huna wisdom. Until 1975 it was illegal in Hawaii to be a kahuna, so there was a cloak and dagger secrecy about the finding of Joseph Kahili, but find him Harry did. Joseph explained that Harry had, in another lifetime, been a Hawaiian kahuna himself. The Kahili family adopted Harry and treated him as a relative. For the next five years, he studied Huna not only in Hawaii but also in New Zealand and Australia.

In World War I, Harry King served as a flyer, probably in the Royal Air Corps. In postwar years, he earned two degrees in engineering and a medical degree from the University of Pennsylvania. He also found time to go to Africa on a filmmaking expedition and was left there for dead when a malaria epidemic struck the crew. Such was the swash-buckling life of this man.

Years later, in Pittsburgh, Harry married a pretty woman of Italian heritage at least fifteen years his junior and set about having a family. Serge was their third child, born in San Diego on February 15, 1938. His parents drove straight through to the coast from Louisville, just for the birth, possibly because Joseph Kahili was in San Diego at that time.

Serge's own psychic life began in Los Angeles when he was seven years old. It was the night of the most spectacular meteor shower of the century. He lay down on the side-walk all night watching this overwhelmingly beautiful sight. "It seemed to evoke memories." He had a vivid vision that aroused his lifelong love for astronomy. I asked Serge if he thought the stars were his home, and he said quite seriously, "I have a strong connection with the Pleiades, but I specialize in Earth."

Another memory from his seventh year was a letter that came from a member of The Organization who said he would watch over Serge's development. Harry read it to Serge.

When Serge was 14 years old the family settled down to farm in the village of South Lyon, Michigan. He was his father's constant companion. "It was a hard physical life, but this was a wonderful period of getting in touch with nature."

Harry initiated Serge into The Organization and trained him for three years in the Aloha lore of Huna and in the elements of telepathy, ways to remove blocks and ways to release energy. The training he gave was casual, given at any time through the day, and not set aside from the rest of life. Harry played psychic games with his wife and all of his children. Serge's training was an extension of this habitual type of practice; but it was deeper and more concentrated. Harry notified the shaman network that Serge was in training.

The Kings were a Catholic family. Serge recalls that they were attending mass in South Lyon one Sunday when his father excused himself and left the pew. A moment later, Serge no longer saw the parishioners and priest. Directly in front of him he had a vision of his father falling down on the lawn of the church. Just then, someone rushed in to tell him Harry had collapsed outside from a heart attack. His father survived for a few more months, until shortly before Serge finished high school.

After his father's death, Serge went into a depression. He was deeply puzzled about his future, but he continued the practices Harry had taught him. He was soon contacted by a man from The Organization who told him he would receive further metaphysical instruction through his dreams. He also had a letter from his father's adopted Hawaiian sister, Ohialaka Kahili.

Serge began reading when he was three years old and always read books ahead of his years; but he was so involved with mastering his extrasensory mental powers and he had such a rich fantasy life that he found school totally unchallenging. In high school, he says, he "majored in pool" and graduated 60th in a class of 64. His SAT scores were high, and he was accepted at Eastern Michigan Normal School in Ypsilanti; but he lacked support or true motivation. After a year of "majoring in ping-pong," he joined the U.S. Marines.

For three years, while serving at Camp Pendleton, California, Serge was given training by his Auntie Ohialaka, a fully trained kahuna. She taught Serge to be in the present moment, to meditate, to concentrate, and to gain command of his emotions. When off duty, he met her at parks or near the ocean to talk. Again, the training was informal, consisting of a review of experiences and suggestions. Ohialaka also encouraged Serge's interest in archaeology and anthropology so he would become familiar with the distant past. Like his father, Serge was adopted by her family. Kahili is his middle name. When he was 21 years old, just before he left the service, he was ordained in the mystical Huna Order of Kane.

Following his military service, Serge was charged with scholarly zeal. He returned to Ypsilanti for one semester as a sophomore and did very well in his psychology and liberal arts courses. Then he transferred to the University of Michigan and majored in Russian studies, including the Russian language. In his junior year, he proposed to Gloria, his high school sweetheart. She was an Army lieutenant serving as a dietitian. They married in 1961 just before her move to Fitzimmons Hospital in Denver. To complete his undergraduate degree, Serge entered the University of Colorado. Colonel David Barrett, chairman of the Department of Asian Studies, became almost a spiritual guide to him. Serge was so impressed with Barrett that he changed majors again, learned to speak Chinese with a Cantonese accent, and graduated Phi Beta Kappa.

By the time Serge graduated from the university, Gloria had left the army and the Kings already had their first of three sons. They moved to Phoenix so he could enroll in the American Graduate School of International Management, known as the Thunderbird School. He earned a second bachelor's degree, in Foreign Trade with a specialty in Spanish and Latin American Studies.

Serge had every reason to think he was thoroughly prepared for a remunerative overseas job in one of the areas he had studied—Russian, Chinese or Spanish—but, mysteriously, he was not hired. He finally accepted a job at infinitesimal pay with the

Catholic Relief Services who, ironically, offered him a post in Africa because his resumé mentioned he had taken French as an undergraduate, a language he could barely speak.

Serge and his family lived in Dahomey, where he worked mainly in the bush, and also in Togo. Three years later he was transferred to the sophisticated city of Dakar in Senegal to be the program director for Mauritania, Senegal and Gambia. All that time he was in training with M'Bala, a Hausa shaman who turned up over and over again wherever Serge found himself, whether he was in a village or out in the desert. M'Bala was a practitioner of a love-based shamanic tradition similar to Huna, and he was part of the international shamanic network.

"I dreamed of him first," Serge said. He actually appeared in the role of a wandering salesman of African art. Serge recognized him as his next teacher because when M'Bala was there, Serge could speak French fluently.

The lessons were unstructured, but through them Serge discovered the power of magic and of the mind. M'Bala introduced Serge to other shamans and sorcerers who demonstrated that emotions have the power to heal. They taught him about the currents of energy surrounding the human body, known in Huna as aka and now known in science as bioenergy fields, which link a person to the environment. "M'Bala taught me the most about mana [love power] and energy," Serge said.

Serge made a business trip home to Pittsburgh to sell some family property. As he was cleaning up there, a Hawaiian man approached him. "It was bizarre. He introduced himself as my uncle Wana Kahili. He said it was time to move ahead and he would continue my training with him. The work was to be mental, a different phase, a period of intensively studying other systems and correlating them with Huna." In *Kahuna Healing*, Serge writes that for three years his uncle taught him about such matters as "love, imagination, beliefs and the nature of success" and profoundly changed Serge's life.

In Dakar's excellent library, Serge began reading in French the works of Mesmer, the Kabbalah and material on Wilhelm Reich's theory of radiaesthesia. He studied yoga and Science of Mind. By 1970, he had "gained detachment" after years of hard work on his self-development. At that time, Gloria did yet not know about his shamanic studies. He revealed them to her shortly before the family left Africa. "By then, it became clearer to me that I wanted to teach, to express this knowledge so that others could understand it. Both the knowledge and the ability to practice shamanism were in place by the time we returned to Phoenix," Serge said.

In 1971, when he was 33 years old, Serge earned his master's degree in International Management from the Thunderbird School. He then entered the private California Western University in Santa Ana, an accredited university without walls, to work on his doctorate in psychology. The family lived in Malibu.

During this period Gloria, too, had a psychic awakening and began helping in the work of expanding the knowledge of Huna throughout the world. "We had classes in our home. I taught metaphysics. The class had a practical orientation. I worked with energy for healing, doing experimenting with razor blades and pyramids. I used energy on our kids to see how it works. Gloria was a regional dietitian who consulted with nursing homes. She taught in the kitchens, and she used the training to create harmony. They had a low turnover while she was on the job," Serge said. He started a mail order business for energy devices, wrote articles about magic under various names for psychic magazines, and did counseling as a hypnotherapist. He also made many trips to the Hawaiian Islands after his return from Africa.

"I didn't go into clinical psychology. Psychology was a bridge for me to interact with the general public. I didn't have a doctor/patient relationship. The person who came to me for consultation was my client, not a patient. I taught self-hypnosis. I wanted to give a person the tools to do something for himself, and I taught my clients to leave me after four sessions."

Serge founded Aloha International, an educational organization through which he certifies shamans and maintains their network. His unusual educational background and experience have given him a global viewpoint. After several concentrated years of teaching, Serge is turning his attention to the Huna traditions found throughout the Pacific. Recently, he has made repeated trips to Tahiti and New Zealand to set up a network among native Huna shamans.

Serge and Gloria King moved to Kauai in 1987. Their home is on property once covered by the old sugar factory and cane fields where the Kahilis worked. Very quickly, Serge developed a headquarters in Princeville and Kilauea, with an office staff who publish the Aloha newsletter. He established a Hawaiian museum and bookstore. He trained a core of assistant teachers who are taking over the task of teaching students the elements of Huna.

Huna is primarily about using the power of the mind and communicating with the forces of nature. It is also about trusting the universe as infinitely wise and loving. "EWOP," said Serge, "everything is working out perfectly," a useful adage that reinforces the affirmative nature of Huna. Serge emphasizes the power of our thoughts to affect the universe. A thought exists and travels forever as energy. Inwardly, our thoughts are the wellspring of our experience, including our own health. Serge explained that the shaman attempts to increase his or her self-esteem and self-confidence by expanding inner communication, a form of telepathy.

Serge said that in this life he has more self-confidence than in any of his other lives. His comment prompted me to ask him about reincarnation. He said that in Huna there are no sequential lives, nor a linear view of time. There is only the eternal present. All lives are concurrent. Serge attempts to communicate with his other lives, particularly those in which he has a high level of self-confidence. He once taught himself to sail a boat by contacting another life in which he is a sailor. One of his ongoing experiments is to practice telepathic communication, channeling through a 14- or 15-year-old girl several centuries in the future (but also simultaneous with the present). "A man is with her who is in communication with me," he explained. Serge is conscious of a parallel life as an artist, and he uses terminology related to artmaking.

Among the most effective lessons of *Haumana*, the first level of Huna training, was the strength test to show the effect of self-criticism on one's body. King told a student to think negatively about herself, and then he pushed her outstretched arm. She had no strength to resist. But when she gave herself inward praise, her arm was visibly strengthened. Often, he said, allergy, asthma, disease and breakdown are begun by our inner self-criticism. Both self-criticism and criticism of others, including the government, weaken us. Serge told us the Huna way is to give praise, to bless with words. "One compliment neutralizes one criticism. Blessing is a way to heal the world." He gave us a three-line affirmative mnemonic to strengthen our inner well-being: "Bless the present. Trust yourself. Expect the best."

Huna psychology describes three inner selves. The *ku* is our child Self who forgets nothing but can always be trained to new thoughts and new habits. The *ku* likes patterns and will repeat a customary response until convinced otherwise. Its task is to protect us, but it always goes toward pleasure and away from pain. If a greater pain can be avoided only by making us ill, the *ku* will make us ill.

The *lono* directs the ku. The *lono* is our conscious, intellectual, reasoning Self and the center of our will power. It focuses our attention and gives meaning to our experience.

The *kane* (or *aumakua*) is our Higher Self, the God within, the source of our creativity and our point of contact with Universal Mind. The *kane* manifests our reality. It accepts our thoughts as if they were prayers. If we monitor our thoughts we can learn what the kane is "hearing." It tries to manifest what we ask for or the nearest equivalent. We may be receiving things we think we do not want in our lives when actually we are asking for them in our daily thoughts.

The three parts of ourselves are totally meshed. Through the *lono*, we teach our *ku* (Serge suggests you give your *ku* a name). To reach our *kane*, we must speak to our *ku*. Huna says you can change your reality. If you convince your *ku* there is a better way, that message will reach the *kane* who will, in turn, manifest a different reality.

Serge described four realities that we often shift between. The first reality is our everyday useful and objective world of separation. The second reality is the subjective level where everything is connected; this is the world of ESP and the akashic records (Edgar Cayce often mentioned these eternal accounts of all events and lives as the source for information that he received in trance). The third level is one of symbols, the dream level. The fourth level represents holism, where all is one.

All philosophy rests upon the essential quandary of Being. Why are we here and why do we die? What is death? In the Huna viewpoint, the state of death is simply another reality. One has no need to be ill at the time of death. There are no accidents in Huna, so one must assume that every death is one to which the soul agrees—this would be in the Fourth Reality, where everything is connected and the entire pattern of lives is known. When our mission is over, we leave. While it is possible to extend our mission, life ends when the mission is completed.

The Huna concept of simultaneous lives implies we are always alive somewhere. Serge believes that Jane Roberts, who channeled *The Seth Material* and subsequent books that deal with aspects of a single Self, was a most important source of accurate information about the nature of reality. Her information is very much in harmony with Huna. "Multiple truths and multiple universes are possible in Huna," Serge says.

To reinforce his teaching, Serge leads his students in workshops on interior journeys. He guides them to close their eyes and go into their inner garden. The garden is a real place created in the imagination. These inner journeys offer an experience to prove that we can change our reality through our imagination. Our imagination is our point of entry to the underworld and the upper world. With Huna techniques, we can mentally change any avenue of our lives, for example: We can mentally visit each other's gardens, perhaps to offer hope or heal a broken relationship. We can recall a sad memory and recreate it in a healthier way. We can go deeply into the underworld to encounter our personal monsters and render them friendly. With our minds we can reach people who have already died.

According to King's teaching, each time we take an intentional inner journey, we are acting as creative artists reshaping reality with the power of our thoughts and effecting changes just as an artist creates form from the materials she or he uses to make art.

Serge adopted the word grok—meaning to completely identify with—from Robert Heinlein's Strangers in a Strange Land. By doing *piko piko* breathing and going inward, we can grok the forces of nature. In the workshop, we practiced grokking the wind. Serge commented that the wind has been everywhere and heard everything, so it is a profound source of information. Such a mystically poetic attitude pervades Huna and adds to the beauty of this way of thinking. It is possible to grok a tidal wave, an animal, another person or an organ in our own bodies. Grokking is probably the single most important mental technique Serge teaches. In Huna, the whole world is a dream world. Everything dreams. By grokking, the shaman can enter the dream of his own liver, or the dream of a tree, or of a friend. Everything is accessible, but Huna shamans do not violate privacy nor cause harm. In Huna there is no evil sorcery.

Serge told us that we could be effective shamans from taking just the first level, but I took the second workshop, Loea, on a weekend in Taos, New Mexico, in the spring of 1988. Shamans, Serge said, aspire to increase their level of Aloha energy, their *mana*, by slowly building up to greater amplitude in order to strengthen the imagination and mental powers.

Our *Loea* training began with energy devices that enhance *mana*. Crystals can be effective, but Serge has a far more pragmatic, unromantic view of them than the New Agers. He said that while a crystal does radiate energy, its significance is mainly what we ascribe to it. Our focused attention enhances the crystals' energy. A crystal retains the energy of the place where it grew, therefore some crystals are more vibrant than others. Massed crystals can put out considerable energy. Each color of crystal radiates a separate frequency.

He mentioned an idea I have read about that the core of the earth might be a giant crystal. My interest in crystals and other stones is enthusiastic, due to their beauty. I like to wear them, give them as gifts, and include them in the shrines I make with mixed materials. Serge carries the shaman set of seven colored crystals in a pouch and uses them in healing rituals.

Loea deals with ritual. A primary aspect of a ritual is the blessing, done by marking or acknowledging all the directions, not only the cardinal directions, but also up, down and inward, to set the place apart as a sacred space. Special objects, sounds and movements also are components of rituals. In small groups, we performed rituals for the workshop group of 45 people. These three-to-five-minute minidramas were memorable for their elegance. When the training ended, I made a commitment of time, resources and energy to go to Kauai and take the next level of training.

Hialoa, the third level of Huna study, took five days. It encompasses subjects such as geomancy, the study of the energies of the earth. Ley lines, the tracks of subtle energy that form a pattern on the earth's surface, are fluid, Serge said, sometimes changing location. Sacred sites are built on them. All roads are ley lines because so many people have traveled on them and invested them with their energy. All towns and built up areas can be considered sacred spaces because of the energy from those who live there. While maneuvering in traffic, it is soothing to think, "I am driving on a ley line."

Serge also discussed clairvoyance, out-of-body journeys and channeling as mental techniques practiced by shamans. Channeling is so prevalent today that it was interesting to hear Serge's description of the Huna attitude toward it. "You can only channel yourself. You channel from one part of you to another." Channeling comes from the *kane*, or Higher Self, not an exterior Being, but the God Within.

Serge's skill at leading the group on mental excursions is so effective that we each had moving experiences with the untapped powers in our own imagination. After each exercise in all Huna training, we shared our visualizations with a nearby person who is our partner. Sixty people took the *Hialoa* session when I did, and all of us presented something original that we had channeled, something we had no reason to expect ahead of time. By the time we finished the week, I felt that cumulatively I had acquired a firm foundation in shamanic thinking.

The Huna idea is to take control of your own mind. The training is just the beginning of learning to live a mystical life. To develop a shaman's ability requires repeated practice of mental techniques. My reason for studying shamanism was not to hang out my shingle and start healing other people. Initially, I wanted to absorb a system of thought that strengthens my own mystical awareness because I believe it will have a healing effect on me. It also gives me immediate access to my creative center. Another reason to take Huna training is that shamanic discipline implies social responsibility. One hopes to become self-disciplined enough through shamanism to serve effectively—using one's own gifts, whatever they happen to be—for the welfare of the planet.

In the late 1980s, Hands Across America, The Hour of World Prayer, Live-Aid and the Harmonic Convergence demonstrated the power of concentrated thought when it is shared by a number of people at the same time. A recent worldwide call for peace and an apparent lessening of conflict has been accompanied by more cooperative attitudes in both the former Soviet Union and the United States. We are witnessing a change of mind on a global scale, and it has a shamanic quality. A responsive impulse, felt by many people who did not participate in any of these collective actions, is resonating in our psyches.

Huna is practical shamanism. It tells us we are effective each time we pause and send out our intention to add Aloha (love-energy) to this planet. As a corollary, each of these pauses to gather in and send out loving energy heals us too.

Without leaving my home, I can use Huna telepathic techniques like a prayer to ask for healing of any condition anywhere. The desire for trying to control the results is not present in Huna. I just send out Aloha energy for the best possible outcome. Acting in concert with a network of others who are trained in mystical shamanism adds strength to such efforts.

Huna principles have influenced my spiritual practice. I try to respond rather than react to the events in my life. Assuming nothing outside of myself has power over me reminds me that I have no power over anyone else. The reality my neighbor is creating is as valid as mine. I used to feel things were this way or that; now I often think they can be both ways at once.

On Kauai in the Huna sessions, when we closed our eyes to enter our garden, my inner image atomized in an overlayer of brilliant dots. This sparkling image has returned to me many times. I interpret it as a sign that "the secret knowledge of all things" means that everything is energy in a pattern. Such an idea is confirmed in science and Huna. The world *is* what we think it is.

In *Urban Shaman*, Serge King presents his fundamental reason for commitment to Huna wisdom:

"Hawaiian shamanism and the spirit of aloha on which it is based represent a way of life with great value for all of humanity. It is a coming together time for all, and the best use of all shamanism, urban and otherwise, would be for the cause of peace, inner and outer. As an old Hawaiian proverb says: *He ali'i ka la'i, he haku na ke aloha* (Peace is a chief, the lord of love). May peace and love be our guide and our purpose as we work on healing the world today." (p. 34.)

My first contact
with Richard Newman was his inquiry
in 1983 about the proposed exhibition of
layering and the Society of Layerists in Multi-
Media. His vita was impressive. The slides of
his mixed-media sculptures, made of
wood, found objects, photography and
paint, were perfect for the invitational show I
was curating. I invited him to be in it.
Newman lives in the small
New England city of Haverhill,
Massachusetts. He heads the Creative
Arts Department of Bradford College, one of
the oldest private liberal arts colleges in the
country. His wife, Rochelle Newman,
an artist and author, is a professor in the
Massachusetts Community College system.
Their daughter Vanessa is a
graduate of Bradford.

ON A BLEAK, DAMP day in October 1983, after a roundabout
journey peppered with interviews, I arrived at a suburban inn near Newman's home. When he
picked me up in his station wagon, my impression was of a youthful middle-aged, spectacled,
bearded and reserved man, almost formal. I was greeted at the door by his wife, and I then
went out with Newman to his studio in a detached building above his workshop.

The altarpieces hanging on his white walls had photo-decoupaged surfaces in a range of
gray values. Smooth mirrored elements contrasted against modeled areas of rich texture.
Other pieces were painted in bright, flat colors that reminded me of folk art. In both forms, the
play of ideas in Newman's sculpture was evident, as was his superb craftsmanship. When I
made a comment about perceiving the meaning of the pieces as "the presence of death in life,
life in death," the atmosphere in the studio warmed with the beginnings of rapport.

R I C H A R D   N E W M A N :   L I F E ,   D E A T H ,   R E B I R T H :
T H E   C R E A T I V E   C O N T I N U U M

Within a few minutes after we met, Richard Newman told me this story:

"In my mid-thirties, I had a vivid psychic experience—like an anxiety attack. I
remember lying on my bed and waking up terrified by the sensation and nightmare
of a succubus who was on my chest taking my breath away. In that moment, I
became completely aware of my own mortality, and I had to face my fear of death.
Then I remembered a suggestion written by Alan Watts to the effect that whatever
you fear, you should make it your life's study. Study it from every angle. Get
totally absorbed in it to the point where it is no longer an enemy, but becomes a
friend. That is exactly what I did. My absorption and fascination with the whole
subject of death became the inspiration and the energy in the center of my work. I
frequently remember a quote from a film on the life of Leonardo: 'All this time I
thought I was learning to live, when I really was learning how to die.'"

Newman's unexpectedly frank admission of the fear each of us faces, but hardly ever
addresses aloud, was a welcome breakthrough. Denial of our fixation with death is such a
built-in facet of Western politesse, it is almost a shock to hear anyone allude to it, especially a virtual stranger.

I heard Newman's story twenty-two months after my father's death. The effects of his
passage had already begun to erode my mother's independence and her mental stability.
While I had turned to my own artmaking to find symbols for death and comforting images I
wanted to share with my mother, she became frozen into the Victorian form of her child-

PLATE 3

"Nature Mandala"
Richard Newman

hood. To her this meant that she must, for dignity's sake, grieve only in solitude and never reveal her fears. Under these conditions, no one could help her.

While Newman guided me around his pieces, I realized that death had a special meaning in his life too. "In retrospect, the death of my father when I was around 30, early in my teaching career at Bradford, had a strong impact. I was very emotionally connected to him. I think now that it took me a long time to deal with his loss and that it was helped significantly by the birth of Vanessa in 1968, a year or so after his death. I have always had the strong feeling that his spiritual presence exists in some strange way in her being. I feel that he continues to watch over me through her in some way."

Newman has taken numerous photographs of the winged head of the death angel commonly found on old New England gravestones. In his darkroom, he controls the tone and contrast of these images. He then composes the photographs according to their values as a surface pattern on his sculpture. The little angel faces aligned along the surface of an altarpiece are ironic symbols of death. He said, "The angel faces triggered something related to the passage I was going through in moving from my thirties to my forties, about the time I sensed the succubus draining my life away."

Turning to his folios, Newman extracted a series of masks created in a photo-collage technique. These collages, which are a continuing part of his art, predate his sculpture. They are intricate and autobiographical. He said, "They touch on the beast that dwells within, the shadow side of life, and polarity." He described the pieces as "photographs with hand-drawn passages, reality with illusion and fantasy, verisimilitude with distortion."

Newman pointed out in many pieces a recurring female presence whom he calls Mrs. Nobody. She is a late middle-aged, undefined person, wearing a winter coat and walking with a cane.

"Mrs. Nobody is my spectre or, you might say, my anima. She travels in my mind or my memory. It was only after reading Jungian thoughts about the anima/animus that I began to realize how important she is to my psychic understanding. She is a universal image and a lot of people identify with her. They see an Ingmar Bergmanesque quality about her.

"My discovery of Mrs. Nobody was a resonant experience. I don't see her image as weak or timid in any way. I see her as more regal, especially since I originally found her in a photograph that showed her walking through a Toronto subway station, with a sign or marker for 'Queen Street' off to the right as she walks toward it. Besides being a personification of my anima, Mrs. Nobody also stands as a guide to the underworld of old age and death. She reminds me now of several aunts I saw often in my childhood. There is another possibility. Someone who claims to be a psychic told my daughter Vanessa that a powerful but benevolent spiritual presence in our house hovers around those sculptural works that have been brought over from my studio."

Both of Newman's revelations—his fear of death and his visualization of his alter ego—burrowed into my mind along with the beginnings of a trusting friendship. Since our first meeting I have seen him in Albuquerque, Ohio, California, Indiana, Maine and Texas in connection with meetings of SLMM. In 1987 he was elected president of the society, and his efforts have been a boon to the welfare of the group. Our contacts with one another deepened when I wrote an article about Layering for the journal *Leonardo*, focused on four artists, including Newman (Vol. 19, No. 3, p. 223-229, 1986). The artists' statements about their widely disparate styles of art showed their similar philosophical worldview.

Richard Newman was raised in North Tonawanda, New York. His father was invalided from the effects of multiple sclerosis. His mother supported the family. There were hardships, but his home was a loving one.

"My family environment provided a very supportive atmosphere for self-expression and discovery. While examples of fine art were not present within my home, there was a pervasive sense of middle-class respectability, a strong sense of order or tidiness (despite the fact of my father's illness), a reverence for things well-made and for working with the hands. I have a recollection of time spent on 'spring cleaning' as a kind of family activity. This sometimes involved stripping and adding new paper to interior walls, which I enjoyed doing. I recall gardening, canning fruits and vegetables, putting up preserves for the winter months. An awareness of the passing of the seasons and cyclical growth was underscored by these activities.

"I frequently accompanied my parents on visits to the cemetery to care for my grandparents' graves and to decorate them with flowers. These impressions have a relationship with my work. So much of my work employs the polar elements of black and white photographs in contrast to bright fanciful colors that Sheli has suggested my early visits to the cemetery may have equipped me with a visual equivalent in the grays of the tombstones set against the flowers and grass of their surroundings.

"My grandfathers, I am told, were a carpenter and a wallpaper hanger. The items of furniture in our house were quite fine pieces, given the income level of my family. My parents had taken great effort to purchase them early in their marriage, before my father became ill when I was in first grade. Since my ancestry is pure German, it does not surprise me that I respond on a gut level to folk toys, Pennsylvania Dutch furniture, tramp art and naive folk carvings. They connect me to a time in the mid-19th century when my town had the influx of German immigrants that included my great-grandparents. North Tonawanda is near the Erie Canal and Great Lakes system, and it was the lumber capital of the East in the 19th century. The Allan Herschell Carousel Factory was located down the railroad tracks from my home. When I passed it regularly on my way to Saturday matinee movies, I used to peek through the windows to see the carved animals in progress.

"My mother sewed a lot, making dolls and simple craft items. My father had exceptional handwriting. Before his illness he was a clerk/accountant who kept the ledger for the local lumber company.

"I had an adopted brother four years older than I who, during my formative years, was interested in classical music and composition. He played several instruments and he introduced me to music. We shared a small bedroom which had his record player in it. This gave me the opportunity to observe his involvement with music. When I had the room to myself, I often mimicked him conducting to the records. He was very good with his hands and built model airplanes, canoes, pieces of furniture and, in his adult years, harpsichords. He reinforced my feeling for the importance of craftsmanship, although I fall far below his standards and expert handling of materials."

In his youth Newman had no private art instruction, but he began drawing cartoons and copies of comic book illustrations in grammar school. In high school, he majored in art and also took mathematics and other college prep courses. His role model of a male artist was the high school art teacher. At the Cleveland Institute of Art, which he attended after high school, Newman benefited from sculpture instructor William McVey who allowed him to observe his professional work methods. Due mainly to McVey's encouragement and nurturing attitude, Newman continued his education at Cranbrook Academy of Art in Michigan where he earned a B.F.A. degree in 1962. He completed an M.F.A. at Cornell University in 1964. He joined the faculty of Bradford in 1965.

Although it evolved into a four-year coed school, Bradford College was originally a women's junior college. Newman has given a goodly amount of his energy in support of women's education. His relationship with Bradford College has been mutually beneficial. He feels that having a working mother freed him from stereotypical thinking.

"I didn't get locked into a notion of specific roles for men and women or a narrow view of a parent's role. Sheli says that's the basis for my receptivity to feminine issues. I've had the luxury of freedom in a low-key, non-competitive environment. I've been able to bring a concept of interconnection between disciplines into the curriculum design here and, at the same time, I've applied the concept to my own work. My art is also interdisciplinarian and layered, in that it allows me to bring my interest in mythology, comparative religion, psychology and craftsmanship all together in one context. It's taken me a long time to get over my art training. I was taught how to make art, but not how to integrate art and life."

Newman described his sources:

"My work emerges from a deep vein of knowledge that links me to a collective past or 'dreamtime' beyond my temporal being. These artistic creations synthesize elements that lie buried and separated in strata of my mind. I perceive the creative impulse as springing from our need to realize and communicate with nature, god or humanity. It derives its energy from our search for wholeness, and its source can be traced to the archaeology of the brain. By this I suggest that an artist penetrates the conscious, unconscious and subliminal 'layers' of the mind to reach archetypal images. My own creative efforts are no exception; they act to blend subliminal messages with conscious thoughts and to connect inner motive with outer expression; they attempt to voice fears, celebrate awakening and illuminate those contradictions which fill my field of vision."

Newman has viewed the job of integrating his art and his life as a psychological job, as if his life were mostly the one he lives in his mind.

"Obviously, my work is very personal and autobiographical. My attitude approaches something close to Joseph Campbell's advice in *The Power of Myth,* when he says to 'follow your bliss.' I rely to a large extent on intuition, but I get tremendous nudges from helping hands. Central ideas and themes persist and re-emerge as I work. They focus the work or hem it in, I suppose, according to one's vantage point. I trust my instincts and see my studio work as a continuum of activity which is directed toward self-knowledge, awareness and inner growth. It is as if it is in preparation for something yet to come . . . perhaps an even greater test or challenge that I may reach in old age. My art is therapeutic in that it allows me to integrate experiences, gives me an arena for playful discovery and supplies an outlet for reverie and reverence."

Newman calls some of his sculptures "monuments," due to their "spatial presence or resonant form," and says they provide him with a format to celebrate and honor the past. He often designs box-type pieces, akin to reliquaries with openings in them, and he believes he might need to put his memories in safe storage. "This feature of my work hints at the value I assign to the unconscious and reveals my psyche's preoccupation with the protection of power objects or experiences."

Newman's family held to traditional German Lutheranism. He was active in the church and Luther League. Although he does not now consider himself religious in the orthodox sense, a religious habit of mind remains. It permeates his work, even to the design of his altarpieces with all their allusions to stately European churches. "Through a collage or assemblage process I lay claim to discarded materials or fragments of time that must be refitted into a new context of meaning." To Newman, the act of making a collage is a testimony to his " . . . primal need to celebrate some belief in resurrection and renewal. I guess you could say that I lean towards a belief in reincarnation. Nature strikes me as a great recycling plant. Why exclude the possibility of humans from such a system? I have no strong vibrations about who I might have been in some other life, but once in a while I have delusions of grandeur and think I might have been a man of the cloth."

Newman makes a habitual connection between his religious beliefs, his mind and his work.

"Man needs to feel a sense of connectedness to the past and present. A full life dictates the need for faith in something and the surrender of one's ego at times to something larger than oneself. This makes us feel most alive. It establishes our purpose for being and fosters a sense of dedication which we can bring to our work and life. I think that mental health is dependent in large measure upon our need to maintain some meaningful relationship with a 'spiritual guide' that stands outside to provide helping hands. Without such a relationship, life is too lonely and dark.

"As a young teen, I joined the church choir, which allowed me to raise my voice in praise of God or a transcendental power. I now use my 'artistic voice' to celebrate myself as much as a larger being. While I enjoy an outside audience from time to time, I feel I am less dependent on it in my middle age. I feel a strength in my convictions as well as commitment to the studio work which I undertake. My religious background was as helpful to me in discovering my identity as my formal schooling. It continues to offer rich memories and directs my search for harmony. I believe it also gave me a valuable sense of communal experience, and this influenced my choice to enter the teaching profession. It provided me with a province of thought and a sanctified place where I could confront esthetic experience. It was evident to my young mind that the church was a place that housed fine workmanship, glorious sounds and encouraged the noblest of efforts. I can remember as a young boy telling my mother that when I was grown up I wanted a job I would look forward to going to. I could sense at an early age that 'work' had to have value and provide an avenue for self-expression and inner growth.

"Certainly my childhood religious experience instilled a sense of mythic meaning as well as mystic belief. This has nurtured my understanding of Art as an instrument of silent meditation and awakening. I feel that Art is a way for each of us to discover our intuitive power and source of inspiration. It can provide a basis for understanding our own humanity and that responsible role we have as caretakers of the natural world. Disciplined activity and heightened sensitivity can reveal a spiritual path for the artist which can lead to a private spring of magic waters. Continual immersion in these waters can heal our psychic wounds, intensify our perceptions and equip us with a Janusian view of life, one that simultaneously looks forward and back. Artists can create a prophetic vision largely because they have learned the value of bathing in these waters, which affords them a clearer recognition of the pattern of life or history."

Newman's mysticism is fed by his reading and his alertness to the events, however subtle, that occur each day, especially in his studio.

"I have constant contact with synchronicity through my work. Whether I am absorbed by an immediate project or beginning to nurture a new one, ideas and materials are channeled to me all the time. I think the mind, when absorbed by a problem or focused on expressive work, acts like a net that traps resources which can serve its identified needs. I think this is common to many artists and plays a part in why we all experience some feeling of control over our circumstances as a result of our creative activities. It also stands as the reason why many of us resist overanalyzing our situation or process for fear we will frighten away the muse and deprive ourselves of its gifts."

At Bradford, Newman teaches a course he designed titled The Nature of Creativity. He uses Herman Hesse's *Narcissus and Goldmund* and Robert Pirsig's *Zen and the Art of Motorcycle Maintenance* to focus on the notion of duality and the need for balance or unity of opposites in art. He finds Bob Samples' *The Metaphoric Mind* helpful also to underscore the need for a holistic view of life. We can glimpse what it might be like to take his course through his broad interest in the basis of creativity in fantasy or enchantment. "Enchantment certainly is missing from most people's lives today. I think this is why so many of us cling to the obvious rituals associated with the holidays. However, we must realize that nature herself holds the power to supply us with an endless source of enchantment. I think the reason folk art feels so innately familiar to me is because it brings religious references into art. Primitive art also expresses an enchanted view of the world through its imagery and form, and it is an enormous inspiration to my own art."

Newman's students are allowed to share his insights and struggles as an artist, which must enrich their understanding of creativity. His thoughts stretch out to encompass his interests as artist and as teacher. Ultimately, his remarks always circle back to the inner core of his philosophy, the concept of unity.

"I'm interested in the recent research dealing with the brain that suggests there is an old and a new brain, and that there's information back there that can be retrieved, which connects us to our past and our ancestry. I have a feeling that childhood experiences are the root of most of our creative effort. I've spent a lot of time trying to get back in touch with childhood, but I am not able to do so consciously."

Newman began his art career as a painter.

"At Cornell I got preoccupied with the mandala as a form. The form had great meaning and resonance for me, but I didn't know why. I just knew that on the technical level it allowed me to explore my interests in color the way Josef Albers makes use of it. I stayed with the radial symmetry of the mandala form for a good six or seven years. Now I realize that this work helped me to re-center my education by healing accidental splits in my thinking. It formed the basis for understanding, in an artistic and psychological sense, the union of opposites or contrary forces.

"I've always had formalist tendencies. Maybe it is because I am of a Northern temperament. Being German by heritage, perhaps I have a fascination with sternness. But, after working with color so long, I wanted a sudden break and I went to the opposite pole of black and white photo-collage. Collage has allowed me to find imagery that grows out of expressionistic tendencies—the other side of the German spirit. In three-dimensional multi-media work, I've made a marriage of the formalist and expressionist extensions of collage and photography. I continue to be interested in the idea of mixing black and white with color elements in the same context. They become like two different realities, the reality of the dream-past versus the reality of the world at present.

"I would say that the primal image in my work is one of a singular and powerful figure or presence, attended to or surrounded by many smaller figures or units. I wonder sometimes if the image symbolizes Christ or some figurehead preaching to the children. Symmetry plays a very strong role in my work and has since the period when I first discovered the mandala form. It lends itself to the concept of a monument that dominates much of my sculptural mixed-media work. The monument form is also tolerant of a complexity of parts and a juxtaposition of polar elements."

How, I asked Newman, is the artist a transformational figure? He replied:

"Picasso once stated that 'Art is the lie that reveals the truth.' Such is the paradox of art. The artist transforms reality by framing and editing his products. He uncovers truth and exposes beauty through a finite and fixed view of nature, though nature is in fact an infinite and incomprehensible process. The artist allows the viewer to take notice of visual details that stand united to one another within a distinct field of meaning, one which is limited and capable of exhibiting visual relationships that encode ideas and feelings.

"I like to employ found objects from many sources in my work. We live in a time of such conspicuous consumption, and our world is so cluttered with useless gadgets and devices. I guess I atone for my guilt about bringing more objects into the world by recycling. But, my approach challenges me to create a new visual construct to extend or alter the original meaning of these objects. To accomplish this, I tap their old associative meaning while also attaching new layers of reference to them as a result of the context in which I place them. Through this process I gain access to my metaphoric mind, and I can then share its expressive capabilities. I have found that any depth of meaning that my studio work can produce is tied to its ability to sustain simultaneous levels of reality and to communicate my mythic consciousness to others.

"My work has never been mainstreamed, partly because it falls between the stylistic cracks, and also because it is multi-media. I've had to find the right form to integrate my experiences, interests and skills, and I had to find the focal point or source of energy to keep me motivated to produce with a limited audience."

Newman's view of art is open-ended because he can find his materials anywhere: from nature, in antique markets, used bookstores, old photographs, even his own work which constantly tempts him to reconstitute it "until I realize when each compositional event has reached its own journey's end." His collages and assemblages are the bridge that lets the past inform the present.

"Art provides a healing force which aids both the maker and the viewer by providing a framework in which to realize faith, union and mystery to discover and chart the meaning of our lives. It offers us a measured area of activity where we can exercise control and seek harmony, perfection or closure. It equips us with a language for communicating our encounter with the world. Through Art's window, we can view the wonders of our surroundings. As artists, we can be touched by the perceptions of others and, in turn, affect others."

Richard Newman's collage/assemblage process is a continuum of birth, death and rebirth; and his work stands as a testament to his belief that, in the final analysis, this life is a mere dress rehearsal for the most creative moment of all when we are born into the future through our own death.

I attended the "Crone Party" in honor of Meinrad Craighead's birthday. The Crone is a woman who upon reaching 50 years of age is released into wisdom and impartiality, but simultaneously can afford to be childlike in feeling delight. When Meinrad's pixieish face brightens over shared humor—she laughs easily—her eyes manage to sparkle even more than her heavy glasses. She's thin as a reed, but not at all fragile. Her physical presence is that of contained vitality. If she speaks, it is to make a contribution. By habit and inclination, she pares things down, so you know if she says it, owns it or wears it, it matters to her. She likes earrings and a bit of Indian jewelry, but she keeps only a cap of hair around her face. From her appearance, you would suspect she is an artist.

MEINRAD CRAIGHEAD was born in Little Rock, Arkansas, the first of three daughters in a family that struggled to make ends meet during the Depression. Christened Charlene, she grew up happily in Chicago and Milwaukee. Educated in Catholic schools until she earned her bachelor's degree from Clarke College in Dubuque, Iowa, she received her Master's degree in Fine Arts from the University of Wisconsin at Madison. For a few years, she taught art and art history in Albuquerque at St. Joseph's College and the University of New Mexico before traveling to Italy to join the staff of the Dominican's Schifanoia School of Fine Art. In 1965, on a Fulbright Scholarship to study art in Spain, she spent the year in Montserrat where the Benedictine basilica held a statue of the Black Madonna. Under its influence, she felt a powerful need to withdraw from the world. Before doing so she went to Einsiedeln, Switzerland. In the abbey there is another famed Black Madonna. While in Einsiedeln, she also visited the tomb of her mother's venerated great-uncle, Bruder Meinrad Eugster, who lived from 1848 to 1925. At age 30, Charlene Craighead entered Stanbrook Abbey in England as a Benedictine nun and took his name, Meinrad. She remained there for 14 years.

Long before I met her in 1984, I knew Meinrad's name through her work that was sold at a religious center in Albuquerque. I went to there to ask if we might have a woman's ceremonial there to launch my book Connecting: The Art of Beth Ames Swart. *I was surprised to learn that Meinrad was living in Albuquerque. She helped me prepare for the celebration and we became friends. A few years later it was natural to turn to her in expectation of the Harmonic Convergence on August 16 and 17, 1987. For a year, a group of us met at Meinrad's little home near the Rio Grande River to celebrate the equinoxes and solstices in rituals she invented. Our grand finale was the Convergence itself. Those of us fortunate enough to be there were offered the privilege of sharing in a stately ceremony of simple truth and rich beauty.*

MEINRAD CRAIGHEAD: VISIONS OF THE MOTHER GOD

Meinrad Craighead says, "I love the dark. It nourishes me. I am a Celtic artist. I am hidden in and understand life out of the Labyrinth. Celtic space is all a fantastic, intrauterine journey; it loops under and over and around, out the edge and back again; everything is the antithesis of Classical space. It is being inside a forest, out of time."

For me and many other women, Meinrad Craighead is a Priestess of the Moon, a font of knowledge and a source of ritual. Meinrad is like a "'wisdom woman,' a Buddha in female form, a woman who realizes that her soul is one with eternal Spirit . . . spontaneously self-perfected, spontaneously self-liberated." (Ken Wilber, in a tribute to his late wife Treya,

Common Boundary, May-June, 1989.)

She is a mystical artist whose vision reflects a profoundly solitary and devoted life. Her art is hermetic. Each image is recognizable, but like a glyph, it refers to a constellation of ideas. An accumulation of these images in a painting is charged with a density of symbolic meaning. In essence, her art is a visual language, created from the depths of her mind, beyond technique. Meinrad says that for her, making art " . . . is an entry to the spirit."

On my wall, frequently in my range of vision, is her painting *Wisdom*, an image of an owl brooding over the white form of the moon, surrounded by the inky night sky. Within it is the darkened shadow moon divided to show its three phases. Meinrad told me, "The moon phases are a constant with me. I never tire of that movement in the universe from light to dark, into light and out of darkness again."

When I first saw the painting *Wisdom*, I knew I had to own it. I felt I had held the image in my own imagination all my life, and here it was, a codification of the wholeness of light and dark, an answer to the yin/yang paradox from a feminine viewpoint. My bonding with Meinrad stemmed from simply knowing her, but this painting deepened my understanding of what her art signifies.

One word that holds true for each of Meinrad's images is power. Strength derived entirely from force of mind and conviction infuses her work. More than for most artists, the language of Meinrad Craighead's imagery is an outgrowth of a daily life in which art is thoroughly infused with the spiritual. She has said, "My whole life is based on my belief in God. I view my artwork as a day-by-day continuous act of thanksgiving to this God of beauty I worship."

Meinrad, though cloistered in a British abbey, was nonetheless known to the art community for her woodcuts, her drawings and the four television documentaries about her. *The Sign of the Tree*, a synthesis of poetry and graphics, was first published while she was behind the wall.

Meinrad's decision to leave the abbey was carried out swiftly. One morning she simply knew it was time to leave. Through friends she was given shelter and time to work on her remarkable book, *The Mother's Songs: Images of God the Mother,* (Paulist Press in 1986). This poetic autobiography and 42 illustrations are a powerful paean to God as Mother, not as a denial of the patriarchal Father God, but as an amplification of a single Divine nature. She explained in her introduction, "My Catholic heritage and environment have been like a beautiful river flowing over my subterranean foundation in God the Mother. The two movements are not in conflict, they simply water different layers in my soul."

Meinrad's sacred images have a glow achieved through layer upon layer of highly diluted ink applied to sanded scratch board and varnished. In form and color they are distinctive, radiant with meaning and purpose. She has created an iconography and style completely her own. The world she projects is inhabited by earthy figures—their mouths, eyes, breasts and hands triumphantly human and metaphorically eternal. They call to mind the goddesses of early fertility cults expressed with a medieval weightlessness and crowdedness of imagery. Femaleness informs not only her symbolism but also her compositions, which frequently are schematics of ovaries and womb. An underlying theme in her work is the gestation, reproduction and suckling of new life, an essential expression of the feminine principle of nourishing. To Meinrad, nourishing means not only giving milk but also passing on knowledge, love and shared experience. Primarily for her, it means making art. Her paintings are her children.

The first source of Meinrad's art and philosophy was clearly her solid and loving family. She says, "It is the basis for trusting people the rest of your life and for not living in fear. That grounding is essential for any kind of creative life. I don't believe in the myth of the neurotic, unstable artist."

"I was blessed with love," she says. She remembers her childhood as a time in which her mother and grandmother were the Wise Women who made God the Mother real in her life. "Memaw and my mother were the role models for my whole understanding of the motherhood of God. Memaw drew me to her especially because she was older and she was a dark woman, dark physically and dark in her temperament. That dark mystified me."

The fourth and last little girl in her family died shortly after birth before coming home from the hospital. Meinrad says,

"I immediately took that child to myself as a guardian angel. Her name was Colette. She was born on the feast of the Immaculate Conception and that was important to me as a child, because I was really heavily into feast days and Catholic ritual, benediction and incense.

"Maybe my parents needed two other children to see that I was different, but whatever I was doing creatively, they knew instinctively to support. Bear in mind there wasn't money—but I always had what I needed, crayons, pastels, paper, an easel which was given to me on my 12th birthday, because I really was drawing regularly from my earliest years.

"I listened to the Tom Rider, Tom Mix and Superman serials in 15-minute sections, one following another roughly from 3:00 to supper time. I would sit there and draw what I was hearing. From the very beginning, I was drawing stories that were coming to me verbally, and doing drawings based on stories I was reading; so the idea of storytelling for the image is very important to me. Consciously or unconsciously, I was teaching myself to draw with facility. Every evening after my father finished reading the newspaper, I would go through it and cut out photographs, especially from the sports page. I taught myself anatomy by drawing from photographs in the newspaper. Later I studied anatomy, but I was always fascinated by the attitudes and movement of the human body. That was like a ritual, a daily habit, reinforced month after month, year after year. I abandoned that after I got to high school.

"Another important thing as a child was the structure of being in Little Rock during the summers and in Chicago during the winters. When I was back in Chicago from roughly September first to June first, from time to time I would make a selection of the drawings that I did in the course of the year and roll them up and send them to Memaw. The real point here, and I only came to know this as an adult, was the fact that I specifically began to associate making art with gift giving. My gifts to Memaw taught me that the talent or the gift or the ability to do these drawings, even the desire to do them, was in itself a gift, and I was giving it back.

"Without saying it to myself in so many words, that giving became, for me, the very definition of religious art. You are given this gift which we call talent, the drive and intuition, and the acquired ability to produce imagery or music; it moves through you and it goes back to a specific receiver. It's a continuous circle.

"Nothing is in isolation. Everything is related. You can't understand being centered, unless you understand relationships. I think that is a profound gift from the Catholic church. The relatedness we have with the saints gives us a living contact with people in history, not just history of movements of bodies and nations and wars and so on, but people who really did live in a particular time and gave of themselves altruistically. To me as an artist, that is significant because I think we give without knowing what the reverberations are going to be. That is what the spirit is. We are asked to do quite ordinary things, but we do them extraordinarily. The extraordinariness of it is in the fact we persevere. I think perseverance is the mystery because there are so many reasons to give up.

"So this understanding of religious art came to me pretty early. And I got better and better at drawing, which of course one does just because of the habit of doing it. I turned to drawing the Christian stories, the New Testament and the Parables. I have always been extra dotty for the wisdom of the Parables. I never tire of reading them, thinking about them or rejoicing in them. They are not only profound literature, but they offer profound spiritual insights into harmony with all of creation. So I really loved doing drawings of The Sower, or Look at the Lily of the Fields, or The Prodigal Son, and other Biblical ideas such as Walking on the Waters.

"Memaw died when I was 12, and my grandfather died a year later. My childhood ended with one axe stroke. Afterwards, my family recalls, I turned exclusively to my artwork; that's all I did. I became quite introverted and surly if I was interrupted. My bedroom was the place where I went to read and to work. And that's the way I remember my time through high school."

In her college years, at Clarke College in Dubuque, Meinrad competed with herself, not with her peers. When asked for a painting a week, she produced more. She recalls:

"I was so eager. I always did well in school, but I hated it because most of what I was learning seemed completely irrelevant. All I wanted to do at the time was to work, paint, draw and read. I was the first person ever in my family—of all my cousins and aunts and uncles—to go to college. I had wanted to go to a local art school. It was my father who insisted I could study art, but I would do it in a liberal arts college, not in an art school. He talked it through with me. It just showed the narrowness of my own vision at the time, my own immaturity, and his understanding of what I needed. I got an art scholarship to Clarke College, which was important financially, and off I went to Dubuque. It took quite a while for me to understand that, in fact, all of the liberal arts courses were necessary to feed the imagery. The habit of books was not something I grew up with."

Meinrad spent her junior year in Vienna at the Academy of Fine Arts, drawing from the live model. "The most important thing about Vienna was the music and the Bosch paintings at the Academia. You know how freezing cold those museums are, especially in winter? So, for me to spend hour after hour, week after week in front of those paintings, you can imagine I must have been besotted by them. Bosch's paintings had an enormous influence on me with their miracle of detail."

Art space became sacred space for Meinrad in Europe. She found she could make no distinction between being in these cathedrals of art history and being in churches.

"They were all cathedrals of beauty and cathedrals of the spirit and I wanted to be in them. In Europe, the immense loneliness of the museum galleries satisfied me enormously, hearing my own footsteps on the cold marble floors. If there were people, if there was speech, it was all hushed as if we were in a sacred sanctum, a sacred space. I found that museums and galleries were places I would go and pray.

"My understanding of the mass is still in some European cathedral—and you know they are usually pitch dark—in some side altar where an old priest in a fiddleback vestment is saying mass on a filthy dirty altar cloth in places hanging with cobwebs and littered with dust."

Our conversation turned from the mass to ritual. Meinrad said, "If you live in the spirit, ritual is as ordinary as breathing. Every act comes out of that center where you live in the spirit. Therefore, every act is a ritual act, an act of thanksgiving directed back to the source. Each of us in the structure of our life should be constantly in the act of celebrating the memory of our own Being in this fantastic gift of life. That is where we have made our mistake. We have abrogated our responsibility to celebrate our own memories."

The subject of memories reminded Meinrad of the Teutonic myth of Odin and the Ravens, which she told to me.

"Odin lives at the very height of Iggdrysil, which is a great World Ash, which dominates the upper reaches of creation, invisible to the world below of course. And he lives there with his two ravens. He is like Yahweh. Having created all things, he lives without communicating with them. However, he has two ravens and every day at dawn he sends the ravens out and they circle round the Earth and see everything that is going on and hear everything. At night they fly back to the topmost branches of Iggdrysil and roost for the evening. Through the evening they tell Odin everything that is going on down on Earth. Now the names of these two ravens are Thought and Memory. One day after he has sent forth his ravens, Odin begins to think, "What if something should happen to one of my ravens? Which one could I live without? And he thinks about this and he thinks about this. Then he finally decides he can live without Thought, but he can't live without Memory."

Meinrad said:

"The myths are filled with insights, but I think this is one of the most powerful insights coming out of world mythology, because without memories we don't exist. At least in terms of our Higher Self, we are our memories. That is why we must celebrate them and honor them, which to me is what ritual is.

"Especially as artists, we have to celebrate our memories. I say artists, but I mean anyone who acts creatively. I think creativity comes out of memory. I say that in *The Mother's Songs*. It's as if we are full of eggs, but the eggs have to be fertilized; and I think it is memory that fertilizes those eggs, which then become babies—the works of art. We are constantly giving birth to something that has literally never existed on the face of the earth before.

"Making art is a journey. As you are going step by step, you literally don't know where you are going. You are moving paint around, and in my case I am moving tools around on the scratchboard surface. And the form is evolving and you are following. It is the form as it is made manifest that is pulling you along step by step. And finally there is resolution; and you think this is it, this is the story, this is where it is coming from. But the artist is always communicating with an audience. If one person looking at my painting says something that identifies the painting in a whole new way for me, it means the painting is wholly outside me, standing with its own life, giving its own energy into the world via whoever happens to see it."

I said, "Meinrad, I think you're an inventor of glyphs that stand for ideas. The glyph grows over a period of time. When the painting is released from you, its inner language continues to communicate with you as well as other people. It develops after it is made." She found the idea stimulating.

"I like the word glyph because it is like making a painting. In picture writing, a glyph has a singular power in itself. All these energies come together to make a final word or statement. A painting also comes one glyph, or image, at a time, so to speak, as you make it, until finally its secret language is revealed to you, letter by letter in a process like unconscious writing.

"The work I am doing now is evolving out of my prayer life specifically in this place. It began in February 1986, when I built that altar out in my yard as an act of thanksgiving for my 50th birthday. Once that fire was in place, I began my morning ritual of lighting the fire to meet the rising sun, so that the fire is lit in darkness. When the sun rises, the fire is calling to the fire in the heavens to meet the fire in the altar and the fire in me. I couple the fire with a water ceremony because I can't disassociate fire and water. My ritual life goes hand in hand, one explicating and one merging with my creative life.

"Now that I have the studio here with seven altars, I come in and make my sacred circle around this space, having done a sacred circle around the fire. Centering myself in those energies means I feel good about going to work. It means that I am prepared to do this creative work. I need all the energy I can have. If I am in the privileged position, as I think all artists are, to receive in order to give, then I want to be as blessed and as consecrated as possible in order to give again. Otherwise, I don't know what empowers imagery. When we talk about powerful imagery, what do we mean, if we are not ourselves empowered to do it? All of this, needless to say, is an outcome of my being immersed in Catholic ritual. Nothing that I do in the morning is that different from the mass. It's an act of thanksgiving, it's an act of praise, it's an act of awe that I am alive. This is my role in life, and I'm asking for the grace and power to do it, which is why we go to mass. We go to mass to be fed.

"I am still in the same river, but I've drifted into another channel of the river. Of course, the river for me is the abiding symbol of my life. The river is the most powerful metaphor for the gift of an artistic life. I think it all springs from that line in Psalm 1, 'Happy is the man who delights in the light of the Lord. He is like a tree planted in flowing water that yields its fruit in due season and whose leaves never fade.' We can truly say, 'Happy is the person who is an artist because that person

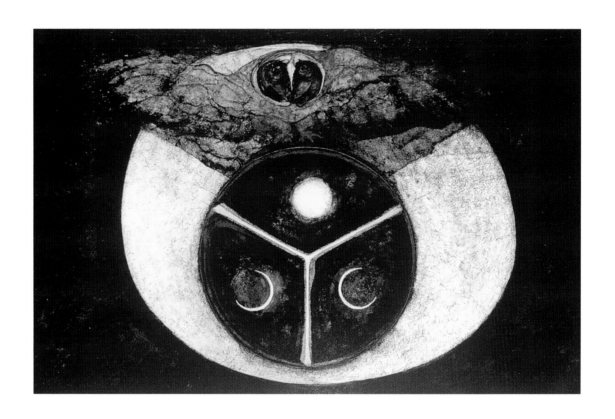

PLATE 4

"Wisdom"
Meinrad Craighead

must constantly live in a state of delight.'

"The artist is like a tree, but the tree has to be planted by the flowing water, and given that, the tree constantly yields its fruit in due season, and the seasonal life of an artist is mystically always in season. We are always ready to give birth."

Meinrad's language of glyphs has changed in her recent book, *The Litany of the Great River* (Paulist Press, 1991). The prose and descriptive imagery in *The Mother's Songs* referred to locations, settings and places. The new works are emblematic, iconic images against featureless grounds.

"My prayer at the altar every morning has become a litany of repeated words and phrases. Some words from the Litany of the Sacred Heart and of the Virgin Mary have become part of this daily litany, which grows and grows. Images have been collecting around the phrases Valley of Darkness, Seat of Wisdom, Arc of the Covenant, Morning Star, Eye of Heaven, Eternal Water, Cave of the Heart, Heart of Fire, Mystical Rose, Shining Valley, and Eternal Presence. I began to realize that what was happening could possibly be the manifestation of my next book, because the images I was seeing were strong central singular figures, which seemed to me the ultimate visual litany. A litany is bang, bang, bang, one strong central image after another."

The phrase "Seat of Wisdom" has prompted Meinrad's *Hagia Sophia*. "I just started drawing a maze and the painting moved out from that center until finally it became the womb of the Mother. As it evolved, the great hand appeared and the beginning of the maze moved right up into her hand. The two owls appeared very late in the painting after the mandorla with the feathers were in place. Sometime after I'd finished the painting, a young boy saw it. He said, 'Oh, Meinrad, you've made a Guadalupe.' That never occurred to me. But I loved the thought that I had done a Virgin of Guadalupe. She had manifested herself."

Meinrad was aware once again of a connection between her painting, *Hagia Sophia*, and the river. She says, "Like Ariadne, the figure weaves the maze with a thread that is both the river and our life. We arrive at Holy Wisdom through the creative life, which is also the Goddess's life. We begin and end in her."

Everyday Meinrad walks beside the Rio Grande. The river is her meditation. "The river imprints every square inch of us. When you are down close to it, the riverbed is a microcosm of the archetypal landscape of the entire Southwest, with little mesas and valleys and small riverbeds within the larger one."

With the help of a woman contractor, Meinrad built her own studio, a separate building from her house. She focused on this task for nine months during which she could not paint. "Every nail you drive in is a centering act, every plank you lay is a centering act, every beam that you measure and get just right is a centering act. You know that wonderful dictum attributed to Thomas Aquinas, 'God is in the details.' A building, like a painting, like anything we are building in our lives, is all building toward the whole. I knew the studio had to be named for and dedicated to a principle or person, a life force that was an extension of my own journey; it had to come out of my experience as an artist, and finally I arrived at this name, The All-Seeing Eye of the Mother."

Having named her studio, the artist evolved its mythology. She says, "We have been created and we are all in the state of being looked at." Her contemplation is strangely entwined with a vision of a goddess that came to her after the studio was completed. One summer evening, Meinrad and her sister who had come for a visit stood near the gate beside the ditch that drains into the Rio Grande a few blocks away.

"We were looking southwest. It was a beautiful twilight during the virgin phase of the moon. Through the cottonwoods, we saw the new moon hanging in the southwestern sky. Quite clearly, I saw a figure standing on the bank of the ditch. She was opening that gate. It was only a flash of intuition but, again, I connected her image with the river. As she opened the gate, in my imagination my dogs rushed to her, as if they were saying, 'Oh, you're here.' I didn't say anything about it; I didn't want to talk about it. When things settled down after my sister left, I got back to my normal rhythm, but I thought a lot about my vision. I realized I had seen the hunter. She didn't carry a bow, she didn't have winged feet, she wasn't dressed as an archer like Artemis with the little leather skirt, yet I knew she was the hunter and that's why the hounds had recognized her. They were going off to hunt too. I found that very exciting. Over a period of days or weeks, I started to paint *The Hunter Comes for Her Hounds.*

"I've always felt the hunter was an image of the artist. The artist is a hunter and God is a hunter, hunting us. We are always being looked at by God, by the Hunter. In my studio, I am in the eye of the hunter. My relationship with God has always been somewhat terrifying. A deeply spiritual Jungian analyst told me, shortly before her death, that the mental institutions are filled with people who have seen too much of God. The gift of God is twice blessed, because it is not only the fact that God hunts me to have me to Herself, but also the gift of being able to give that energy back that prevents the energy from imploding in me.

"I feel the hunter appeared to me very strongly when she did because my studio was just finished. I wanted her to watch over every aspect of my life. The hunter became another aspect of the eye, the eye that hunts. Obviously, the main tool of the hunter is the eye watching, wide open in absolute silence.

"When I started painting the hunter, a really quite violent face appeared. To my amazement, she was holding my binoculars that I keep on my work table for watching the birds. The binoculars are a fantastic way to understand the hunter as the ultimate see-er. The see-er does not come with bows and arrows; she does not come to kill; she sets out to seek. The seeing is the slaying. To be seen is to be so purified that one is slain in the process, because the layers of the old self literally fall away."

Meinrad insists, "My usual role is to be as withdrawn and quiet as possible in order to make the images." Yet her calendar is often full. She is visited by collectors, friends, writers and women who turn to her for guidance. Her books, lectures and workshops have made her well-known in the new spirituality movement. For their well-being, she advises people to tell their own memories and stories, or better yet, to draw them. "Memory and dream language are the same to me. When you tell or write a dream, you are translating into another language, but if you draw your dream you stay in the same language."

In my mind's eye, I see Meinrad Craighead on her land under the cottonwoods in the bosque, visiting her altars, entering her studio and beginning her painting as an act of prayer. Her art is a gift to the world, but it is her dedication to doing holy ritual that makes her a priestess-shaman, an artist of the spirit down by the river.

*M*y route to meeting
Linda Tellington-Jones was circuitous.
Texas layerist Delda Skinner
told me that her daughter, Eleanor McCulley,
had a friend with a gift for healing animals. After a
series of phone calls to Delda, to Eleanor and
finally to Linda, I explained my project and
why I wanted to interview her for this book.
In a lyrical voice with an easy laugh, Linda said she
understood the connection I am making between
artists and others with the gift of the spirit.
An element of trust was there before we met
in person.

"I can hear animals and I love to pass on
what they tell me," she said, and then she related an anecdote about being
part of a shipboard expedition to British Columbia in support of a
scientist who studies the sounds of orca whales. On the evening of their arrival, they
were sitting around a campfire in the darkness when they heard a "whoosh"
sound nearby in the water. Glowing phosphorous lit a huge orca who was only ten feet
off the beach. Linda received a message from this whale's sound-making, which
she translated into a moving poem. "Speak ye to those of your kind who cannot hear
with your ears, who cannot see with your eyes." The orca pleads with people to behave
responsibly toward all species.

THIS WAS THE MAGIC part of our conversation, but I also discovered that Linda, who is an idealistic pragmatist and an effective organizer, speaks about her work in a very down-to-earth way. As a project director with Esalen Institute's US/USSR cultural exchange, she has been to Russia several times a year to demonstrate her Tellington-Jones Every Animal Method (T.E.A.M.) techniques. In 1985, she founded Animal Ambassadors, International under the aegis of Esalen to contribute to the cause of peace and understanding around the globe. Through this organization, she has developed programs for schools and zoos and worked on wildlife rehabilitation.

LINDA TELLINGTON-JONES, ANIMAL AMBASSADOR

Linda Tellington-Jones is the discoverer and inventor of T.E.A.M., the Tellington-Jones Equine Awareness Method, known also as the Tellington-Jones Every Animal Method, and also The Touch That Heals. She says, "My work is really teaching people how to train horses and other animals with behavioral difficulties. I train people. We are working with all kinds of animals, with Wild Life Rescue, Endangered Species Breeding Programs, with cats and dogs. I do not call myself a healer. I teach a type of work that anyone can do to heal themselves or animals."

On March 7, 1989, I drove north of Santa Fe, New Mexico, along the Rio Grande River into Casa Las Barrancas and parked outside the compound where Linda lives between travels. Linda's comfortable apartment is at one end of an L-shaped adobe hacienda. Her mementos and her personality give the place its warmth. Her small, well-organized office is the center of the international network she has founded. Her own energies are assisted by those of her younger sister Robyn Hood, who edits the T.E.A.M. newsletter from her home in Edmonton, Canada, and also teaches the training around the world.

Linda is in her early fifties, radiantly healthy and cheerful, youthful, friendly and straightforward in manner. She is small in stature and wears her blonde-gray hair in a short pageboy style. Her light aquamarine eyes twinkle. We sat for hours in the communal kitchen while she told me her story.

Linda Tellington-Jones (née Hood), the oldest of six children, was born in Edmonton, Alberta, Canada, in June 1937. "I want to show you some photographs, because I believe that many of us were influenced from the very beginning in what we are going to do," she said. She held out two snapshots of herself, one at eleven months playing with a bear cub's ear and a later one of herself riding a spotted calf. She was under three when her family settled in Yellow Knife in the Northwest Territory.

"There were things I remember as a child that shaped my life. The first winter in Yellow Knife, there was not enough housing so we had to live in a tent with wooden walls and a floor. I remember a scene of a little deermouse standing on the wooden floor. The family cat was attacking him, and my mother was insisting that the cat leave that mouse alone. My mother and both grandfathers could communicate with animals.

"Growing up, I was deeply involved with horses. I rode to school from our wheat and pig farm near Gibbons, Alberta, for four years. We didn't have any other transportation. I don't think I missed riding a horse more than ten days a year from the age of six to fifteen. I'd ride at least three horses every day after school. Between the ages of eleven and fifteen, I trained horses for shows.

"It was normal for my parents to be around animals. My mother's real father, Will Caywood, trained horses for the Czar in Russia. My grandmother was with him in Moscow, but she got tired of him traveling all over the country with race-horses and she came home. She divorced him and married his brother George Caywood, who was a real frontiersman and pioneer.

"I didn't meet my real grandfather Will until he was 82, and he came to live with me and my first husband, Went Tellington, on our ranch in California. In the 1960s we had the Pacific Coast Equestrian Research Farm and, connected with it, the International Pacific Coast School of Horsemanship. We wrote syndicated columns in horse magazines. Will shared secrets with us that he had learned from the Gypsies. For instance, his Russian Gypsy translator taught him how to read a horse's personality by the cowlicks on its head. It's like finger-printing, like a brand or marking. You can't change the swirls on a horse's forehead. We did a survey of 1500 horses, going about it from a scientific point of view, to check out what the Gypsies had said. My husband and I wrote a paper on the results in our column. That information is now used for official identification of horses in this country for breed registry. The horse world usually keeps secrets, but I was raised to be open. Went and I believed in a philosophy of sharing our research."

Linda was 15 years old when she met Wentworth Jordan Tellington, 36 years old, an ex-army officer, an engineer and an explorer. She was 18 years old when she married him in 1956. Linda said, "Thanks to him I believe that my creativity had an avenue for release. He's a brilliant man, ahead of his time. He taught at West Point. At 19, he gave a piano recital at Carnegie Hall. He is a writer, and he has won awards for his photography. He was my teacher and mentor. I admired him. I feel like he raised me."

Although Linda was not a college graduate, she and Tellington both taught at the Chadwick School in Rolling Hills, California, near Los Angeles. During their four years at Chadwick Linda studied liberal arts at the University of Southern California. Tellington served on the advisory council of the Rand Think Tank working on bioengineering.

The couple left Chadwick to open their research farm in Badger, California, where they conducted a nine-month residential program in horsemanship. "We had the first training school with actual reading lists and course assignments. My husband ran the school with the same discipline they use at West Point. That's why it worked so well. We were involved with 100-mile endurance racing and researching massage for horses to help a horse recover after a hard performance. I was used to using my hands in my work with horses."

Linda contributed her lifelong experience around horses and her family heritage to the Tellington massage system. She and her husband worked together night and day as teachers, researchers, writers and managers. She explained:

"When I was growing up, George Caywood lived with us and was always around. He had worked with race horses. Both he and his brother Will said that horses talked with them and they knew when they were going to win. They worked over the horses with their hands and their grooms did, too, for ten minutes a day. They were giving horses a whole feel of their body, which allows them to be more athletic, more confident. So, I grew up sharing a very physical connection with horses.

"Since I was a child, I remember operating at a nonverbal level. Went was a student of mysticism and he had an excellent library. I know I picked up all kinds of information from him that he wasn't aware he was giving off."

By way of introducing her own psychic life, she told this childhood dream: "I was out in the woods on a moonlit night and I found a small stuffed horse with hand-shaped wings. I picked up the horse and started to stroke it and suddenly the horse said, 'It's nice that you stroke me, but if you would do circles on me I would come to life and fly you to visit your animal friends.' As I made circles the horse grew to life-size, and I became aware of a circle of animals surrounding the small clearing, all waiting to talk to me."

From the age of nine, Linda has had a recurring dream of another life lived as an Indian on the Great Plains. She believes this is the source of her interest in the earth and animals. "I think it's the reason I feel as I do about circles and the oneness of life."

In 1969, on the first day of a new school session, Linda overheard a student named Birchel Jones telling classmates that he could remember before he was born. He said he saw his father and grandfather walking together beside the San Francisco Opera House, and he chose them as his family. For a time, he was at a Catholic seminary studying to be a priest, but he dropped out. Linda was intrigued by his remarks. That afternoon she showed the class of students around the farm as part of her regular duties.

"We walked to the edge of a cliff overlooking our ranch. Suddenly, I had this feeling that I was going to pick up my arms and fly. I could feel myself doing it, and I had to force my hands to my sides to stop myself. I thought perhaps the student standing next to me had caused me to feel that way. It was Birchel Jones.

"I managed to get through the afternoon, but something had really shifted. That night was my customary student interview evening when I brought each student in for 15 minutes, starting late in the afternoon. Jones was the last to be interviewed. He came in around nine o'clock and sat down beside me on the bench in my office. I opened my notebook on my lap, picked up my pencil and turned to look toward him. His eyes held no emotion, but my abdomen started to spasm and I just went out of my body. I felt myself flying very fast over a marsh and lake, mountains and forests. I could feel my physical body leaving earth. Ahead of me the clouds seemed to form an eye and I shot through that eye.

"Then I came back and looked at Jones. He said 'Are you all right?' I said yes, but I wanted to go back out to wherever I had been. This time, I saw a pulsating black ball. I returned, left again, and saw a black neon hand blocking me, flashing off and on. Then I heard my husband calling me and Jones said, 'He needs you.' I walked into the house without doing the interview or speaking to him again. It was one o'clock in the morning. The next day I was disorientated all through the day while I was teaching. That night I was again out of body and thinking, 'I'm not ready to go.' I did not speak to anyone about what I had experienced. I thought I was pregnant and then became sure that I had been implanted while I was 'out there,' seeded with information. I think now that I went home to my universe.

"Over the next few days, I wrote a lot of poetry. What came into my mind was the word reincarnation. I had never thought of it before. I knew I was carrying a seed of information that would unfold as I was ready. Then books were given to me that I needed to read. The first one was by Ruth Montgomery, about our families and reincarnating in groups. After my friend Kai de Fontaney gave me Jane Roberts' *Seth Speaks*, I bought Roberts' *The Nature of Personal Reality* and read the first 91 pages nine times. It changed my life."

About nine months after her out of body experience, Linda had another vision at Prescott College in Arizona. She was there as a consultant with their Outward Bound program helping people overcome their fear of horseback riding. She was to give a lecture on endurance riding to about 250 people. "It seemed such an opportunity for me to give them something inspirational about nature, but what?" she recalled. Before the lecture, she stepped out onto the desert as the sun was setting. "I just opened my arms and let the sun fill me. I thought nothing. As I walked in the door, everybody stopped talking at once. I started my lecture and afterward people came up and said it was so beautiful. I'd love to know what I said—something about our horses giving us the opportunity to experience God in nature. On my way home, driving across the Arizona desert, I had a flash of insight that I had come to this planet to make humans aware of the importance of animals in our lives." The brief moment of inner awareness confirmed for her that her life has an ultimate and profound purpose. She has never forgotten it.

Linda's marriage became increasingly loose-knit, finally fraying in 1970 when Tellington left the farm for San Francisco. She found a manager for the school, and divorced her husband. From 1971 to 1974, she was married to Birchel Jones, who is eleven years her junior. (She keeps Tellington's and Jones' names in appreciation for their part in her professional and spiritual life.) Throughout most of their brief marriage, Jones trained to compete for the Olympic pentathlon while Linda trained horses and managed a farm in the Los Altos Hills south of San Francisco. The University of California at Santa Cruz asked her to start the first horse management class in the Adult Education Department. Thirty-two students were needed to break even; 96 showed up. She repeated the course and 142 students came.

One evening in 1972, one of her students led a psychic exercise. In the midst of it Linda felt a spiraling light coming from her own solar plexus. She could control the feeling and "spin her energy." It felt as if she had awakened all the cells in her body. Since that time she has continued to practice, and now she believes she spins her individual cells. She has harnessed this ability to increase her physical energy by allowing spiraling light to spin outward from her solar plexus.

Despite the excitement of psychic discovery, she wound up working so hard on the new farm that in two years she was burned out and in need of some serenity and solitude. Her friend Kai invited her to visit Esalen, in Big Sur, California, to relax. Then she talked her into taking a workshop in the Sheldon Alexander technique for self-awareness from Alana Rubenfeld.

"Alana gave us a large piece of paper and a crayon and told us to draw a picture of how we saw ourselves. I drew the outline of a Buddha figure cross-legged. I thought I saw myself as contained and complete, but when my turn came to explain my drawing, I realized it meant I was empty inside and closed to the outside world. I was stunned by what my higher self said. I felt I had shut down and didn't feel emotions at all.

"When I went back three months later for another workshop with Alana Rosenfeld, I stayed seven weeks. There was a very young man named Roger Russell there. He looked like a wood nymph and was so shy he couldn't talk at all to anyone. You remember I had learned to turn up my energy in my solar plexus; I had also learned to turn it the other way to slow down my vibrational rate. I wanted to slow down my vibrations enough so I would be totally nonthreatening to

Roger, to just be there. I didn't talk. I finally got so quiet that I started hearing the grass speak to me."

Esalen became her source of wonder. She had visions of past lives. She could see people as they were in another life. At one point, she felt herself shrinking likeAlice in *Alice in Wonderland* to the size of a fairy. That sensation may have inspired the trip she took to Ireland with Russell. They also visited Ursula Bruns at her Equine Test Center in Reken, West Germany. Bruns had previously spent a month at the Tellington Pacific Coast School of Horsemanship. Linda's contact with her was soon to deepen.

"In 1973 I remembered my vision of 1969 with its sense of purpose. I realized that it was time to move on, to be challenged creatively. I knew I had to actively find a way of bringing to humans the importance of all animals in our lives. I spoke to the Dean of Adult Education at Santa Cruz where I had been teaching for two and a half years, and asked what I should study to make a difference in the world. He said, 'Linda, a university is for people who don't know what they want to do. You do know what you want to do. Just go around the world and whatever you need will come to you.' That's when I closed down the farm, sold 65 horses and all my equipment at auction."

She and Birch Jones parted as inevitably as they had married. From 1973 to 1981, she shared her life with Roger Russell.

Linda again visited Ursula Bruns."She is one of the most creative, genius women in my life, an expert horsewoman, a journalist and a photographer. She asked me to give a demonstration at Equitana, the world's largest equestrian trade show where 30 countries are represented. Linda and Roger demonstrated riding without bridles or saddles. In the following weeks, she was invited all over Germany with extensive press coverage. Bruns asked her to stay a year and do a pilot training program, government-sponsored, for German riding instructors. Linda actually stayed in Germany for five years, working and refining her Tellington-Jones Equine Awareness Method with assistance from Bruns and Russell.

Russell sent for information about the Feldenkrais system for retraining habitual human movements. Moshe Feldenkrais, an Israeli, developed "awareness through movements," a way to reorganize the human nervous system through very gentle, nonhabitual movements. Linda was so interested in the material that, beginning in 1975, she traveled to San Francisco each summer for four years to study with Feldenkrais.

"It is not a structural system. It is about moving the body. One aspect of it is functional integration in which the practitioner moves your body in nonthreatening ways to bring a new awareness to you and to give you new ways of moving, breathing, walking, so that your athletic ability is increased. Moshe talked in terms of activating unused neural pathways to the brain. In this Feldenkrais work, I've seen many people who were paralyzed walk again because they learn to use other neural pathways. It's not magic. His work is really a philosophy.

"One of the books we were required to read for the Feldenkreis course was called *Man and His Nature* by Sir Charles Sharrington. Two sentences in that book changed my life. He wrote, 'Imagine if you cut out a portion of a neural pathway. Given enough time, those two ends often find their way back together.' He asked, 'How do they know that they belong together?' The answer, he said, is that every cell in our body knows its function within our body and within the universe.

"I read that during the first month of the first summer's training. I thought at that moment, all I have to do is put my fingers lightly on those of another person and allow the intelligence of my cells to speak to their cells, to show them another possibility for function." Discovering the intelligence of the cells was a crucial insight in Linda's development of the Tellington Touch system.

Linda expected to adapt the Feldenkrais method for use with horses and to train others to use it. However, it takes too long to learn.

"I wanted something I could teach in an hour. After I got that key about the cells the first summer, I was always experimenting, developing this system for the horse. One day, I was working with the wife of a veterinarian and she said, 'Oh, Linda, I would love to do what you do; but what should I feel in my hands, cold or heat or what?' I said, 'Nothing, just put your hands lightly on the horse and push the skin lightly in a circle.' I have no idea why I said that. But sometimes when I said these things I would have a vision of a Chinese man with a long white beard standing there putting words in my mouth.

"That's the first time that I ever pushed the skin in a circle. Before that I just put my hands on and felt the body and moved my hands a little bit here and there. The circular movement is not Feldenkrais. Feldenkrais is just very gentle manipulation of the body with the intention of activating the unused neural pathways.

"I have developed a method of working with horses without force, in harmony, which means there is understanding with the horse. Wherever there is resistance, instead of seeing it as intentional resistance, what we do is look beyond that and give the animal an avenue to relieve tension. The official Tellington Touch is 15 different ways of using the hands. The basis of the touch is the circle. You push the skin or muscles in a very gentle circle. It's making a contact and making the surface move. All of these touches have animal names. I just did the Clouded Leopard touch on you. (She had cupped her hands and used the pads of her fingers to make a series of small circles on my arm with hardly any pressure. It tingled.)

"I taught all over Europe for five years, but in 1980 I got the feeling that I had to go back to the states. I came home to start a center. I was guided by some advice from a channel at Esalen named Jenny O'Connor to a piece of property in California out in the boondocks down by San Luis Obispo.

"At that time, The Nine came into my life. The Nine said they were extraterrestrials from the star Sirius who had come to help in the evolution of mankind. The Nine are really one entity. At first, I experienced them and I heard them in my head. Now whenever I need them I feel their presence just as I feel the presence of many masters. When I first started working with The Nine, it was through Jenny O'Connor doing automatic writing with them. One day at Esalen in May 1982, I sat up with her all night and at 5 o'clock in the morning they asked me to channel for Jenny. That is when they started coming into my head constantly. I was not in an altered state because I wanted to make a conscious transformation and not simply bring through information in a trance. When we were in communication there was a change of vibration. I could tell the difference between my thoughts and theirs."

In 1982 The Nine told Linda to go to Australia and "Look around and see what you can see." In early July, on the Great Barrier Reef at Cairns she met Peter Caddy, the founder of Findhorn, and Helen Rubin, who was organizing his workshops. When The Nine directed Linda to the outback near Alice Springs, she received a sense of the area ahead of time. Through Rubin, she found that her destination was Ayers Rock, which the Aborigines call Uluru, the Center of the Universe.

Rubin agreed to go to Ayers Rock with Linda after the forthcoming six-day One Earth Gathering, which Caddy, Rubin and Linda attended together. Linda recalled:

"All 250 people there had one minute each to introduce themselves. David Barados, a world class anthropologist, got up and said, 'I am here from the Philippines and I am to hook up with any Star People and three others I am to meet.' My ears picked up at 'Star People.' I subsequently discovered he had been working through a channel in the Philippines with The Nine and they had sent him to Australia too. He somehow recognized my connection with The Nine.

"When five of us left for Ayers Rock, one of them was David. We drove for five days. We reached the rock and we climbed it to spend the night on top. When we came down, we had an amazing experience. Until that time, I had not done automatic writing myself, but I felt a prompting for all of us to sit down with paper and pencil so each of us could try automatic writing.

"My message was that I should tell David to ask me a question. He asked The Nine to show us the chakras of the planet. The answers I received came to me as mental pictures of specific power places on Earth. All of us were successful at automatic writing."

In 1984 Linda led another group to Ayers Rock. She wanted to connect with its direct channel to the universe. Again, she spent the night on the rock and then went out into the desert for messages. "I learned that by traveling to sacred places we release information planted there in the earth and it raises the vibration of our DNA. Then, by our traveling around the planet contacting others who are ready, their cells pick up our higher vibration. Even by reading about this, the information comes through and has this effect."

Linda's spiritual breakthrough and her discovery of the Tellington Touch to quicken the intelligence of living cells have been synchronistic.

"I was so much into horses that I didn't get into a spiritual awakening until I was about 20. I remember being at Vesper Service at Chadwick School and crying all the way through it. I felt then I was making a connection to God.

"My parents lived by the Golden Rule. I always had the background belief that God would take care of us, but I was raised without Jesus as an intercessor. I felt Jesus was my brother, but I had my own direct channel to God. I just stayed away from church for years. But now the basis of my being is the connection I have with Jesus, a personal connection through experience. When we talk about what makes a difference on this planet, it is the recognition that he was a human being with the **courage** to stand up and say what he believed. He's my model for my waking up to know I am more than this human body.

"I began to connect to the universe, to have a cosmic perspective. I began to see my body as made up of cells in which information is stored about every human being who has ever been on earth. In that memory is a lot of negative information. Pain, anger and guilt live in the human body. When we feel depressed, it may not be only *our* depression.

"It is very important for people to know this. When we feel anger or sorrow, we can consciously choose to release it. This idea came to me in Australia in 1984 with a mental picture of literally shoveling all these little pains, angers and sorrows out of my body. Then I received the awareness that I could make room for joy and unconditional love. These are not seeded in the human form on this planet because we have chosen our separation from the Source.

"I experience the connection with the Source from outside this universe, from a place where we know our oneness and our connection with all things. We lose this awareness when we choose to come to this schoolhouse of Earth. But joy and unconditional love can awaken the nucleus of the cell. The secret of the universes is in the nucleus of our own cells. To go into our own cells is like going into other universes. Through our cells, we are all connected to the Divine stream of consciousness."

Linda went to Russia for the first time in 1984 after reading an article about a group of psychologists who were allowed to interview a number of schoolchildren there. "I felt in my mind that I had to go there to take in the Light. It wasn't The Nine but my Higher Self that said go. Since my grandfather had been in Russia and I had taught about the Soviet Union in my social studies classes at Chadwick, I thought if the psychologists can go, I can go. Jim Hickman, who was then the director of the Esalen Soviet-American Exchange, said, 'Why don't you come in with us and we can make some connections?' They had been going in for years, before citizen diplomacy became popular."

By prior agreement, Jim Hickman and another Esalen director, Dulcie Murphy, met Linda at Pyadagorsk, the site of a huge Arabian horse auction. Her ostensible reason for going to Russia was to work on one of their top stallions, who had severe arthritis, in order to show the Russians how he might live longer. However, her efforts to make a prior professional contact were unsuccessful, so she traveled to the auction as a tourist. She was met by an Intourist guide who was to take her tour group to Pyadagorsk.

"I was afraid since my grandfather had worked for the czar they'd throw me out of Russia, but I started talking to the guide about him. As it turned out, the guide was an amateur trainer at the Hippodrome Race Track where my grandfather had trained horses, and she was clearly thrilled by our connection. My true goal was always to make contact with Russians at a grassroots level. Everyone told me I was nuts, but here she was being open with me before we had even arrived at the hotel. She invited me to train in the Hippodrome and in Pyadagorsk, and she introduced me to the head veterinarian.

"After we returned from Pyadagorsk to Moscow, a Russian named Joseph Golden, who was known to everyone in the Soviet-American Exchange, arranged for me to give a demonstration at the race track. The trainers got really excited and said if I came back the next day they would have 50 vets and trainers there, and they did. They came from all over, even from Leningrad. I gave a three-hour demonstration with a racing stallion. They asked me to come back and spend more time teaching them this work. Four months later, I returned to Russia to teach a group of veterinarians who now use the Tellington Touch extensively in their work with horses.

"I was terrified at first, but on the third trip I shared more with one of their top people, Elena Perestrova, a professor of chemical biology of the University of

Moscow and president of Athletes for Peace—and a top Olympic athlete. I told her I felt I was here to make a difference on the planet. I was here to awaken cellular intelligence. She knows cellular biology, and she knew exactly what I was talking about. I've now made many connections with the Academy of Science and doctors in Russia, not just with their horse people. Russians are so far ahead of us in what I consider the true universal connection to the self. They are truly connected to the Earth and the universe. They are attuned to the unseen. It is such a pleasure to work with them, I can't tell you.

"I've been going to Russia three or four times a year since 1984. In 1987 I was there in Red Square for the Harmonic Convergence with Chris Griscom, three of her children, and Harriet Crosby from the Institute of Soviet-American Relations in Washington, D.C. A couple of our Russian friends were there, too. We did a ritual, planting crystals all around the Kremlin wall. We dug up a little dirt and pushed them in. Lots of people have been burying crystals there for years. We had a little ceremony. By previous arrangement, we were also hooked into other people who were doing the same ceremony all around the planet.

"In Gorky Park in Moscow, I work with a large spiritual group called the Healthy Family; there are about 400 members who meet there. Five years ago, their leader had a vision that she was to open people to their star memory. I was with their group in 1985 when I had the vision to begin my Animal Ambassadors, International program. I founded it under the umbrella of Esalen Institute in my role as a Project Director for the Soviet-American Exchange."

The afternoon of our interview was waning. Fascinating as it was to speak of Russia, I wanted to pursue a question that had been in my mind since our phone conversation. I asked Linda if her experience with the orca whale was unusual for her. It seemed as if her work is mostly done with domestic animals, and the orca is a wild animal. She said:

"I had already worked with an orangutan at the San Diego Zoo and a snow leopard in Zurich. Gigi Coyle had organized the Orca Expedition around the research of Jim Nolman who has worked with music and communicating with animals for many, many years. The people Gigi invited were part of his research project; and we were paying his way while sharing, experiencing and being there to see what would come out of our 'dance' together.

"When I went to British Columbia in 1985, I had just finished my first session with Chris Griscom in Galisteo, New Mexico, where I had been teaching. It had really opened me. [Chris Griscom is the founder of The Light Institute. Shirley MacLaine worked with her to remember her past lives.] So when I was on the orca expedition, instead of just writing messages from The Nine which I had done before that, I started getting words directly from the whale. My purpose in being there was to listen, to hear what the whales have to say. It's not like I expected it, but the message I received from the orca was the second time such a thing happened to me. I had received an earlier message from a 1000-year-old Morton Bay fig tree. I've read it to thousands of people.

"I have learned that my connection to Earth Mother and the breathing I do as I make the circles in my touch system came to me from Atlantean times. I made an agreement at that time to come back and teach a special type of touch which would awaken memory in anyone who used the touch.

"For years, Atlantis held no interest for me; I didn't want to hear about it. Subsequently, I did a regression and saw myself at the end of Atlantis as a woman standing on a huge aquamarine stage. I was saying goodbye to all the people I'd been working with to keep alive a connection to the Divine stream of consciousness of Oneness."

It grew late as I listened to the enchanting story of Linda's life. Throughout our conversation, my comments revealed the struggles I had made to free myself from feelings of guilt. Just at the end of the long afternoon, Linda took time to give me a gift of words.

"When we polarize, we separate; when we make something wrong, we inhibit the other person's possibility of seeing what we have to share. I think that one of my roles is reminding people of the values of the conservative and conventional traditional paths.

"I totally appreciate that the church has taught that we are not the center of the universe. I acknowledge that religion has kept the concept of God alive while we are in a state of separation on this planet.

"I choose to stay clear by listening to the Earth, listening to the animals, to the trees. When I say listening, I mean experiencing these things, being one with the wind. That makes me open to the other unseen teachers we have around us. A number of times when I have given public presentations, I've had sensitive people say they have seen the masters around me, and one of them is Jesus.

"I work a lot with those who have been extremely abusive to animals, to circus animals, to zoo animals, to bears, to elephants and certainly to horses. People do awful things, prodding them with electric shocks in a punishing way. The T.E.A.M. work is about simply giving them other possibilities to find their own choices. We just give them an opportunity if they choose to take it, not to make anyone wrong in what they did before. That's hard for a lot of people to grasp. But, they are *me* yesterday. We do these things because we don't know any better.

"As networkers, we can weave our experience with others. I've seen the darkness in myself. We all have those forces in us. When we acknowledge that we are all one, we see ourselves in each other. Rather than remain separated, I give my will to the Source. I am willing to take the responsibility to do what I can to weave back together, to bridge the separation.

"I just wrote Went a letter to officially thank him and to tell him that what he taught me and what we did at the research farm has spread around the world. It's not ended. It goes on."

Linda Tellington-Jones is a most unusual woman, blessed beyond measure with insights and visions. She is one of the most effective women I know. Through her work and her Animal Ambassadors, she has created an international network of understanding based on a universal concern with the treatment of animals. I wanted to see her "in action." It was therefore with considerable expectation that I went to Santa Fe in May 1989 to watch her make a three-hour presentation of the Tellington Touch in support of the Santa Fe Animal Humane Shelter.

She treated a cat, two dogs and a pony while sitting down as often as practical on a chair placed on a table so everyone in the audience could see what she was doing. With a firm grip she held each small animal and soothed it occasionally with sounds and words, as she touched the ears, back, tail and gums of these aching creatures. The moment when they relaxed was dramatically obvious. All the while, Linda kept up a continuous explanation for the entranced spectators. She climbed down from the table to treat the pony who hung his head in misery. From his tail to his ears, she used the circular touch until suddenly he defecated, shook himself and lifted his head vigorously. It was like watching a miracle.

In performance, Linda is an active ambassador, a bridge between animal and human. As she treats the animal, she is reaching across to people who feel a kinesthetic reaction to her movements and to her intimacy with the animal she is touching. She has enormous presence, professionalism and vitality. The visionary inner person lights up her public persona, but it does not intrude into the practical teaching she shares wherever she travels. She has an admirable ability to combine visionary knowledge with her work in the world. It strikes me that this is what the mystic is all about, to do ordinary things in extraordinary ways.

Linda fits the description by Jean Shinoda Bolen of the Virgin Goddess: "Artemis as Goddess of the Hunt and Goddess of the Moon was a personification of an independent feminine spirit. The archetype she represents enables a woman to seek her own goals on terrain of her own choosing . . . Artemis as a virgin goddess archetype represents a sense of intactness, a one-in-herselfness, an attitude of 'I-can-take-care-of-myself' that allows a woman to function on her own with self-confidence and an independent spirit." (*Goddesses in Everywoman: A New Psychology of Women,* 1984) Bolen says further that Artemis has an affinity with the wilderness and undomesticated nature. "Women who follow Artemis into the wilderness characteristically discover themselves becoming more reflective. Often, their dreams are more vivid than usual, which contributes to their looking inward." Artemis finds relationships secondary, whereas career and creative projects are primary. Precisely to this point is Bolen's comment: "She is likely to have an on-the-move lifestyle, which she enjoys."

Linda Tellington-Jones is the mystic Artemis and the healer. She has come to a place within herself of unconditional, unspecified love. I believe she carries this awareness of love with her as she moves from country to country, an ambassador to the animals and a conveyor of messages to humans. I will not forget her message to me: we can make our choice without making the "other" wrong, without separation, without guilt.

*O*ne Saturday in 1985,

I attended a Book Fair and there

on a table beckoning to me was a book

covered in acetate with the word

Atlantis visible on the cover, my old trigger

word. Of course, it drew me closer.

The full title was Exploring Atlantis, Volume I;

underneath it was Volume II.

I bought the first one and went home to read it

through. On Sunday the fair continued

and I was there as soon as it

opened to get the second book.

That is how I "met"

Dr. Frank Alper.

ALPER PRESENTS *primary material about the uses of crystals in Atlantis. In Volume I are his sketches of Atlantean patterns used for placing crystals of different types around a person to heal various physical problems. Some of the patterns require a copper wire to connect the crystals, making a circuit that increases the effectiveness of energy generated by the crystals. His material has been copied by other authors, sometimes without credit for the source, in subsequent crystal books. The only source, the only reference Alper makes, is to his own channel. His information, though esoteric, is specific in detail.*

Alper's descriptions of the continent and life in Atlantis were so convincing that his name became important to me. Not too many months passed before I saw an advertisement for his workshops and tapes. It included a photograph of him showing a man with white hair, soft features, and glasses: a genial-looking man. The idea that I would one day meet him settled itself into my mind.

When writing this book became a compulsion I could no longer ignore, I wrote to Dr. Alper and received a warm and welcoming letter back from his assistant, who advised me to visit Phoenix in time to hear his end-of-the-year channeling on December 17, 1988. I was told Dr. Alper would make time for me to do a two-day interview.

His meeting room is a chapel and his ministry is to the Church of Tzaddi, a nondenominational metaphysical church. Just before I met him, he had returned from a teaching tour in Germany. He has given annual summations since 1976. Although he does not make predictions, he does answer personal questions. The audience was expectant. He spoke to us through more than one entity, but mainly through Adamis, the name by which he describes his soul. His message included "Allow the truth of others to be. Your truth is inside and is only for yourself."

FRANK ALPER: CONSCIOUS CHANNEL

In Frank Alper's presence, you are aware of his unusually even energies. No purely masculine descriptive word exists that connotes his state of awareness. I recognized a relationship to Alper in Marion Woodman's remarks about the crone: "She has nothing to lose. She has no investment in ego . . . She's the kind of person you can honestly talk to, profoundly trust. She has no reason to persuade you to do anything other than be who you are . . . She has the kind of wisdom that takes life with a grain of salt, smiles at the divine comedy . . . I have known four or five crones—two of them men. Their love was palpable. No advice." (Barbara Goodrich-Dunn's interview "The Conscious Feminine," *Common Boundary*, March/April 1989.) One of those men could have been Frank Alper. He exhibits that poised balance between male and female energies that Woodman ascribes to the crone.

Alper was born January 20, 1930, in Brooklyn, New York. He was the second of three children in a middle-class family that was culturally but not religiously Jewish. Frank remained intensely shy and solitary in all his activities through his college years. "I very rarely got any advice or counsel. I was left alone to do whatever I chose to do. I was always aware that my thoughts and my mind were very different than those around me. My mind was always an adult's mind, never a child's. I was more comfortable with adults."

In leisure time, he sculpted, painted and became skillful as a cabinet maker. He was a competitive, at times professional, tennis player. At Brooklyn Tech High School he prepared for engineering studies, but he did not pursue that career. He majored in business at New York University with minors in psychology and fine art. He always lived at home and made no friends. Though he graduated in three years, he felt no satisfaction from his achievement.

During the Korean War, Frank enlisted in the Air Force. He was assigned to a camp in the Finger Lake area of New York as the assistant to a clinical psychologist. The six-week program they developed for rehabilitating AWOLs had an eighty-five percent success rate. Frank was so intrigued by it that he hoped to become a clinical psychologist himself when he left the service in 1954. But after he thought it over, he made a practical decision that he was already too old to begin such a long educational process. Instead he opted to go into his father's clothing manufacturing business. He married unhappily and had two sons and a daughter. He thinks now his time in the service was the beginning of his own training for the role he has filled for over two decades—that of a conscious channel.

From 1954 to 1969, Frank did everything he was expected to do in business and family life. In his circle of relatives, he was the pillar of strength who was supposed to solve everyone's problems, although he had no confidant. He did not know what was wrong with his life, but it all soured in the mid-1960s when his father retired. He took over the family business, eventually sold it, and left his marriage.

In January 1970, "two weeks shy of 40," with his current wife Helene, he escaped to Phoenix, Arizona, where, he says, he felt at home the moment they arrived. As they drove into town, nearly penniless, Helene suddenly remembered a person she knew in Phoenix. They called and were invited to come right over.

The moment Frank walked in, the husband of Helene's friend took him aside and asked, "Where have you been? I've been waiting for you for two years." Frank was completely mystified. The man guided him into a bedroom, and for the next ten hours he told Frank that he was to become a spiritual teacher and he was about to undergo a painfully intense training period.

"Everything I had done in my life had been successful, but it never meant a thing to me. I had all these holes inside. Something was missing in my life. I was never at peace,"

Frank explained.

The stranger told him, "You have been brought to me so that I can enlighten you as to the truth of your existence. I am not here to teach you. You will never have a teacher. You're going to do it all yourself." Recalling that evening in 1970, Frank said, "And every word this guy spoke to me was like he had a trowel with plaster and was filling up a hole. When I walked out of that room it was the first time I had an inkling of what the world was about. I never saw him again."

That night, as Frank lay sleepless in bed, he had a vision: A parade of little men in full color were walking by, waving and smiling at him. He jumped up and wakened his wife to tell her he had just had a repeat of a dream that had frightened him very much in his childhood. At that time, his parents told him to go to bed, close his eyes and not look, so he would not see the dream again. "I felt such guilt because I had shut that door." Through channeling he learned that on the night when he had first had the dream, when he was eight years old, his present soul entered his body as a walk-in. This is a theory he accepts as possible. He has no recall of his life prior to that age. The return of this familiar dream was exceptionally important coming as it did the very night of his first illumination about the purpose of his life.

In his book *Universal Law*, Frank gives a new interpretation to basic tenets of the Judeo-Christian world, particularly the Ten Commandments. His essential idea is that the time for suffering, guilt, sacrifice, abject obedience to someone else's truth, self-condemnation, judgment and shackles accepted from outside oneself is over. Before he found this truth for himself, he endured emotional and mental suffering through a long period of self-doubt.

By day Frank worked at his job designing women's sportswear, for which he has a real gift. In the afternoon and evening, he learned about metaphysics by word of mouth and from classes. He did not study metaphysical books; instead, he practiced metaphysical exercises as often as possible. He did not receive a single confirmation that he was on the right path.

"One of the things that helped me was my background in business. I was able to cope. I started teaching simple meditation classes, drawing upon my experience from the time I was in the service. I always was interested in people. Meanwhile, I was such a mind-person it took me about eight months to learn to meditate because I was afraid of letting go of control. I could not close my eyes and see colors or images. I never remembered my dreams. I thought something was wrong with me."

A vital experience convinced Frank his path was valid.

"One night my wife was having her period. We were in bed. She was having severe cramps and she asked me to place my hand on her stomach. A few seconds later, she said, 'You healed me. The pains went away.' When she said that, it was like an atom bomb went off inside me. My hands turned the color of your jacket, a real bright red. For three days, I could not shut it off. The skin peeled off my hands. I'd had a bolt of energy and a healing. I knew that healing was what I wanted to do. Well, I started developing techniques to increase my healing energies. Everything I started I completed. I had a burning fire in my heart that came and never waned. It's still as strong as it ever was."

Frank met other people in the esoteric field. One of them gave him a pendulum for a gift, and he decided without much hope to try it out. To his astonished joy, it worked for him, and he received answers that led him to automatic writing. "I sat down at a table with pen and a pad, and the minute I picked up that pen, my arm flew across the pad and it started writing. The first words that came out were, 'My name is Aaron and these are the names of your masters,' and he listed twelve high masters for me," Frank related.

The dam had broken. He now was in contact with King Solomon, the head spokesman of his inner teachers. He received volumes of information and he began doing readings for people. "It was an evolution. It came to a point that when I was doing my writing I knew what Solomon was going to say. I put down my pen and had a conversation with him in my mind," Frank said.

While Frank was meditating, Solomon gave him a proposition. If he would submit himself to a short period of testing and if he survived, he would be able to consciously fulfill the purpose of his soul on earth. If he failed, he would be spiritually barren for the balance of his life. Frank refers to the next three years as a crucifixion of his emotions and his whole reactive system. Night and day he heard a voice whose frequency of energy was different from his own. Within his mind, this voice continually told him what to do, questioning and teaching him. He was forbidden by his guides to share this experience even with Helene. Each afternoon after he left work, Frank was directed to review his day in a search for spiritual lessons. "Somewhere inside, I knew my mind was okay. I had been isolated so long throughout my life that I had a very strong mind."

There came a time when Solomon told Frank to call some people together and "channel" for them, which was not a word in common usage at the time. Frank asked eighteen friends to gather together and lend him their support. "I sat down and channeled for them and it was wonderful. Even then, when I first started channeling, I could feel the difference between the energy frequencies of Solomon and whoever else was there with me." Gradually, he realized that he could channel any information he sought. "So I started developing the *universal channel.* At this point in time I can channel anyone in the universe or beyond, up to the Creative Mass." Demonstrating his ability to channel brought Frank an enormous emotional release.

Frank's primary speaker is Adamis, whom he defines as his own soul. Many others speak through him, including the entity who named himself as Solomon. While channeling, his voice alters slightly and he speaks fluently. He is always aware of what he is saying. He explains that he made a pact with his teachers that they would never ask him to go into a trance.

Having found his ability, Frank Alper began applying his training to the healing of other people. To do so, he needed a structure and credibility for the information he was sourcing. In 1974 he founded the Arizona Metaphysical Society. On January 23, 1977, he was ordained by the Mother Church of Tzaddi, which conferred upon him the title Master Physician or Doctor of Divinity, hence his use of the title doctor. His own branch of the Church of Tzaddi was chartered January 22, 1980. Most of Frank's work is done by counseling others. He teaches through workshops he calls Carousels. He sets up and encourages centers around the United States and in Europe, he writes books and he channels.

The content of Frank Alper's channeling is extraordinary. It is cosmic in orientation, yet it is grounded and extremely practical. Mainly, it is directed at methods of healing oneself and others. His work is concentrated on the lost civilization of Atlantis, which he describes as a forerunner and warning to the society coming into existence at this time. He channels details of technological discoveries made by Atlanteans and the ways they were misused, particularly in genetic research. Just as other contemporary channels are saying, Frank states without equivocation that many people alive today are reincarnated Atlanteans who have returned to help build a new society. Frank told me:

"Any creative endeavor is channeled, whether it be music or art or theoretical science. We have the capacity to tune into energies and to convert them into reality for ourselves. That's how channeling works. One of the greatest misconceptions about channeling is that people think we are literally hearing voices talking to us. We are, but we're not; because all channeling comes in the form of energies. When the energies reach our brain they get converted into our language, our thoughts and our phraseology.

"The channeling process is based on trust, but it takes time to develop that trust. If any doubt is there at all, the material comes to you in a distorted manner. I train people to be channels. It's a slow progressive process. The first thing I tell them is, 'You are going to get in your own way. Your emotions, your wants and needs are going to interfere.' I don't believe we are merely serving as a vehicle for Spirit. When I open my mouth and something comes out of it, I, Frank, am responsible for what I speak, whether the Spirit is saying it or not.

"To this day, I have no visualization. My pattern of growth was to go from the bottom of the ladder to the top without going up the steps. I bypassed all psychic energies. I have never had psychic experiences. I still am not able to do anything psychic at all. I went from nothing into soul consciousness, so to speak.

"When I do soul life readings, I make a connection between my mind and the soul of an individual. I relate to the person what his or her soul wants them to know about their life's purpose. I just help people get on with what they are here to do in their lives. I never channel for notoriety. For me, channeling is a tool. I channel to make masters available to people. When I channel and people experience their master, a frequency opens and afterwards they can channel that master themselves. Also, I channel to teach people not to be in awe of Spirit, to understand that Spirit is just as they are, although now the Spirit doesn't have a body.

"Now the channeling is an evolutionary process for me. I became aware of different levels of my soul. It didn't happen all at once. I wanted to know my soul's name, and my guides gave me the name Manfred, with some information about him. I was excited, but I felt there was more to come. Six months later, they had additional names to tell me. They did this three times. One day in 1983, I was just sitting at my desk and the name Adamis came to me. That was the completion of everything."

Frank explained that Adamis is an Oversoul, connected to millions of souls, not just to his.

"Once Adamis was revealed, a total unity started coming to me and the channeling changed. Before you begin channeling, energy-wise, you are at zero, feeling nothing. As you start to channel, you experience the energy frequencies of the different masters, of power and love—by a lightness of being. When you go around the circle 180 degrees, you are at the apex, you feel the unity of the soul. But when you get all around the circle, 360 degrees, you feel nothing again, and that is when oneness has occurred. When I'm channeling now, I don't feel anything at all regardless of whom I'm channeling, although those in attendance feel a great deal."

I asked Frank why we have this capability to channel, yet we seem to be screened from it and cannot discover it without extreme effort. He replied, "If you didn't have the screen you couldn't survive here. Your soul is a pretty sensitive frequency trying to integrate within a vibrationary planet of much lower frequencies of emotions. Your soul is completely incompatible with these frequencies; therefore it has to have a dense structure to shield it. That is the function of this body, to shield the soul."

So why, I wondered, do we come here at all? Frank said he could answer that question easily. "The ancient masters used to say our mission is to be conscious that what emanates from the physical body is the total expression of our soul. We are here to add elevated energies to this planet as a stimulus for people to grow. So in the final analysis, we don't have to go out and teach; we don't have to say a word. We just have to be that beacon of energy we are. That in itself is a stimulus to raise the frequencies of Planet Earth. Earth is in an evolutionary stage, just like everything else. Around this planet has been installed a karmic school. Not all planets are karmic planets. Some are just service planets." Alper's explanation of karma differs from other seers'. He believes karma is the life experience we choose to have. Karma allows our soul to grow or to be damaged, depending upon our own freely made decisions.

Usually, Frank Alper gives precise answers to questions. Mine had to do with what is special about the earth and is there to be an Armageddon, in his opinion. He stressed that Earth's mission within our universe is not unique.

"You have to realize that within our galaxy alone there are over 100 million civilized planets. Within our solar system, Earth's energies are only now at Level 6. We went into the Age of Aquarius on March 23, 1985. On that day the Planet Earth underwent a vibrationary elevation, from 5.5 to 6. All of the people on Earth whose energies are at 5.5 found themselves incompatible with their planet. So we see increased crime, mental illness, divorce, war, dislocation. The end result, which will be the catastrophe, is that their souls will not return to earth. Another planet has been prepared at 5.5 where they can go to continue their growth. The souls that are coming in are at Level 6 and higher because only compatible souls can incarnate here. Each time the planet evolves, more and more higher souls incarnate here. Many master souls are coming in. From a logical point of view, that level of soul would not incarnate if the world were about to disintegrate. Master souls don't need that kind of experience. They are coming in in droves; they are coming to serve. They are coming in aware. It was channeled to me that now is the time for us to keep open the minds of one generation of children. If one generation of children remains aware, within three generations, we will all be aware.

"Since I've become involved in this path, I won't say I've become more religious, but I've become more aware of God and of myself in relation to God than I ever dreamed I could be. When I talk personally about religion I mean my relationship with God. Many times people come to me and say 'I want to grow but I don't believe in God.' I say it doesn't matter. Do you believe you have a soul? And they say yes. That's all you need to believe. I know from experience that the moment they acknowledge they have a soul, they believe in God. There is only one reality and that is there is a God. Your concept of it and how you relate to it is fine. There are so many different paths of temporary truth that lead to ultimate knowing, it doesn't make any difference. The commandment in the Bible, 'Love your neighbor as yourself,' has nothing to do with love at all. It means I don't even have to like you. I certainly don't have to associate with you. But I have to allow you to be who you are.

"I'm here in the capacity of a World Teacher. My work is very different from what it was. I'm not involved with metaphysics per se anymore. I'm a spiritual teacher. I'm always looking for techniques to help people with their needs. Someone said to me, what is it exactly that you do? I said, in essence I teach people how to love themselves. I teach them how to feel love. Most people have never done it. They experience emotions. That has nothing to do with love at all.

"When you open your mind, you break through the limits of the earth's frequencies. In my counseling, I use a lot of affirmation techniques. I try to get people to know they are not a child of the earth, but they are a child of the universe. That's their home. I believe that I am one of approximately fifteen per cent of the population who are higher souls here to serve. That is why people come to me and others who are like me. Essentially my work is to help teachers discover who they are."

Frank Alper is an exceptionally creative man. One does not have to agree that his information comes from an outside source, a higher entity or the Creative Mass itself, to appreciate the extent of what he has set down and explained in his books. In his three-volume work *Exploring Atlantis*, most of the recorded channeling sessions relate to the functions and uses of quartz crystals. He says that prior to any earthly Atlantis, a planet by that name, and with the same energies, was destroyed. His material reads like an ancient legend. He gives very distant dates for the surface life of the original earthly Atlantis—around 90,000 years ago—and he says that 77,777 years before the Christian Era, both Atlantis and Lemuria, a continent in the Pacific Ocean, sank. Aliens from other universes came to repopulate Atlantis under the sea. Perfect crystals, huge in size, were manufactured to supply the power for this civilization. The crystals were lowered into tunnels that attached the continent to the surface. Frank claims that there is still a network of tunnels beneath the surface of the earth that connects continent to continent. The second earthly Atlantis was a city protected by a magnetic dome beneath the sea. The third Atlantis was a continent-wide civilization on the Earth's surface. Alper postulates that there were numerous other experimental civilizations on Earth besides Atlantis and Lemuria, and there still are, beneath the poles, for instance.

Frank Alper mentioned Space Brothers, the Space Command, Space Ships and the responsibilities of these extraterrestrials. They are to detoxify atomic explosions set off on earth to prevent pollution of space and to avert the human use of space for destructive purposes. Their visits to this planet have been going on for eons and will continue to do so. He prophesies that they already have made numerous contacts, and these will be recognized in a relatively few years.

These are exotic statements and they intoxicate the reader's own imagination, but Frank has also channeled technical information that could, conceivably, be tested. In his first book about Atlantis, he gives 24 chants in written form that can be heard on an available tape. In the third volume, he repeats the chants and connects them to color rays whose descriptions he has channeled. One of them, a silvery pink banded in gold, is a ray used in healing. His color ray descriptions are inspiring for artworks as well. Frank links specific color rays to certain patterns of quartz crystals for healing. He tells the circumstances in which each of the rays is most effective. In the third volume he depicts designs for fan-shaped devices on which different colors of gel or plastic film are stretched for use in healing. Again, he correlates the use of these color "paddles" with certain patterns of crystals to place around the body. He predicts that within thirty years, our doctors will treat an illness by exposing a patient to a single frequency (representing a color, a sound and a crystal frequency). Healing will be immediate. He has channeled that within the next hundred years, most diseases will virtually disappear as will lower level intense emotions; simultaneously, vibrational frequencies will continue to rise, and increased spiritual awareness will become dominant.

In Volume II of his series, Frank describes a series of crystal pyramids in the ancient world that were constructed in a band around the earth for purposes of exchanging energy and information beyond and within this planet. Although the pyramids are largely destroyed, their energy patterns still exist and continue to operate.

In Volume III, he lists four major places where world energies and information for "total enlightenment" are stored beneath invisible structures of pure energy. One of them is in the Himalaya Mountains, another is the Great Pyramid, a third is a "mountain of magnetics" in Arizona, and the last is in New Zealand.

Many of our contemporary science fiction imaginings are, Frank indicated, truths that apply to the ancient civilization of Atlantis. Dematerialization—what we jokingly call "beaming up"—was a fact and will be again. He does not agree with Edgar Cayce's prediction that Atlantis will literally rise again in this century. Frank believes Atlantis is allegorically rising again as an elevated frequency in the minds of people now living who were once a part of that civilization. He thinks there are more advanced souls on earth at this time than ever before, and each of them is charged with bringing about the rising frequencies that will characterize the Age of Aquarius. Armageddon, he said, is taking place as a spiritual cataclysm rather than a battle. It is not necessary, in his view, for the evolution of the earth that land masses be destroyed—as they would be if Atlantis physically rose from the sea. The idea that destruction will occur due to man's sins is a fallacy. Much that is wrong in our present world is the result of our own actions. The challenge of this period of Armageddon is to recognize our problems as essentially spiritual in nature and to create spiritual solutions by a change of mind. This change is to be global in nature, not private. Each of those who are awake, he says, is to serve as a center of truth for those who are still asleep. In the future, there will be no seers or prophets because everyone will become a source of his own truth. The entire planet was once the Garden of Eden, and it will be so again.

"My whole purpose is to help people develop their own philosophy. I give them a foundation from my concepts, but I always tell them I don't want them to believe a word I say, just to acknowledge that it is my truth. I do a lot of energy work on people, guided imagery, meditation . . . and rebirthing. To me, growth is the continual elevation of energy frequencies. Spiritual growth comes from becoming more receptive to higher frequencies. I've counseled about 2,000 people. People come for a maximum of six sessions. Energy either works or it doesn't work. I don't use my own energy. You never use your own energy. If you do that you become drained. I channel universal energy or God's energy or magnetic energy. Sometimes, depending on the situation, I use crystals. Crystals don't heal, but they do create energy fields. Most of the time, when I'm giving someone a healing, I use the crystals to restrengthen their energy system.

"To find one's truth, one must be free. Growth can be nothing but joy. When a soul finishes serving God, that God-soul becomes part of the Creative Mass. This is the final step of existence. It's like taking a drop of water and placing it in a bucket of water. That soul loses its individual identity, and it becomes part of All That Is; and yet when it has the need to be isolated, its identity is still there. The Creative Mass itself grows by the addition of this soul. I believe that every single soul that is created eventually serves as a God. That is the final step of soul expression. We are trained for that all the time. We are consistently learning to be Creators.

"Your soul was created by God out of a single energy cell. There is always a fairly equitable balance of souls created with female vibrations, male vibrations and androgynous vibrations. These are the basic trinity in the construction of God's soul and the basic construction of all souls. We are in a trinity. So even though your soul may be dominantly a feminine soul, which means that a good portion, more than half, of your incarnations are female, that doesn't mean you have not incarnated as male. We incarnate as both. Like I say to women all the time, don't call yourself a single mother; you're avoiding part of your energies. You are a single parent who is capable of using your masculine strengths and feminine softness. To me, a woman who walks around dressed like a man in order to feel more powerful is less effective than a highly feminine woman in her own feminine power. The reality of you is your feminine power, not your masculine power.

"Let me tell you what is happening on earth. The seeds . . . they are part of new root races that have already incarnated on earth . . . [They] have been incarnating sporadically on earth for the last 30 years. I know two young people who are now in their twenties who are part of these root races. They have known from the moment they were born what planet they came from, who their souls are and exactly why they are here. They have what we would call super powers. When they were five and six years old these kids could lift up a refrigerator with one hand. They are totally telepathic. Both the boy and the girl have large physical structures. They are both six feet five inches in height. Their heads and brains are large to be in proportion to their physical bodies. We as a physical race have started to grow in preparation for housing the larger brain that will offer greater capacity for consciousness in the future. You have seen visualizations of space beings with very large heads and functional bodies. They do not have the senses we have, and they are not involved with emotions.

"In my philosophy, our senses are not gifts from God. They are obstacles that we are to overcome. Every time we see someone who is blind we feel sorry for them, but we will learn to see without using our physical eyes. We have to learn to sense without touch pressure, to hear with our minds. This is how we will progress.

"Let me give you an example. There's a man named Dr. Bernard Jensen; he is called the father of nutrition, and also the father of iridology. He is brilliant. He has been knighted. He is almost 80. He came to see me once and he couldn't believe all the colors that I have described. Later, he called me from Russia and said there had just been a discovery made. We have been teaching that the eye has 40,000 rods and cones, or perception centers; but the Russians confirmed that the eye has 130,000 rods and cones. I started laughing. He said, why are you laughing? I laughed, I said, because where do you think psychic vision comes from? How do you think blind people can learn to see?

"I train blind people to see color, to see images. There are 100,000 rods behind the eye that are lying dormant because we have not activated the parts of the brain that bring them into active use. I have a 30-year-old client who has been declared ninety-eight per cent blind since birth. Since he came to me he has learned to do visual readings. With his eyes closed, he sees colors, images, pictures. A friend of mine teaches blind people to cross streets. One man was afraid of doing it. I explained how he could teach the man to sense energy. This kid has become so confident that he knows who has entered a carpeted room by their energy frequencies. He knows where objects are. He has become like an animal with a sensory antenna. He achieves things that people who can see cannot do. What I'm saying to you is: our eyes are obstacles to overcome.

"The function of those who serve in the Space Commands is to provide guidance for us. At the present time, while people are sleeping at night, they are receiving energizing treatments. Their bodies are literally bombarded with energy and are taught by information implantation. They are not aware of it. A verbal key is given and, when the situation arises, then they become aware of something. I, because I am aware, will lie down when I am tired and ask these beings to take my energies aboard ship and cleanse them. It is like taking a vacation from human energy. I see lots of ships in the skies over Phoenix.

"I screen the people who come to me. When a person who has had no experience with metaphysical growth asks for a private session, I don't do one for them. They are not ready. They would not understand what I am saying and their acceptance would not be there. I would rather not risk stopping their search. My clients have to be those who have been on their path and exposed to growth. They have a sincere need to know more about themselves and why they are here. I always deal from their strength. I am not involved at all in psychic energies. When someone comes to me I establish an energy connection between my mind and their soul. I serve as a vehicle for what their soul wishes them to know at that time. I'm like a guidance counselor. Most of the time they will receive information about their soul: how long it has been in existence, what it has done, its karmic progression to this point, and some past life expressions both on and off this planet. I only give them information about the experiences their soul had in past expressions that contain tools that apply to this life. Other information about past life experiences only feeds the ego. I relate to them the reason and purpose for their soul's incarnation—what did the soul come to do, what karmic lessons are they to learn, why have certain things happened to them in this life. I try to bring peace into their mind about those things in their life that have not been resolved.

"I ask questions. The reason I ask the questions is that it helps me lock into those patterns of energy where they need help and to lock out incidentals. I don't allow them to ask questions until I'm done. Their answers serve as keys for me. Sometimes I discuss future incarnations, especially if people are close to the end of their incarnation here. I can only do that if the energies for those incarnations have already been set into place. I always give people a soul vibration, a resonant sound, the frequencies of the nucleus of their souls. It is a permanent mantra for them. It never changes. When they chant it, it helps them come into soul consciousness in a much shorter period of time because the resonance from it helps them to change their conscious energy patterns. I chant it for them. I just know these things. When I do a reading for them later, different past lives might come up. I will do follow-ups but never more frequently than a year apart.

"Souls are created all the time. There are souls that cease to exist. Souls do commit suicide. They don't want to exist anymore. Their energy just disperses. Souls are created by two sources, by God, and also by Ascended Masters who have reached the point of evolution where they serve as the Spirit Core. A soul that is an Ascended Master serves to guide planets. It retains the core of its essence, and it divides the outside portions of itself into souls. This is where the idea of soul mates comes from. When the point comes that the core of an Ascended Master reaches the ultimate frequency, it breaks free and serves as a God, a creator or a head of the universe.

"What I have inside of me is energies that have been on earth 74 times. Everyone who comes to me has been with me before. Once I energize someone or heal a person with my energies, the energies of Adamis are available for them, not through me, but by means of their own channel to Adamis, to the Source.

"I really believe the soul who walked on earth as Christ—and we have all been Christed—is an Ascended Master. Within the universal hierarchy, his soul was not the highest Ascended Master, but when he came to Earth, he received a projection of the feminine aspect—the Sananda energies of God—to give him that extra charisma to draw people to him. This has happened to every world leader, from Abraham and Moses, to Ghandi, Churchill and Mrs. Roosevelt. Although their charisma is not to the same capacity as it was with Jesus, it is of the same source as his very highly evolved soul. A walk-in occurred when Christ was 22 seconds old, because there was no female on earth who could carry his energies. Twenty-two is the spiritual number of completion. What I believe—what I'm telling you that was told to me—is that because Jesus disbelieved who he was, he was transported by the Space Brothers to different lands, so that he would understand who he was and learn. In the eighteen missing years of his life in the Bible, he was teaching. He was in Tibet. Tibetans claim they have his fingerprints and that he became an initiate. There isn't anyone who hasn't doubted. There isn't any avatar or seer or prophet who isn't portrayed as having one imperfection."

We had had a long, serious discussion. Just before I left, I mentioned to Frank my feeling that Christ had meant to cleanse the Judaic practices of his time, rather than to begin a totally new church. I expected another sober reply.

He agreed with me, and said, "All of the disciples and the first three popes were Jewish." But then Frank chuckled. The last thing he said to me still makes me smile: "There's a wonderful Christmas card that shows a Santa Claus with a black beard, who says:

"Roses are red, violets are bluish,
If it weren't for Christmas, you'd all be Jewish."

PLATE 5

"Another Song—Innocence"
Melissa Zink

*I*n 1980 I saw Melissa Zink's work in an Albuquerque gallery. Her small clay figures were posed in a trancelike state, dreaming within an interior stage set that could have been designed for a surrealist play. Something about the somber stillness and imaginative content of these three-dimensional scenes remained in my memory, accompanied by a sense of awe. Here was a fresh approach to plastic form.

I wanted to meet the artist. Several years later our mutual friend Leslie Crespin, introduced me to Melissa over lunch in Taos. I was as intrigued by the artist as I was by her work. Our first conversation revealed her familiarity with and love of literature. I have followed her work over the last decade, never ceasing to be intrigued by it.

From the beginning of my work on this book, I hoped to include Melissa Zink. I explained to her that I was making a comparison between artists and seers. She agreed to work with me, and we have met sporadically by mail, phone and in person over the years. Each time we have connected, I have enjoyed her point of view, which is absolutely original and often delightfully funny.

IT WAS QUICKLY apparent to me that Zink refrains from using words that one might call emotionally inflated. Although I see her as a shamanic artist and view her work as laden with prophetic insight, I respected her reserve to such an extent that my first efforts at writing about her seemed destined for the dry pages of an academic art journal. Rather than dwell on the transformative aspects of her life, I devoted paragraph after paragraph to art analysis. Admittedly, I am fascinated by the development of her artwork, but Melissa Zink—the person, the woman, the artist—seemed to be missing. I started again.

Deepak Chopra tells us that "Knowledge of any kind gets metabolized spontaneously and brings about a change in awareness from where it is possible to create new realities." (Creative Affluence by Depak Chopra, p. 39.)

The challenge of Zink's life was the long delay between her art education and the opportunity to develop her talent. For more than twenty years, family restrictions held her back from becoming an artist. Once she claimed her freedom, her creativity was released and she found her own voice. Her story demonstrates the potency of the creative impulse as a way to knowledge.

MELISSA ZINK: OTHER KINDS OF LOGIC

Melissa Zink (née Ellis) was born in Kansas City, Missouri, in 1932. In the psychological sense, she had a difficult childhood, though she was raised in physical comfort. Her mother suffered from multiple sclerosis, undiagnosed for twenty years, and the family home was controlled to some degree by her serious illness. Her mother would say, "You'll have this after I'm gone," implying that she was close to death. Despite these expectations, Mrs. Ellis outlived Mr. Ellis by ten years.

Mrs. Ellis was preoccupied with religion, and she underwent a series of conversions. She became a Christian Scientist, a Fundamentalist and then an Episcopalian in a process that moved her steadily toward more ritual and dogma. Finally, Mrs. Ellis became a Roman Catholic during Melissa's freshman year in college. Meanwhile, Mr. Ellis, while indifferent to religion, was prejudiced against Catholicism.

Mrs. Ellis taught herself Greek in order to study and compare versions of the New Testament, but in Melissa's self-revealing judgment, "She was looking for confirmation of her beliefs, not for broadening them."

Melissa's father had a depressive personality and seemed disappointed to be a successful banker rather than the lawyer he had intended to be. His presence was also a controlling one, in that decisions were often suspended because he spent two weeks of each month on business in Texas. The household he left behind was filled with women: Mrs. Ellis; Melissa; Susan, a daughter 13 years younger than Melissa; the housekeeper;

and a maid. The housekeeper was a Fundamentalist who competed with Mrs. Ellis for the allegiance of Susan.

Melissa told me, "The disagreement between my mother and the housekeeper was carried on with silent fury, which made it more disturbing since nothing was ever clearly stated or resolved."

Within this cloistered, coercive home, Melissa developed contrary beliefs, fiercely held, and at odds with the adults who dominated her life. Her independent views did not really protect her. She still said, ruefully, "I bought a whole suitcase full of old-fashioned male values."

"Before I went to school, I never had any playmates. We lived in a pleasant, residential part of the city, but my parents were private, conservative people and their friends had no children. I learned to play by myself."

For most of her girlhood, Melissa was the only child. She amused herself by building dollhouses from shoe boxes, shirt cardboards and the dividers from shredded wheat boxes. She made clothes for Storybook Dolls and placed them in these rooms that she decorated with cuttings from wallpaper books. She did not play with the dolls nor talk aloud for them.

"I was trying to explain to my husband [Nelson Zink] that if you don't play with anybody, you don't talk. It all goes on in your head. Something about dressing the dolls and making up settings for them, that was the story."

At a young age, Melissa knew she wanted to become an artist, but her parents were concerned that the artistic life could lead to immorality. While reading an old family volume of Wordsworth and thinking about Romanticism, Melissa recently found this passage noted by her mother in 1942:

Rapine, avarice, expense
This is idolatry; and these we adore
Plain living and high thinking are not more
The homely beauty of the good old cause
Is gone; our peace, our fearful innocence
And pure religion breathing household laws.

Her parent's fear of corruption was softened by their natural pride in Melissa's ability. On the one hand, they gave her art materials. On the other hand, they discouraged her aspirations to become a painter.

"I was commended [for artmaking], but they didn't want it to be important. It was okay if you did it as a kid, but they wanted me to have status as an educated person and to be married. Anything else you did was fine, but it was subservient to your role as wife. I received two conflicting messages from my family. 'What other people do has no effect on us' and 'Beware of what people think.' My father found art 'not respectable' because artists lived lives that did not conform to our standards. He based his opinion on the lives of notorious artists such as Picasso. But in a way, since my parents had so little respect or interest in it, art was all mine."

Books were and are Melissa's constant companions. They are the guides to her imagination, her entry point to other times and places. She has a special fondness for France and England from 1830 to 1940. She is widely read, retentive and absorbed in visual images called up by words.

Melissa's father read to her from E. B. White's *Treasury of Humor* and opened a "window to another world" that helped to stimulate her ambition to become a writer. Years later, someone asked why she did not write and she answered, "I wanted to be a writer when I was young, but I found that all I did was describe things and it seemed a lot easier to make them."

When she was 14 years old, Melissa told her family that she did not believe in God. Her dismayed mother asked if she wanted to see a psychiatrist. When she turned down the opportunity, she was sent to finish her last two years of high school at Emma Willard, a prestigious preparatory/boarding school in Troy, New York. It proved to be a boon.

At Emma Willard, Melissa first knew the pleasure of friendships with girls who were as intellectually curious as she. The school gave her a stimulating introduction to the life of the mind that has nourished her ever since. She recalls wryly that her instructors gave her the impression that she was "unusual, but not gifted."

After Melissa's graduation, her parents were lukewarm about her attending the Rhode Island School of Design, and she was not sure enough of her art ability to plead for it. She opted for Swarthmore College in Pennsylvania, which had no visual arts program. Her liberal arts curriculum at Swarthmore left her feeling "second-rate" because she did not pursue historical research, which was the implied goal in all her art history courses. Those college years are one source of the bruised self-image she suffered from for the next two decades.

At 20 years of age and less than a year before completing her degree in art history, Melissa dropped out of college to marry Bill Howell, a tall, attractive man from St. Louis. While he completed his education at the University of Chicago, she was given advanced placement to work for a master's degree in art history. The couple moved to Wisconsin before she could finish the program.

In 953 the Howell's daughter Mallery was born in Wisconsin. The family lived in New York City for eighteen months, and then moved to Kansas City in 1957, where they opened an art gallery and framing business. For the next ten years, Melissa worked behind the scenes of the shop. She became an expert at gessoing (plastering), gold-leafing, antiquing and designing frames. She also gained mastery of power tools.

In spite of the demands on her time, Melissa entered the first year course at the Kansas City Art Institute. This did not please her husband. Just as her parents had forestalled her study of art, Howell did not want her to be an artist. He told her she had no understanding of three-dimensional form.

A further obstacle to finding her way as an artist was the strong influence of Abstract Expressionism on the faculty of KCAI. Her studio courses were in conflict with her idols from the history of classical art. Holbein, Bosch, van Eyck, Memling and van der Weyden, whom she admired to the point of worship, were all figurative artists whose drawings are sublimely well crafted.

"I like line," Melissa explains, "but I was not one of those people who was born knowing how to draw."

Practice has been Zink's best teacher. However, time to spend on her art was so extremely limited, she began using smaller canvases; and finally she put her painting aside.

Friends convinced the Howells that they would like Silverton, Colorado, a mining town with a craft-conscious youthful population. They moved there and set up another frame business. For Melissa it just seemed to be a continuation of her work running the family shop; yet, the move to Colorado was healthy for her psyche.

"There is some kind of primeval chord or resonance about mountains. When we are going through a major change, walking in the mountains is a particularly important way to get us in touch with that change. You need all those elements— the physical aspect of the mountains, the way they smell, the activity of walking outdoors and thinking—to make the change.

"The mountains in Colorado gave me a lot of strength. I could get a topographic map and make my way by myself to the top of the mountain."

Strength from just being free in the mountains helped Melissa to end her unhappy marriage. In 1975 she married Nelson Zink, a psychotherapist.

Melissa has had three last names, Ellis, Howell and Zink, but it is only as Melissa Zink that she has come into her own as an artist. For nearly 20 years she has enjoyed partnering and support for her development as an artist. She praises the role her husband plays in her late-blooming expressive life.

The Zinks stayed in Colorado for three years and then they moved to Arroyo Hondo, New Mexico. The first home they built was a solarized one beside the Hondo River. They moved away, Melissa said with a smile, because "The river dried up for the summer and that was enough to offend me."

The couple has lived for the last ten years in an adobe-style house beneath a large willow tree in Embudo, adjacent to the Rio Grande River. It is a perfect sanctuary for creating art, and it is also a sublime place for Nelson Zink's patients to come for their psychotherapy sessions in the seclusion of the countryside.

Everything Melissa needs for her life is contained in this space by the river. The comfortable, book-lined home supports her love of reading. Her kitchen is a well-equipped place any one would crave.

In 1988 the Zinks built Melissa's studio in a new wing. It is uncluttered, very white and light with ever-changing views of river bank life directly outside the windows. Outdoors are the various gardens she enjoys tending. She has to force herself to leave home even for a brief time.

Melissa's opening to her creativity coincides with her relationship with Nelson and their happy marriage. They were visiting Santa Fe on a holiday when they began talking about her desire to be an artist. She told art historian Margery B. Franklin, "I wanted to be recognized . . . And I had to be able to say that before I could do anything really . . . Without Nelson, I doubt if I'd still be alive. I was a very frustrated painter . . . "

Nelson Zink had some clay and he asked Melissa if she would like to try it. "I couldn't make a decent pot, but I made a little tiny head, and I rolled out some clay and made a bandage to wrap around the eyes. Nelson came in—one of those wonderful serendipitous events—and he said, 'That's terrific. I really like that.' If he had said nothing I don't believe I would have continued."

Her advancing career dates only from 1977, shortly after she began sculpting small figures with clay. She says disarmingly, "I didn't know how to do eyes. I thought they looked terrible, so I put blindfolds on the figures and it made them seem intriguing." By dint of intense self-teaching and practice, Melissa now creates egg-smooth clay portrait heads with subtly shaped, expressive features that seem like a distillation of her own strong nose, linear mouth and round eyes.

Clay gave Zink a means to create figurative content at a time when the prevailing and accepted form of painting was abstraction. "I couldn't find my way to paint. I found my way by making the things I painted. Now, I'm moving back to painting through sculpture. The two forms are thoroughly intertwined. It doubles my expressive possibilities. I choose three dimensions for one kind of feeling and two dimensions for another."

Under her nimble fingers, clay is mutable, taking on the substance of delicate, long-fingered hands, soft flesh, draped cloth, gleaming metal, stone, leather, pottery or tile, depending upon the illusion she is trying to create. Her clay modeling extends in any direction she cares to take it.

Melissa's technical precision in her several mediums allows her to give exquisite form to fragments of memory. Many of her thoughts are echoes of cherished books, reflections of art history, and revelations of her own fantasies. She has reached back into her girlhood to recapture the strong sense of individuality and control she once had in her solitary playroom. The size of her ceramic figures almost matches the scale of her homemade dollhouses—which sets her work apart from the huge scale of much feminist art. She resists the temptation of giant size as well as the ugliness and obfuscation often emphasized by the art marketplace.

Zink said in prepared remarks for a gallery talk: "I want to make it clear that the representation of what I see dimensionally has very little to do with the external world. In other words, representing a tree for its directly perceived beauty is not my intent. Rather, a tree functions as a symbol, as a sign."

She leaves clues to the sources and meanings of her signs in her titles. In *D.H. Lawrence: A Biography in an Analytic Mode,* the clearly recognizable figure of D. H. Lawrence bends forward in a chair, too depressed to put on his second sock. Across a wall, he appears again sagged across his mother's lap in a Pietá pose, craving the maternal love his mother denied him.

Far more goes on in this piece than craftsmanship animated by wit. Zink's enthusiasm for the descriptive nature of Lawrence's writing became her sympathetic meditation on the personality of the man himself, and she invoked his experience with uncanny perceptiveness.

Recently, she has portrayed men more often than women. A number of these figures are bald, which accentuates their vulnerable humanness. She comments, "I have thought about this often. As I was able to move away from directly autobiographical work, I began to model more male figures. For a while, in response to feminist thought, I wondered if that was a betrayal, but I realized that for hundreds of years men have been portraying women. It seemed like true freedom to be able to turn the tables."

When speaking of her masterful work of 1989, *The Inevitability of Order*, Zink said, "For four or five years, there has been a lot of discussion of chaos and entropy . . . What we had thought of as decay can be seen as another sort of order."

In the long 103-inch piece of painted red wood, she built varied niches to house Christian figures of a priest and a fish repeated in a series of permutations. "By focusing on one single point and drawing all of one's energies from that, we can convey some kind of order," she said. The work seems connected to the fears generated in her childhood home, preoccupied as it was with dogma and death.

Zink has been reluctant to identify her inspiration with metaphysical language. However, her work and her thoughts are in transition, and she has moved closer to a transformative viewpoint.

"I feel I know less every year than I knew before, so I have to be a little more open. I see there are primary patterns to the way humans think. We set up models and then try to fit our experience into the model which happens to suit us. I have come to the point that I don't think my model is better than another's."

A case could be made that all of Zink's work is the visual equivalent of words. The connection between her art and an abstract concept she calls simply "the book" is so strong, I asked her to distinguish the phases of her work in terms of literature. The detailed tableaux she did from 1977 to 1987 she compares to Proust, the archetypal rememberer/describer. She feels her work since 1987 is more akin to Primo Levi, an Italian Jew who survived the Holocaust. In Levi's book *The Periodic Table*, he presents his autobiography in chapters of crystalline simplicity subtly linked to his profession of chemistry.

Zink says, "Everything I have done has been so complex, but now I find myself going the opposite way, toward simplifying, something I never thought I would do, because life is so complex." She is trying to surrender control of her creative process and just let her mind cast up its own associations. Her selection of elements for a piece thus becomes a function of her unconscious.

"I used to take an idea and analyze it. Now, when the idea comes, I watch it in my mind without trying to manipulate it. I stay in the dream or unconscious and let the images happen. I make my judgments on a kinesthetic or emotional basis, not an intellectual one. Nelson thinks the nonconscious mind operates from a logic that is different from our conscious mind. I am trying to work with this nonconscious kind of logic.

"Why does something move us? I've settled on expressing what moves me, but I hope it is not too arcane. One always hopes it will move someone else. I'd be very unhappy if no one ever saw my work. We are really dependent on the fact that other people exist. We are a tribal unit, like insects.

"When I say we are insects, that's not a pejorative. We are only another life form. I find some great comfort in that. Maybe it is because it reduces the importance of what I do to just a human activity.

"Although I decided against actually doing it, I spent some time considering a piece about beetles. It had to do with the work I think of as 'book pages.' These pages are references to a number of elements in my life: my Mother's Bible work, when she wrote concordances in the tiniest handwriting; Victorian illustrations and science illustrations of the 19th century, of which I am very fond; and also my love of Islamic manuscripts. For about fifteen years, I have had a super book on beetles with gorgeous illustrations of their overlapping, iridescent wings. Suddenly, I had one of those magic flashes when I saw all of these things combined.

"I had made a page with a sculpted relief of a hand holding a piece of paper, but I didn't use it. I kept thinking of the word 'mandible.' I could see it on the paper the hand was holding. I don't know why I thought of it, but I'd been thinking about why Islamic manuscripts are so wonderful and why I respond to them. I can't reproduce their content or pattern, but I kept wanting to replicate my feelings about those manuscripts, like a little tickle. I wanted to get behind the feelings. Is it the ornateness, the calligraphy, the little human beings, flowers and tiny details of the illustrations? For some reason, that question is part of the logic.

"I made a connection between 'mandible' and 'manuscript.' I thought of doing a series of labeled parts such as 'elytron,' the forewing of the beetle. Instead of imitating the idea of Islamic manuscripts, I could use beetle parts. In the end I incorporated the word mandible in a piece which says, 'Join the sundered mandible.' The piece I did not do led me to the one I have made.

"I have faith in this other kind of logic. If it feels correct to put apparently disparate things together, which I cannot logically defend to you, and if it moves me, then it is going to be all right, and hopefully it will move someone else.

"I am interested in new brain theory about connections, which implies that the more connections you can make, the better thinker you are. The illumination of connecting is that by allowing myself more connections, having faith in that, the logic of it is valid."

Zink teases her mind, her thinking-machine, with deliberate games. One of them is to play with her computer. She feeds lists of similar words into the machine and then she receives back from the software such grammatically correct, but illogical, phrases as "The Rats of Ambiguity."

"I am interested in phrases in which the meaning must be created by the reader as opposed to accepted meaning. In the Rats example I was interested in different types of nouns. Rats you can put in a wheelbarrow. Ambiguity you can't."

Zink seizes upon words as a title for a book "Page." The pages are two-dimensional wall pieces from which three-dimensional elements emerge. They are far simpler than her earlier tableaux. "I only want enough content to resonate so that we recognize that it has the look of a book. The only message is, thoughts in the context of the book, a form which equals imagining for me."

Water Dog's Tale is an actual book Zink has written in the form of a fable. She begins with:

"The blissful Flowering Spirit lives in the Mystic Garden where, instead of rules, there were grand celebrations and everyone was equal. The Oldest Inhabitant spent her days feeling the mysteries of life and sharing her visions. The only rebellion known to the garden came when serpents arrived with their packs filled with facts and logic. Their message was the omnipresent truth of death. When they left, the inhabitants of the garden were confused by unfamiliar fears."

To paraphrase the story, Water Dog convinced the community that the beauty of the garden outweighed the power of the serpents' symbols of pain and suffering. Water Dog's temperament, however, was far more introspective than that of the other garden dwellers, except for the Oldest Inhabitant. She restored the serenity of the garden for her neighbors, but her own state of mind was affected by the words of the serpent, and she became gloomy. The garden could no longer make her happy.

Water Dog prepared to leave. The Oldest Inhabitant saw her and said, "Some must leave before they can return." For a long time Water Dog lived alone beside the river under the willow tree. She surrendered to the river and the nearby hills. For long moments, she could hear the voices of the trees. She became familiar with the eddies and flow of the river and attuned to her surroundings. As her knowledge increased, her bleak emptiness faded away. She was one with all of time and nature.

At last, a delegation from the garden asked her to return and take the place of the Oldest Inhabitant. She then found a happy ending.

"The happy ending was, of course, death without fear. I don't think that most people equate that with a happy ending," Zink said.

At the end of Zink's book, her friend Dolores LaChapelle has written a statement in which she calls Water Dog's Tale a "Taoist story which came right out—just as it is—in one sitting." LaChapelle believes Zink has been transformed because she has found her own place under the willow tree beside the river.

The transformation Melissa Zink has undergone is similar to that of a shaman. For years her true self remained shadowed by conformity to the social structure of her upbringing and the obligations to others that blanketed her creativity. Once freed of these restrictions she encountered two openings at the same time—a loving partnership and a sense of her own power as an artist. The self-propelling evolution in her work grows by way of periodic integration of knowledge. With each step she alters the form of her work to account for a more encompassing synthesis. At some point in her process of growth, Zink began shedding fears and concentrating on "the things I love," and this too is a shamanic experience.

The shaman has an intuitive point of view, closer to the intuitive feminine than the analytical masculine. Psychologist Alberto Villoloco, in the PBS program "Thinking Allowed," explained the components of a shamanic path. First, he said, we have to follow the spirit of the serpent and "shed our skin," to leave the past behind. Then we must follow the spirit of the jaguar by confronting our fear of death in a place of power. "Fear is the greatest enemy of the shaman." Until we disengage from our own physical self, knowledge is just experience, not power, he explained. The person of power dares to take a chance.

The shaman is often called "the wounded healer," and also a prophet who serves as an example for others. Melissa Zink's story is that of the wounded healer made whole through her art.

"I only realized two or three months ago that I really want to be happy," she said.

*M*einrad Craighead vicariously introduced me to Barbara Hand Clow months before we actually met. Between meeting and interviewing her I read Eye of the Centaur: A Visionary Guide into Past Lives, *and* Heart of the Christos: Starseeding from the Pleiades, *the first two volumes of her* Mind Chronicles Trilogy. *These books are taken verbatim from the tapes of forty sessions of past-life regression conducted by hypnotherapists. In a foreword statement for the first volume, she wrote,*

"The goal of this series is to experience and chronicle the story of humankind since the Primeval Fireball as coming from the depths of one human mind, my own." In the Preface to the second volume, she elaborated, "As for where my material really comes from—past lives, primordial memory bank, or simply from creativity— I do not think it makes any difference . . . All that matters is whether it strikes a chord."

CLOW'S BOOKS CAN hardly fail to strike a chord. With absolute candor she shares sexual, magical and ritualistic material recovered from her innermost mind. The events are so convincingly described in such an emotional tone that the reader is moved to access personal fantasies—and this is her intention. Through her own experiences with past lives, she hopes to enable others to reach the deepest levels of their own consciousness.

Heart of the Christos begins with Barbara's unforgettable memory of a total lunar eclipse in 1472 B.C. She describes an event during her life as Aspasia, a Minoan priestess, when she offered to undergo a hierogamous, or sacred union in a tantric initiation. "The Moon darkens. I hear the movement of men's bodies as they pass around in a slow circle behind the stones [on which she lay] . . . My legs are spread, and I feel the chilled and damp breeze from the sea cooling my moist woman being. . . . The priest in black moves his erect phallus into my virginal body and I am ripped by a pain that gags my throat and shocks my heart . . . My brain explodes with saffron color, and my soul cries . . . this is wrong!" (p. 5.)

Beyond the gripping effect of Clow's memories, her books are a challenge to read. Separate typefaces identify a cacophony of voices, all of them in one way or another her own. Normal book type indicates a transcribed past life. Italics are used for Barbara's memory of her own life, while a contemporary font serves for her commentary. The sentences slip from tense to tense, from life to life, from outer description to inner experience. Her past lives group themselves as they were received, around a central core of sustained soul experience. In Eye of the Centaur, Clow shares vivid accounts of serving as the male priest Ichor, initiated into the cults of Osiris and Horus during the time of the Pharaohs in Egypt. The female/male personifications who wield the strongest influence throughout her soul lives are Aspasia, the Priestess of the Oracle of Thrace; and Isaiah, a prophet of Biblical times. In vivid detail she recalls being castrated in Rome. She tells the story of the Court Jester, the Victorian Lady, the Assyrian prostitute who lost all value to her father because she was raped, and, among others, the Renaissance astronomer whose main interest was science. Overshadowing these dramatic glimpses of her historical lives are her equally compelling revelations of this life as Barbara Clow: the visions, disconnections, bleed-throughs of past-life memories, suicide attempts and a schizophrenic breakdown.

BARBARA HAND CLOW: SPIRIUAL TEACHER

Heart of the Christos is the account of Barbara Hand Clow's journey through the underworld in search of her own shadow. Far back in time and far out in space, from the Paleolithic period on Earth to life on other stars, her psyche brings to the surface mythic tales of magical possibilities. Entwined in this material as asides or brief introductory passages are evocative connections with her current life. "I was meditating in the blinding sunlight of August 1987 in the Temple of the Quetzal Butterfly. I also existed simultaneously two levels below. An intense macrocellular reorganization was occurring. I shifted in my body, which felt like carbon being pressed into diamond, and I was myself then as I had been in 6700 B.C." (p. 112.)

Late in the fall of 1990, Barbara Hand Clow and I settled down for a long-planned conversation in the living room of her contemporary adobe home in Santa Fe. Before I could ask a question, we talked animatedly of her life and life itself, touching upon a mutual concern—the effect of television and films on the education of children. She observed that all of us today, adults and children alike, are encountering our past lives in filmed images, rapidly bridging into consciousness material that otherwise could take a lifetime to discover. In effect, she thinks of film as a tool to quicken self-awareness and transformation. Her upbeat view of filmed imagery is an important clue to this versatile, creative woman. Her roles of mother, wife, astrologer, artist, author, editor, spiritual teacher and ritual leader are all packaged in a glamorous blonde who is entering her fifties.

Finally, I began my interview, asking logically, "Were you brought up in a nourishing family?" and unlocking the story of a life marred by abandonment and abuse, hidden within the appearance of privilege. Barbara Hand was born in Saginaw, Michigan, in 1943, the result, she said ironically, of her father's home leave from Australia where he served as a medical doctor during World War II. "I was a child with outrageous, bouncy energy. My mother couldn't handle it."

Barbara's mother socialized to assuage her loneliness. She left the care of her son and baby daughter to the nanny and maid. Barbara's memory begins when she was five months old. She was lying in her crib, blinded from an eye infection, frightened and uncomforted through four long days and nights. She recalls riding on a train when she was 18 months old with her aunt who was taking her to live with trusted family friends. Meanwhile, her mother moved to New York with Barbara's older brother. After her father returned from the war, the family reestablished their home in Saginaw. In September 1946, her mother gave birth to a second son, Bobby. Shortly thereafter she sent for Barbara, who was now three and a half years old. Mrs. Hand had not been able to visit her infant daughter. She was ignorant of the fact that her friends had abused and raped her daughter. Barbara was thirty years old when she learned that her mother had been seriously ill throughout the war. It was only when she became aware of this that Barbara could forgive being abandoned by her mother.

Remembering her reentry into the family, Barbara said she didn't even know who they were. In *Eye of the Centaur*, she describes herself soon after returning to the family: "The reality I was born into was very bland, and the people around me seemed to be dedicated to living a 'normal' life . . . I was a wild little girl which upset just about everybody . . . If only they could have understood how hard I was trying to please them! But I didn't fit. I was in the wrong place. I felt like I'd been dropped out of a tree in the middle of everybody's life." (p. 69.)

In a fundamental way, Barbara remained outside her family, like a changeling— essentially different from them, depressed and mildly schizophrenic, by her own account. When she was five years old, she tried to commit suicide. She told me this story: "My mother was standing on one side of some train tracks that ran behind my school. I remember seeing her like a mirage. I saw a train coming and I became fascinated by the train wheels. I couldn't resist jumping in front of the train. Mother was screaming. The train knocked me toward her. I had a nasty bruise and swollen bones on my hip. I clearly wanted to be crushed under the wheels." In later years, her mother could not recall the incident, although she did remember that Bobby also was hit by the train in a similar way. The near tragedy was held within Barbara's memory as a genuine suicide attempt, a desire to leave the life she led.

Even as a young child Barbara was exceptionally sensitive to and aware of the numinous. Inwardly she was living in what she calls spherical time or Dreamtime. "Sometimes I could see blue-white energy around objects in the house or around the trees and rocks . . . The land was alive with Indian spirits . . . " (*Eye of the Centaur*, p. 40.) She heard inner voices, was aware of other lives and had visions.

The family home was situated beside a large Catholic cathedral that was built over an Ojibwa, Chippewa and Potawatomi sacred site. Before the earliest priests cut it down, the sacred Great White Oak Tree of the Great Lakes grew on this spot. Barbara was attracted by the energies she felt in the cathedral and, though forbidden to do so, she attended mass as often as she could. "From the age of 6, every time I went to mass I felt high." When she was 12 years old, Barbara asked her family's Congregationalist minister, Who was Jesus? He told her she could think he was the Son of God, or just a great teacher, or whatever she liked. "He didn't have any answers," she said. For the next seven years, she had no church affiliation.

The central figures of her childhood were her father's parents who lived eleven miles away in Bay City. Twice a month for ten years, she spent the weekend with this intellectual, professional couple. Her grandfather was a lawyer who aspired to be a Classics scholar. Her grandmother held a master's degree in Latin and was a great-niece of Susan B. Anthony.

"My great-grandmother—my grandfather's mother—was a full-blooded Cherokee. When we were kids, it was just not acceptable to be an Indian, so in the family this particular grandmother was a shadow figure. Her son, my grandfather, was my teacher, beginning when I was five. He had a fine library and he put me on a reading program. By the age of 12, I was familiar with the classics of

Western literature, as well as Greek, Egyptian, Sumerian and North American Indian mythologies. My grandfather Hand felt I needed an esoteric education. For years, I could not understand why I knew how to follow the Dreamtime. All my life, I've had this amazing knowledge that I've watched unfold. I thought that, because my grandfather was a 33rd degree Mason, the knowledge he gave me must be Masonic; but I studied Masonic material, and it was not there.

"When my second son was 17, he had a blood test that showed an enzyme found only in Native Americans. Then I began to wonder. My father and aunt kept complex genealogies. [On both sides, the Anglo family has been here since 1640.] Once I studied the genealogies, I realized that I am one-eighth Cherokee. Then, I went back and registered with the Cherokee tribe. In the last few years I've learned that what my grandfather taught me were the ancient Cherokee teachings.

"I'm so grateful to be part-Cherokee because I understand things from the indigenous point of view. If you look at reality the way an indigenous person does, it's possible to receive a teaching when a butterfly lands on a plant. In other words, everything unfolds for you as it is occurring."

Barbara never formally graduated from high school or college. She enrolled in summer school at the University of Michigan in Ann Arbor after her senior year in high school. While there, she met the founder of the Port Huron-based Students for a Democratic Society (S.D.S.). In 1962, she married John Frazier, who was an aspiring writer as young as herself. Together they converted to Catholicism. The newlyweds moved to Seattle, where a year later a son, Tommy, was born. Barbara enrolled as a full scholarship student for two years at the Jesuit University of Seattle to study philosophy. She completed a year of psychology courses also, but she said, "I wasn't interested in graduating. I couldn't see any point to it." She founded the Seattle Committee to Stop the Vietnam War and also worked with S.D.S., spending the next several years as a political agitator. The couple visited San Francisco during the heyday of Haight Ashbury.

In 1968, they moved to San Francisco just before the birth of a second son, Matthew. Barbara founded the Déjà Vu Jewelry Company, a strangely prophetic name. "I have always been a good designer," she said. The business grew to 20 employees. She also studied stained glass making, and that craft was her major interest after her younger brother Bobby joined and expanded the jewelry company.

Though San Francisco was exciting and charming, Barbara worried about her older son's education. She took the boys to the mountains and started teaching Tommy herself. She had recognized from the beginning that her marriage would inevitably end, and she was planning how she might live on her own. Most of this time John Frazier spent on the road selling jewelry while she lived independently.

She opened a stained glass studio in Nevada City, a town that became a historical landmark; and she contributed to its restoration. Among her projects was the renovation of her own Greek Revival house. Later, she sold this home to fund her next move when she accepted an invitation to join a craft guild in Massachusetts. Again she was motivated by finding a fine school system for her sons. Frazier drove the van across country and helped her settle in Amherst, but at that point they parted amicably. She sought and won an annulment of their marriage by the Church, followed by a civilian divorce in 1972.

In the following year, Barbara's reputation as a glass artist attracted the attention of Gerry Clow, a reporter for the *Boston Globe* who also was a crafts editor for Little, Brown and Company. He asked her to author a book on stained glass that he expected to edit. Their book, *Stained Glass: A Basic Manual,* was published in 1976, two years after they were married. The Clow's have a mutually supportive and loving relationship. Gerry immediately took on the role of father to Tommy and Matthew. In 1976, the couple moved to Chicago; and Gerry joined Rand McNally. He was the third generation of Clows to hold a position in that publishing company. Christopher Clow was soon born there in 1976, followed by Elizabeth in 1978.

Barbara maintained a professional stained glass studio in Chicago, but she also explored her second avocation of astrology, which began in California in 1967. Although she had never seen one before, she had spontaneously read an astrological chart to a group of friends who were professional astrologers. Their response made her take the incident seriously. She began studying astrology texts and doing readings, at first only for her family, but eventually for others.

"I went into it gung-ho. It was the only thing that answered questions of personality conflicts for me. It defined what people were. I began an intensive analysis of my family and my parents, who were both Pisces. Through a number of years, I tried to understand reality based on astrology. It worked. I found my life and the lives of those around me improved as a result of doing things astrologically. I was never interested in astrology as a predictive tool. I was only interested in the way astrology explains the psychological makeup of an individual and the interactions between people. I use it as a healing tool.

"Because of my struggle to become sane, as a result of my early abandonment, I had read Jung, Freud, and most major psychology sources during my twenties. In the 1970s, I became a psychological astrologer and teacher. When we moved to Chicago, I did some financial astrology, and I was on television programs. By the late 1970s, I was well known for giving astrological readings, and I was getting some profoundly therapeutic results with astrology in three-hour sessions. I contemplated becoming an analyst utilizing astrology. In 1981, I studied for a year at the Evanston Jung Institute, but I found analysis too slow and expensive. I wanted a faster and more direct way to help people reach the deepest level of archetypal exploration. Astrology does not deal with processing the contents of the subconscious mind, although it can be used to direct such deep exploration. I needed to find a method for doing that.

"I intuited that with past-life regression under hypnosis, a person might reach a deep level of the subconscious more quickly and cheaply than by analysis. I made an appointment at Mundelein College and presented my idea for graduate research into past-life regression."

Barbara was accepted in the Mundelein master's degree program in Creation Spirituality headed by the controversial former Dominican priest Matthew Fox. She entered the program with the clear understanding that she would report on the results of her own sustained past-life regression under hypnosis as a basis for comparison to Jungian psychoanalytic therapy. Once she was accepted, Barbara engaged Gregory Paxson to conduct twenty hypnotic sessions. Together, she and Paxson developed her thesis—that past-life regression provides a fast means to discover the hidden contents of one's own mind, and the material brought to awareness has profound effects on an individual's self-understanding. She created her book *Eye of the Centaur* from her master's thesis. Paxson wrote in his introduction to the book, "In times when high spirituality was seen as a technical capability [these ancient lives had to do] with practical service at a literally spiritual level." (p. 2.) He developed the idea further in the passage, "In the training of adepts, Past-Life Regression serves as a shortcut, allowing the trainee to recapture the steps toward mastery already taken in previous incarnations. This same act of remembering opens a doorway that enters into the realms of higher vibration, the understanding of those realms of our source, and a working relationship with the Beings of those realms." (p. 4.)

Paxson noted that Barbara witnessed the ongoing progression of her soul as a conscious energy field, entering a body to grow, departing the body at death and returning for yet another life. The personalities she encountered are connected in a holographic sphere of time. If there were a single word to link these earlier selves, it would be *service*. The identity which she filled often in her past lives was that of a priest-like adept. In Barbara's present life, the notion of serving as teacher or priestess rapidly awakened as a result of remembering lives of service under hypnosis. She was soon to make a major change of residence and occupation which would encourage her to serve in this life as a spiritual teacher.

In 1983, shortly before she was due to graduate from the master's program at Mundelein, Matthew Fox sold the Clows the largest interest in Bear and Company, a publishing house he cofounded in 1980 in Santa Fe. The Clows moved to Santa Fe a few days after Barbara's graduation. Around this time she received in a dream the concept for her *Mind Chronicles Trilogy*. All three titles appeared to her at once, and she registered them with the Library of Congress. *Eye of the Centaur* was first published by Llewelyn in

1986, and subsequently by Bear. *Heart of the Christos* was published by Bear and Company in 1989. The third title of her series, *The Signet of Atlantis*, published by Bear in 1992, was in embryonic form at the time of our interview.

Since moving to Santa Fe in 1983, the Clows have spent all their vacations at sacred sites around the globe. Their first trip was to Egypt. Drawing upon the teachings she received from her grandfather as well as the instinctive material she reawakened during past-life regression, Barbara has conducted ritual at sacred sites around the globe. In Mexico, she identified the sacred site of Teotihuacan—"where the tree god comes to Earth"—as her special temple.

Entering the publishing business has brought Barbara Clow into contact with extraordinary people who have become her teachers and colleagues. José Arguelles approached Bear and Company with his manuscript *The Mayan Factor: Path Beyond Technology* in October 1986. Arguelles is the visionary who identified, organized and inspired the worldwide Harmonic Convergence of August 1987. Barbara worked at top speed to publish his book in time for it to reach the public before the scheduled convergence. As the Convergence neared, she felt drawn to participate ceremonially at Teotihuacan. To make plans in conjunction with native leaders, she made a preparatory trip. When the time arrived, Gerry, Barbara and her son Matthew spent a week in Mexico. At the Harmonic Convergence on August 16, 1987, she first met White Eagle Tree, a teacher in the Cherokee Sweet Medicine tradition. Since then they have been teaching together at sacred sites.

As she told her extraordinary life story, Barbara's round eyes grew wider and her energy level seemed to increase. She revealed the quick, fertile way her mind moves from one subject to another when suddenly she wanted me to see samples of her son Chris's art. Five fully realized images, each entirely separate in style, were created by Chris when he was 13 years old while he was at the Interlochen Summer Camp where he had gone to study music. We also looked at Elizabeth's altar of sacred objects. Barbara accentuated her belief that in a family attuned to the sacred, children can bypass much of the hardship of initiation and reach through to their inner awareness easily and quickly. Mothering is never far from her consciousness.

As we returned to the moving story of her assertive spiritual leadership among native people, I was more than a little astounded. It is one thing to recognize your own spiritual knowing and another thing entirely to claim it and have it be accepted by others, especially tribal wise men. The discussion led us to her membership for six years in the Banana Clan, associated with the Hopi Indians, and founded by a Frenchman, Robert Boissiére. Boissiére once lived among the Hopi. He moved to Taos and married an exceptional woman of enlightenment from Taos Pueblo, who has since died. In his book, *The Return of the Pahana: A Hopi Myth*, Boissiére mentions the vision he had after World War II that inspired him to found the Banana Clan for non-Indians who would align themselves in spiritual practice with Hopi prophecies. The Hopi permit the Banana Clan to have its own shrine on Second Mesa in Arizona. Barbara has co-celebrated ritual there a number of times, and she led New Moon Lodge in the Banana Clan kiva for several years.

Barbara said, "The indigenous people have been awaiting the point when the white people in Western cultures who took their land—people of European background and consciousness—would be ready for their teaching that Mother Earth is the teacher, and anyone who attunes to the mother will receive the correct knowledge. But it was always understood in their prophecies that the invader would come and oppress them first."

In March 1989, Barbara attended the Mayan Initiatic Openings of Ceremonial Sites in Mexico with her son Tom. Just prior to this trip, her doctor found she had a breast tumor and recommended an immediate biopsy. By this time, however, her trust in native wisdom was so powerful and sure that she told him her tumor would be healed in Mexico. After two weeks of ceremony, she participated in a White Brotherhood Healing ceremony conducted by a group of Mayan spiritual teachers at Chitzen Itza, and her response to it was electric. "My kundalini energy was so strong afterwards, I was paralyzed. Tommy and I were on our beds in our hotel unable to move until 9:00 the next morning, and then the paralysis let go. When I got home I checked again with my doctor, and the tumor was gone. I asked him if he wanted to know why, but he said no."

Through service, Barbara Hand Clow has found her social purpose.

"There is a planetary effort being made to awaken sacred sites through conducting ceremony and to release the knowledge held at these places. Major breakthroughs in my consciousness occurred at the Mayan Initiatic Openings of 1989. The Mayan medicine man Hunbatz Men led us on the journey. The main leaders agreed that it was time to create ceremony at temples, and we all created ceremony together. We started at Palenque, where Alberto Ruz Buenfil created a ceremony with the Lacandon Maya, who have been the guardians of Palenque for the last 1500 years. Hunbatz Men and Alberto Ruz Buenfil have had a powerful effect on me. Along with my grandfather Hand and White Eagle Tree, they are my most formative teachers.

"In ancient days, the sacred sites were the pulse of the planet. In every tribe, places that had telluric force were determined by the healers and teachers. Their temple structures were built around those sites. People were the interfacing, unifying unit between sacred earth and cosmic laws."

Clow has devoted her energies to restoring that holistic relationship.

Robert Boissiére writes, "In order for humanity to regain control of its destiny, such knowledge must be rekindled." (*The Return of Pahana*, p. 98.) Barbara Clow's personal discoveries have rekindled in herself memories of ancient mystical ritual and symbolic truths. Just as she sought and then practiced her knowledge of astrology—in a sense creating herself as an astrologer—she has enacted the role of spiritual teacher directly from the force of her experience. In this regard, she suggests that after transformative revelations occur, a way opens to use them in service to the respiritualization of the earth. There was a time when spiritual awareness penetrated daily life. Barbara places it in the period from 10,000 to 1,500 B.C., when human beings lived intuitively and listened to their inner voices. The Goddess culture was still intact then and "People breathed and interacted with the sacred sites," she said.

Clow posits that we are witnessing a revival of the intuitive abilities of early man, but they are combining with the fruits of evolution in the clarity of the rational human mind. "What's happening now is the reemergence of the neolithic mind." In her words, "As the right-brain, numinous consciousness is reemerging, it is within the context of the developed left brain." Thus, for the first time, we will have a chance to surmount the duality we are plagued with in our present state of consciousness. Avatars such as Pahana, Quetzalcoatl, the Plumed Serpent god of Mexico, Christ and the Buddha are models who represent the unmet aspirations of people to become fully aware and fully human, to be both rational and intuitive in a state of at-one-ness.

When asked what is her most important contribution to the bridging of our dual mind, Barbara Hand Clow did not mention her work with ceremony. Instead, she said, "I am the teacher who brought the teaching of Chiron. This will be the new way of consciousness on this planet." (Chiron is a recently discovered minor planet in our solar system.) Clow's exegesis on the subject of Chiron furnished me with a matrix from which I can better understand the onrushing demands in my own mind to seek new prophets. In Barbara Hand Clow, I clearly found a prophet who illuminates my quest.

A planet does not begin to affect ordinary human beings until it is sighted, Clow told me, even though sensitives may have been aware of a planet long before it makes its official appearance to our technologically aided eye. Chiron was officially sighted in 1977 between Saturn and the outer planets. By 1983 Barbara had developed a method of working with Chirotic energies in her astrological readings, and she felt called upon to explain her intuition about its planetary significance. In her book *Chiron: Rainbow Bridge Between the Inner and Outer Planets,* she presents her theories for professional astrologers based on hundreds of natal charts in her files. She states that Chiron rules Virgo and the sixth house of the zodiac. The non-astrologer will find many revelatory nuggets within the technical explanations of her book. For example, she writes that Chiron's sighting was accompanied by a "planetary eruption of communications from other realms," and its appearance is a marker that we are recapturing skills that once seemed normal before the rise of Christianity. "The eruption of channeling, divination, and multidimensional skills is ruled by the planet Chiron." (p. xiii.) Clow has often found that people had a significant change in their lives around the time of Chiron's sighting, between 1977 and 1979. She asked me if that had happened to me. Yes, I had my fiftieth (crone) birthday in 1979, and those are the years when my insights came together leading to the founding of SLMM and to the writing of this book.

Barbara Clow believes that the Chirotic effect on human behavior and evolution will be a rapid increase in a feminine way of knowing, which she equates with intuition. With the deliberate intention of demonstrating a nonlinear, nonrational mode of communicating information, she writes whole passages in a stream-of-consciousness style—as if William Faulkner had returned in female form. Separate ideas tumble forth as apparent non sequiturs, but the reader is able to make leaps between them. Reading without analysis allows this material to seep into mental recesses where it seems to remain in memory as discrete images, recoverable from one's intuitive right brain in much the way she recovered them herself. Eventually the ideas she suggests yield their fruit.

Undergirding Clow's urgent and passionate explosion of words is her lifetime habit of study and creative synthesizing. She brings to her work a familiarity with myth and a knowledge of symbolic language. Her prodigious intuition is not to be confused with romance. Clow does not romanticize either myth or astrology. She mines them for useful information, believing them to be storehouses of data we can apply to our present life.

In Greek myth, Chiron is the centaur, half human, half horse. He is the great teacher and healer. The arrival of Chiron in our psyche in the late years of the Piscean Age indicates we are to have an accelerated mythical unfoldment. Our new Chirotic consciousness will be less fixed in three dimensions, more attuned to the fourth dimension of spacelessness, timelessness, and emptiness because the energy of Chiron bridges the inner and outer planets. Having never studied astrology I found these ideas new to me. I learned that the inner planets deal with temporal matters about one's present personality, whereas the outer planets fill a role in the eternal spiritual journey of the soul. The sighting of Chiron connotes the beginning of a higher vibration on Earth and the possibility of our mastering magic. "Mastery is the conscious evolution of self with magical forces," Clow writes. (*Chiron*, p. 2.) In addition, she believes "The actual sighting of Chiron may hint that the power of the priesthood may be over with, that anyone can learn the sacred sounds and words to enter into the revelation of the secrets." (p. 9.)

However, she warns, "At this critical juncture, we are in grave danger of falling into atavism or reversion to a more primitive state of mind unless we define the new bridging energy according to our present reality instead of the distant and de-energized past."

Barbara explains one of the teachings associated with Chiron has to do with our understanding of illness: "Chiron, by transit, will often identify the maximum pressure times in a lifetime which are also the illumination times. Those times are often when the relentless pressure of Saturn can be left behind, and the electrical healing potential of Uranus released. Chiron rules crystals. Crystals can be great healing tools because crystals are frozen white light in hexagonal rigid Saturnian mineral form. If you have a past life trauma or illness some place in your body, during each lifetime your higher self will try to push through that point, that density. That is, you will get sick in that place until you clear it, until you can turn that place to pure crystalline white light. Each incarnation is a chance to clear past life blocks and become whole in this lifetime . . . " (*Chiron*, p, 6-7.)

Barbara believes that Chiron is the "gateway to the least resolved and deepest fears lurking within each one of us. It is the key to facing death with awareness." (*Chiron*, p. xx.) When fears are faced, the personality is "remarkably illuminated."

In summary, she said,

> "For us who are working with new consciousness, the point is to stop trying to identify the enemy or the victim, and switch to a new paradigm, which is: begin with yourself. The key or core teaching for me is that I must heal myself in order to build a world in which my daughter will not be raped as I was.
>
> "Chiron is the wounded healer archetype. The Chirotic principle is that if one person heals a deep psychic wound it becomes a planetary healing. In other words, when something shifts in one place, it can shift universally. When the wounded healer shifts to a place of being healed and trusting, it is immensely powerful. Chiron represents the synchronicity principle: As above, so below. I coined the word Chirotic and it is now in the language. The psychologist Jean Houston uses the term Kairotic. We agree about it and started using the words at the same time."

Barbara finds her own role in defining the meaning of Chiron symbolized by her maiden name, Hand. She cites Robert Graves who pointed out that the name Chiron derives from the Greek word *cheir*, which means hand. In her present work, she is expanding her relationship with Chiron from astrology to ceremony. "I keynoted the Conference of the Wounded Healer in Niagara Falls at Summer Solstice of 1990. Native American healers from the United States and Canada attended it. In my book *Eye of the Centaur*, I described my vision of the Great White Owl landing on the Sacred Tree of the Great Lakes. In Niagara Falls, I released the Great White Owl and the Sacred Tree to be empowered on the etheric plane. The Great White Owl can now fly again, protecting the forest and protecting Mother Earth against invasion. The very day that I gave that teaching, which had been planned a year in advance, Congress passed the Spotted Owl legislation. As above, so below."

Barbara is confident that her *Liquid Light of Sex: Understanding Your Key Life Passages* will bring into popular understanding the role played by three major transits in one's life. When one is approximately thirty years of age, Saturn returns to its natal placement in one's horoscope. The main concern of the individual under the influence of Saturn has to do with finding one's way in the material world.

At approximately the fortieth year of one's life, Uranus is exactly opposite to where it was at one's birth. This event provokes a mid-life crisis, when the basic electrical energy of the body, the kundalini energy, rises to its most intense levels of a lifetime. "When people hit mid-life crisis, the electric body is so charged it creates a magnetic field of oscillating waves that travel at the speed of light," Clow explained. The main spiritual transformation of a lifetime, accompanied by the most doubt and pain, occurs at this mid-life transit. Clow's book is meant to teach the reader how to pass through these crisis points to the best advantage.

When one is fifty years old, Chiron returns. Chiron is, mythologically, the opposite of Prometheus who sought godlike power. The Chiron archetype seeks healing, to be healed and to heal others. If Chiron triumphs upon its return, the Promethean complex is overcome and the ego loses its control.

Barbara cites the work of astronomer Percy Seymour as a reinforcement for her astrological theories. Seymour has written that astrology works according to the principles of solar magnetism. Barbara Clow bases her theories on the practical work of reading thousands of natal charts, plus her studies in the wisdom of India and the mechanics of subtle energetics medicine. "The reason astrology is helpful is that if we know in advance the path we will be traveling, we can anticipate and create better realities for ourselves."

Barbara said another planet was sighted by satellite in 1983. She thinks the planet will be named Nibiru in honor of Sumerian sources. "Nibiru is on a 3500- to 3600-year orbit and was last in our solar system at its perihelion around 100 B.C. to 1 A.D. During the previous return in 3600 B.C., Nibiru was completely chronicled in ancient Sumerian sources . . . I even believe that the Star of Bethlehem was probably Nibiru rising as Christ incarnated, since the symbol for the Star of Bethlehem—an eight-pointed star—is the same as the Sumerian symbol for Niburu." (*Chiron*, p. 18.)

Beginning in her girlhood, Catholicism provided a grounding for Barbara's spiritual education. "The Catholic Church has been the mainstream of Western intellectual thought for the past 2000 years," she said; but now that Chirotic energies are influencing the planet she sees that changes of profound consequences will affect the church. Because of the entrenched position of the hierarchy which prevents women from full participation in the priesthood, the church is pitted against the global impulse to release the feminine aspect of human nature. Modern churches that are organized around a principle of separation—separation of men from women, humans from God, and God from nature—will lose power as we reach the new millennium if they resist the Chirotic transmutation's essential require-ment that individuals must balance polarities and overcome duality. To assist in this unification, sensitives around the world anticipate the arrival into consciousness of a new avatar; and this sacred persona, Barbara thinks, might well be a woman.

Based on astrology, Barbara Clow made a prediction at my request. The United States is ruled, she said, by Uranus. Due to the conjunction of Neptune and Uranus in 1993, she expects this country to soon undergo its own mid-life crisis, a social upheaval leading to a more compassionate governmental system. "The country is going to go through a complete grassroots revolution. There is no way to go through this level of rapid change without suffering. I think we're already seeing terrible levels of inner anger manifesting as cancer and autoimmune diseases."

In 1948, when she was five years old, Barbara had a vision in which she "ascended to the higher planes" and fused with her higher self. This mystical insight was too much for her to understand then, but she finally gained control over it, and she claims, "I have chosen to stay with the alignment." (*Chiron*, p. 28.) Her decision implies the acceptance of responsibility for what she knows and for her actions on behalf of what she perceives. Barbara Hand Clow's power is in her creative insight and her ability to make daring syntheses of information. The importance of her work is sure to grow as more and more people delve into her books and integrate what she has discovered.

Barbara found her own way to serve when she participated in the Harmonic Convergence. "I took on my power then as a ceremonial teacher during the pipe ceremony with White Eagle Tree at Teotihuacan. I don't know for how long it will be, but when I am called to do ritual at sacred sites, I'll be there. I am involved in a planetary shift. I gave up questioning whether I should or should not do something. What I am supposed to do, I will do. One of my biggest issues is how to be in the power, to offer it and give it, and yet not to be in control. The protection we have is in knowing we are really in our truth. We offer it to others. It does not matter if they take it."

*W*hile curating the invitational show Shrines and Sacred Places, I asked
Susan Halsten McGarry, editor-in-chief of Southwest Art magazine whether she
knew any artists who were expressing a sacred theme. She suggested Pat
Musick who lives in Arkansas. Musick sent two painted wood sculptures
for the show. As we took Pat's pieces from the cartons, I was struck
by their strong physicality and the power of their allusion to the
shelters of woodland Indians. We stayed in touch. She became a
member of SLMM and sent me catalogs of her touring exhibitions.
As we grew better acquainted by mail and phone, I sensed
a prophecy in her work related to human connections
within nature through time. We discussed
Artists of the Spirit, and our mutual
interest led to a taped interview for this
book. We did not meet in person
for another two years.

PAT MUSICK'S RESPONSES to my questions revealed that her art is rooted in a concern with unity and universal symbols. However, she emphasized to me that she limits her field of vision to history and now. She avoids speculations on the future or an afterlife. Her early influences were Sartre, Brecht, Ionesco, Beckett and Camus. "My worldview has been formulated to an extraordinary degree by existentialism. One of the strongest messages I get from this philosophy is the importance of personal decision in our universe, which often seems to be without purpose. I believe my individual efforts are an important determinant of my existence. That worldview informs my art," she said.

From her choice of words, I realized Pat Musick offered me an experimental model of a way to fit into my vision not only herself, but also other artists I consider prophetic who are put off by mystical language. She speaks precisely for herself, her words grounded in professionalism. Her experience amplifies the notion of prophecy as a normal part of an artist's life, not something wispy and vague.

Musick holds a doctorate in psychology from Cornell University. She has taught at Syracuse University, Cornell University, the State University of New York at Oswego and the University of Houston at Clear Lake. She has authored books and articles about creativity, art therapy, symbolism and the practice of teaching. Her research is focused on "repetitions of human behavior as they are reflected in historic art." In her artmaking, she strives to express classic polarities, such as "heaven/earth, light/dark, man/woman, good/ evil." Although her art is based on the discipline of figure drawing, her style has grown increasingly expressionistic and abstract in recent years. By virtue of sustained concentration, she has achieved a synthesis of art and psychology with a compelling integrity about it that is entirely personal. The fact that she has reached this level of education and maturity in her art is something she secretly hoped for but had little reason to expect in her younger years. Harsh experience has fueled the development of Musick's inner life and driven her art into its present channel.

PAT MUSICK: IN THESE FOOTSTEPS

Pat Musick (née Tapscott) grew up in Los Angeles in the 1920s. She remembers secretly yearning for the ideal of stardom and the Hollywood syndrome surrounding her contemporary, Shirley Temple. Pat and her younger brother were raised in a middle-class, cultured and strained household. Her father collected old European oil paintings, fine books, Oriental rugs, crystal and tableware. Her great-uncle on her mother's side, Ashe Davis, was an artist whom she visited at the age of 12 years old on a trip to Iowa with her father. Of this visit, she says, "His overpowering paintings of larger-than-life religious figures greatly affected my childhood determination to pursue an interest in art.

"My parents noticed my ability to draw when I was very young. Encourage it? No, not at all, but my mother's twin sister spent a considerable amount of time with me, encouraging me to draw. I did not get parental praise . . . if anything, I got discouragement. I have no recollection of attending a museum as a child. It was not until I had initiated all the effort solely by myself to get an art scholarship to the University of Southern California that my parents finally gave in, with great misgivings.

"In an overall view, my childhood home was kind of hellish. It was one that Eugene O'Neill could have done justice to, with an enormous amount of conflict and self-interest. The self-interest expressed and fulfilled by the four family members was one of the ingredients that fed my stubborn pursuit of an art career.

"My home was also a place of sensitivity to the classical 'tragic artist' concept; the artist who is misunderstood by society, who is introspective and deeply mournful. I remember the influence of my cousin who introduced me to poetry on the same trip to Iowa when I visited the family's farm. He took my brother and me down to slop the pigs at night. Once the job was over, we sat on the fence and watched the pigs eat. Then, he would recite Edgar Allen Poe. It was something that burned into my brain; and I never forgot, not only the fact that I was introduced to a new artistic medium, but the sensitivity and fineness of soul of the individual who was speaking it.

"My father's brother had what today we would call a psychotic episode. Emotionally, a tremendous amount was made of that event. My father flew back to Iowa to rescue him from the clutches of his wife and the doctor, who were going to subject him to electric shock. Dad took him back to the farm where he made a slow, painful recovery. That psychotic tendency was generalized in the minds of the entire family. Who would be next? I was the identified possibility because I exhibited the same level of sensitivity prevalent in my father's family, rather than the level-headed coolness exemplified on my mother's side.

"One of my parents' techniques for having me achieve suitable behaviors was to make dire threats. 'Don't smoke or you'll get TB.' 'Don't do this or you'll have a nervous breakdown.' At some young level, I became aware that a breakdown was an expected potential in me. In tracing my path back, I would say my interest in art therapy probably came from the unconscious realization of this expectation. Later, it became the foundation of my belief that the terminally ill, the psychotic or the mentally retarded individual, through the making of art, gains control over his or her own destiny. That is the basis of my teaching of art therapy.

"There is a time when you are directing the pencil or crayon, making it do what you want it to do, making it achieve what you want it to achieve, when you have control over life and you forget that you are going to die of cancer in six months, that you are locked into a psychotic condition or that your intellectual level gives you slight chance of progress. I must have sensed that because I knew when I was drawing as a kid, for that moment I was in control, and the fears, doubts or concerns about what my parents might think, disappeared. I was thoroughly invested in that activity.

"As a child, I knew instinctively that the racial prejudice in my home was wrong and that I would reject it the rest of my life. Because of that rejection, I began to seek out information about minority groups to help me understand and to have a better appreciation of who we are in God's world.

"For two years after my brother was born when I was four years old, my mother was ill. A Navajo woman from the reservation came to help with child care and to live with us in a program that our Presbyterian church had developed for Navajos to learn English. Part of my earliest memory of art and drawing are the endless hours I spent watching her weave beaded belts, headbands, anklets and wristlets. The patterning, color, lines and forms she made absolutely intrigued me. Frequently, I find that in creating my work, aspects of her imagery creep in. I particularly respond to the snake formation. When I see it, in the Navajo, Aztec or Mayan symbology, or the related Greek and Roman key, I resonate to something that I can't express in words, some unknown power."

At the end of three semesters, Pat dropped out of college to marry Jack Musick. While he finished college, she supported them by working as a secretary, but she continued to study art in evening classes at Chouinard Art Institute. Jack Musick's profession was coaching football. Pat, Jack and their three daughters lived for ten years at Dartmouth College and then moved to Cornell University.

At Dartmouth, in her thirties, Pat had several years of therapy with the late psychiatrist Margaret Antonison who led her to an internal aphorism that sustains her still, "Negatives can be turned into positives." From this intensive inner work, Pat came to see her child-hood as one that nourished certain aspects of her creativity and fueled her tenacious spirit to maintain her path as an artist. She says she loves her parents, now deceased, very much and remains grateful to them for the gift of her life.

"While we were at Dartmouth, I had my first awareness of education as a lifelong process. I audited liberal arts courses and took art classes without credit. When my girls were all in school, I studied with Paul Sample, who became a lasting influence. After five years, he said, 'It's time for you to get your feet wet and call yourself a professional.'" Pat studied figure drawing for eight years and felt most comfortable expressing the human subject. At the time, she customarily drew figures with charcoal and graphite worked into ink washes, and painted in oil on canvas.

When Dartmouth established a visiting artist program, for which Musick was not eligible, she watched through the windows while Frank Stella, Robert Rauschenberg and Hans Hoffman taught studio classes; and she attended their lectures. She visited museums in New York every other month and became familiar with Abstract Expressionism, which was quite foreign to the representational style she had been taught.

"I looked at, questioned and tried to learn from abstraction. For an hour or two several times a year, I studied Picasso's *Guernica*. It was a real breakthrough for me when I began to understand and respond to what Picasso was doing, not only thematically, but also technically." Jackson Pollock and Mark Rothko became heroes for her, too, once she had started to "see" their work.

Yet, she did not become an abstract artist herself. The entire question of abstraction versus realism was an unsettled issue for her. Something she heard in 1984 from the octogenarian Louisiana sculptress Clyde Connell supported the gradual change Pat has made in her style, and it also challenged her.

"As an artist," Connell said, "you cannot move too far from the central innermost core of your being in the making of your work. If you do, it will show. It will not ring true." Musick's work was still largely figurative until the mid-1980s, but she has moved steadily away from a narrative, figurative approach to a more symbolic expression of what that "innermost core" of her being is about.

In response to student unrest during the Vietnam War, Cornell University opened a program whereby minority students could get credit for field work or "life experience" and apply directly to graduate school without an undergraduate degree. Pat heard about the offer in the media, and she immediately applied for the same privilege. Through the good offices of her mentor Jim Maas, she was accepted. By that time, she had spent far more hours in classes than an undergraduate degree demanded. She was a professional artist, albeit her first priorities were her children and her husband's career needs. After a year of probation, she concentrated on a master's degree in design with a minor in psychology and then went straight on to earn her doctorate in psychology in 1974. Many years later, she asked Maas why he had vouched for her, and he said he knew her creativity was so deep it would carry her through the academic requirements of his department and add something to the program in the process. His prediction was realized later in her teaching. "I was able to bring to my painting classes the psychology of perception and various issues of how we perceive images, to provide a level of understanding not usually achieved in studio courses. Conversely, I introduced my psychology classes to an understanding of creative problem solving, of how artists create and think, [and] of motivations for creating. This approach is unusual in such courses."

Even before graduation, Pat started teaching. She relied upon her original insight to combine psychology with the field of art therapy. From 1974 to 1976, she developed an innovative curriculum in New England universities, and she was offered a part time position at Syracuse University teaching art therapy in special education. But then her life was abruptly altered.

"The night I discovered my husband Jack was having an affair, I found myself at three o'clock in the morning crawling around on the floor of the kitchen. The childhood projection of a psychotic episode was right in front of me. I 'saw' this huge black pit in the floor, and as I looked down into it there was nothing but black, black, black . . . I was on my hands and knees right on the edge of the pit. But I reared back and sat on my buttocks and said to myself, 'Nobody on Earth, not Jack nor anyone else, is going to make me step into that pit.' I stood up on my feet and from that day on I began to be myself in a way I never had been before.

"It's necessary to understand, I believe," Pat painfully but forthrightly explains, "that my love for Jack probably died when I discovered he was having an affair. However, I had not resolved the problem a year and a half later in 1976 when he was diagnosed as having a fatal brain tumor, with death expected in six months. Standing on my own two feet gave me the strength that was responsible for getting me through the passage of his death in rather tough circumstances. What seemed to be negative is something to be grateful for, because without that experience I am not sure I would have known myself as I do.

"In Samuel Beckett's play *End Game* Clove asks, 'What is there to keep me here?' and Ham answers 'The dialogue . . . that is what keeps us from self-annihilation, or stepping into the abyss.' What pulled me back from the brink of the dark hole that night so long ago was the dialogue, the chance for interaction, the opportunity to exist in relationship to others, the glory out of all the tragedy and woe, the ultimate glory that being alive is.

"At first, my children were not aware of the personal struggle Jack and I were having. The feelings others expected me to have were not there. I ended up taking care of him. He was handicapped almost immediately from the diagnostic surgery, and steadily declined until he ended up in a wheelchair. He survived for 18 months, and it was hell. I felt very sorry for him, but I also felt that I was locked into some giant prison from which I might never escape."

The immediate problem for Pat was to support herself and Jack. She applied to a number of universities. The only job opening in her field was on the faculty of the University of Houston. She moved there in 1976 with Jack, leaving behind her support system of family, friends and colleagues. "I moved radically within a three-month period of the diagnosis from a secure haven into the unknown. Fortunately, I found great warmth and support."

Even before Jack's death, Pat had to learn to live alone for the first time. She arranged for his care as his condition worsened. Meanwhile at the university, she developed her curriculum in art therapy, creative problem solving and psychology. During the final two months of his life, she visited Jack at the Veteran's Administration Hospital where he was transferred once their health insurance was exhausted. Following a series of strokes or brain seizures, he slipped from a conscious state of mind to a "conscious thought process, but somewhere else." Pat says:

"I would walk into his hospital room, and he would be talking to someone either at the ceiling or toward the foot of the bed. When I asked him who he was talking to he described a little girl about four years old with blonde hair. We had been godparents to a child in Hanover, New Hampshire, who died of leukemia at four and a half. I felt certain it was Emily he was talking to. Jack was not a Catholic, but he manipulated his fingers, very much like using a rosary. He began to push off the bed covers, though the room was quite cold, and I asked him why he did it. He said, 'Because I can't go with *them* if I have them on.' 'Them' was definitely a group of people he saw even though he was blind. He communicated with them and he reached up toward the ceiling as if he were reaching out for them to lift him off the bed. One of the group was an older, heavy set man I identified as Jack's father. At one point he described a library full of books. I never saw what he saw. After he died, I asked the doctor if these were hallucinatory visions, and he assured me most definitely not. He had seen this happen too often in people whose brains were not being destroyed by cancer. I had used Elisabeth Kubler-Ross's books on death in my classes, but I had never really believed in these experiences of the dying until I watched Jack.

"My mother's twin sister Louise predeceased her by six years and Mother missed her sister, who was an extension of herself. Before her own death, she had an awareness that it was imminent. The night she died, she went into the bathroom and put her hair up in curlers, dressed in her best nightgown and lay down on the bed with this incredibly beautiful smile on her face. I feel very convinced, after Jack's experience and Mother's, that he saw what he described and that Louise reached out her hand to Mother and helped her to that other place. I'm saying that I really believe this. It is a reassuring thought to have witnessed the possibility that there is a place after death for the soul, but it is not a thought I think about often.

"You will notice that these transformational events were very much in the present time. In other words, they were not mystical events. They were not mythological. They were not mysterious. I feel very strongly about the importance of that in my life, the fact that the major transformations occurred as a result of the here and now, the experience I was living through, the moment of my existence.

"However, the life/death polarity informs and motivates the painting that I do. It is the underlying structural subject of all that I create. The fact that each of us has such a small moment in time, particularly when one considers not just the length of time mankind has existed, but all of time since the cataclysmic birth of the earth, this small period of 70 to 80 years we spend here, and what we do with it is something of total fascination to me."

Through her graduate school years, Pat had time for only an occasional drawing or pastel. She closed her studio completely before her move to Houston, but a few months following Jack's death, she bought an easel, paper, charcoal, pastels and ink and put them in her kitchen where she stared at them until she finally made some ink blots on paper. However, she had been away from her own art so long she felt blocked, and for a few months she could go no further. Then, on a beautiful sunny day as she drove home from the university, she saw through the windshield a cloud pattern almost identical to the ink blots she had made on her paper. A moment later, she saw a figure emerge within the pattern.

"I was so excited that when I got home at 6 o'clock in the evening, I rushed to the easel, picked up the charcoal and worked on the figure for five hours. The completed drawing was so right and so wonderful, I was ecstatic. I was back in business again. After that, every day as soon as school was over, I worked on a drawing. I carried it around the house to look at it, leaned it against the dresser so it was the last thing I saw as I went to bed and the first thing I saw by the dawn's light from the window. It was a powerful, potent, creative period. It poured out of me in gushes. Probably, I had been storing up images and ways of expressing them all of those years. Though I was totally unaware of it at a conscious level, my mind, heart and soul must have been growing and developing. What came out was so much better than the last thing I had created before putting my studio to sleep."

Musick completed 27 of these drawings she called *The Lovers* and exhibited the series in Houston in 1978. Again, she turned the negative ending of her life with Jack into a positive reflection of the love they had originally shared. The drawings also referred to her rediscovery of love with Gerald Carr, the astronaut who was in space for 84 days in 1973. She met him at a singles group held at her church, and they were married in 1979.

The last oil paintings Pat did at Cornell prior to entering the doctoral program in 1972 were influenced by Alan D'Archangelo, a teacher-in-residence she much admired. In his senior thesis class he advised her to work very large. Her first effort had been an eight-foot

PLATE 6

"Barren Storm Diverted"
Pat Musick

portrait of Jack. Almost a decade had passed since that high point was reached, and it was intimidating to her to think about regaining it, but her goal was to get back to painting. In 1984, she added color to her drawings with oil sticks. Musick loves the sensation of drawing on paper in charcoal, feeling it crush beneath her fingertips, and she found that drawing on canvas with the oil stick was similar, so she started working on canvas instead of paper. Her work grew larger and flatter, with little articulation of form.

One day, while teaching a course called "Creativity," she had a brainstorm. Perhaps as a result of her admiration for Frank Stella, she thought if she could cut up her large flat canvases and lift portions of them above the surface, she might reassemble them in slightly different form, creating a more dynamic movement. Several of her students helped her engineer ways to separate and lift the parts. Within a brief time, she found that oil sticks on canvas were not satisfactory for what she was doing; and she experimented with acrylic paints on plyboard, which she cut with a jigsaw and assembled on different planes, separated by spacers.

"I would say that around 1985 I probably reached the first stage of growth and development of that technique," she says. In 1987, she used this method to create a sixteen-piece series called *Indian Wood Songs*. In an interview with *Eleven x Fourteen*, a Houston art paper, she said, "When I use a jigsaw I find myself connecting to my past, cutting into layers of my life . . . The interstices, the spaces in between, hold the passing of time, changes in perception, understanding, love, anger . . . "

Pat gave up her position with the university when she and Carr moved from Houston into the Ozarks not far from Fayetteville, Arkansas, in 1986. There they built a home, a studio for Pat and an office where Carr runs CAMUS, Inc., an international aerospace business specializing in space habitat design. Their marriage gives them mutual caring and room to be creative in their own endeavors. Pat is intensely aware of time passing, and there is an urgency in her desire to go as far as she can in developing her art, its technology and its meaning. "I have no ambitions to be a star, but I want my art to be the star. I have set that as a goal I want to achieve," she said.

One of the first independent actions Pat took after Jack's death was to purchase a time-share condominium in Cancun, Mexico. Living six weeks a year in proximity to the pyramids and temple sites of the Mayans affects her psyche and her art. "I love the temples, and the mysterious feeling when I walk through the jungle and come upon a structure that is such an artistic accomplishment, with such power and complexity, a richness and sheer endurance our modern architecture lacks."

Worldwide travel is a frequent requirement of Carr's business and Pat often accompanies him. She has stood in the cave at Lascaux and felt her connection with artists of 20,000 years ago. "The Lascaux cave thrilled me because this early feat of man's engineering and artistry relates to the very same activity I am involved in now."

The matrix from which Musick's art emerges is the web of connection she feels with indigenous cultures, particularly that of Native American peoples. A possible Indian ancestor, four generations ago, gives her a slight claim to a relationship. Living in the woods of Arkansas, she feels this link especially on her morning walks with her dogs when she imagines that she is following in the footsteps of Cherokee women who once inhabited the valley. "I am sure all this is related to the imprinting with the Navajo woman who took care of me when I was a young child. It seems I resonate to a primitive drum, the heartbeat of a culture embedded in nature," she said.

Pat created a multi-leveled series of cut and painted wood pieces titled *Lore and Legends* that illustrates the creation myth of the Cherokee. In reflection of her identification with the culture, she painted her own face as she looked in her youth on nude, pregnant, female bodies. On bisected masks, she also painted herself in middle and old age. Pat wrote in the catalog for the show that toured in 1987, "The [everyperson] figure tries to place herself in relationship to the past, particularly to the mother-grandmother mask figure, and to the future—represented by the soon-to-be born child. The paintings are metaphors of this [birth-life-death cycle] experience."

Donald Harrington commented in that catalog, "The paintings in this exhibit tiptoe on a tightrope between painting and sculpture." In her current work, Pat no longer tiptoes. She is frankly involved in sculpture, upon which she again paints, but the three-dimensional quality is paramount, and the size of her work is as long as 20 feet.

Pat has two male studio assistants. Because her work is often monumental, they assist her with the weight and size of the constructions. One helps with the wood and canvas work, and the other with the metal fabrication. Her husband engineers the suspension of the pieces from the wall and has designed the crating and packing system. Her materials—native Arkansas stone, cedar, oak, steel and glass—are combined into abstract renderings of her vision of life.

"Not only are the planes of the constructions moving off the wall and being lifted into space, but I am creating a three-dimensional form like a giant slab of rock. We have a lot of rocks around where we live on a bluff overlooking the river, and there are great slabs of limestone that have been heaved up over time. I wanted to put that effect into my constructions. Each stone is like a swath of paint across my mental canvas."

Musick's work is an expression of time and space in a symbolic/literal manner that works well as art and as a sign or communication. "I use aspects of the natural world, such as the exploration of forms, textures, colors, hidden crevices or protrusions in a cave to serve as metaphors for nurturance, for the expression of love and for birth. I use the sense of tension, tearing and destruction in nature to talk of the struggle with pain and unhappiness in events that seem to literally sweep us away in a whirlwind."

Musick refers to German psychologist Erich Neumann's essay, "Art and Time," in which he describes four stages in the artist's relationship to time. Stages are not delimited, and individuals can move back and forth between stages at various ages. Pat simplifies his concept by saying:

"In the first stage the artist's role is to portray her unconscious because this is the material most directly available to a young artist who is just beginning to express and create. By staying close to the center of her being, she can be the most truthful. In stage two, the artist looks at the surrounding society and culture and reports on them, frequently assuming the role of critic. It's my perception that many of the currently fashionable painters—Eric Fischl, David Salle, David Hockney, for example—are reporting about the conditions of our culture in a critical voice. The artist, according to Neumann, moves on in stage three to become a prophet of a better way. Finally in stage four, the artist takes a transcendental approach to the work. It is my understanding that he means the work transcends barriers that inhibit communication, such as time, age, geographical location, religious preference or political ideology. This is a stage of synthesis when the artist draws upon her earlier experience and forms a work of transcendental communication."

Musick has analyzed her long career, with its decade-long hiatus, based on Neumann's paradigm, and finds that her evolution fits his description. After her early explorations of herself, she was in her second, "critical" stage when Martin Luther King and Kennedy were assassinated. In that time of national despair she needed to affirm that violence is not a uniquely American failing. She found examples of assassination, of burning men and of manhunts using dogs from Mesopotamian wall carvings, dated from 3000 to 500 B.C., and incorporated those ancient wall carving figures intertwined with modern day figures in a series she called *Continuum*. Today, her theme is love.

"Love of mankind, love of nature, love of life and love of the opportunity to exist. I am looking for ways of being one of those great 'oldies but goodies,' to synthesize the works of stage one, two and three, to actually create a work of transcendent power.
"One of the most transcendent concepts I know is Jung's notion of the collective unconscious. I see it as being asexual, generic to all mankind. It is appealing to me to think that deep within each of us is a personal unconscious and, at a deeper level, a collective unconscious capable of communicating over time. Jung believed the collective unconscious is not revealed to us in any didactic way. Rather, the communication comes through words, visions, extrasen-

sory means and through art.

"When we stand before a work of art created centuries ago, if it rings a bell with us, touches a familiar place of understanding in our soul, the collective unconscious has spoken across all barriers, has transcended and transformed our experience.

"That concept is one of my motivating factors. The idea that I am, in this present moment, making something that may, long after I am gone, have communicative power with people who may encounter it is a tremendously happy thought for me. My drive is to produce an art object that will serve as a beacon or a guideline, as a communication, a moment of understanding with a person who stands in front of it, who says, 'It's not important that I understand what I see; what is important is that I see what I understand.'

"I'm not a very subtle person. I am very direct and prefer to have things out in the open and on the table. Honesty is one of the most important human characteristics, I think, and lack of it is devastating when I find it in any of my encounters. A critic said I hit people over the head with my paintings because they are so direct, immediate, powerful and honest."

In a few short years, Pat and her husband have organized four traveling exhibitions of her work. One of these was a series of three-dimensional works in large scale called *Huracán*, which expressed her reaction to the effects of Hurricane Gilbert.

"As I flew away from the Yucatan, my overwhelming impression was one of beauty. Along with the devastation, sadness and bleakness, there was an incredible beauty in the way tree limbs bent, twisted and interlocked with each other. It was a powerful statement about existence." As she frequently does, Pat wrote a poem in blank verse on the same theme as her paintings.

Gilbert

I could not get away from the destruction.
It was complete.
Everywhere I turned my vision was assaulted by the
twisted   torn   bleak   barren
paradise.
This was more than a hurricane. This was a visitation from the gods
to the neon and false turreted temple mejor. It was Babel repeated
and Noah's flood; its source, one of the three Mayan gods. Huracán,
the god of creation, made man and woman. Now his media, sticks,
bones and mud, had been hurled into violent debris.

I could not get away from the destruction.

It was complete.

So I was not surprised to find myself turning to my media—wood, plaster, wire and paint—to try to create the beauty which Huracán had wrought.

broken   bent   splintered twisted   torn

fractured   furious   achingly painful beauty.

Pat Musick is a woman with a clear faith. She says:

"I believe in a God that gives birth to life, my own included; and then, very much like the mother who needs to release the child once it has been born of her body, God gives us the opportunity to struggle and define our own existence. What I am concerned about is my life right now, and how to live it the best way I can.

"I consider my work a statement of living between the poles of birth and death. Each of us is given a period of time through which we can direct our lives. It's a short period of time, and each of us has his or her own responses to it. My response is to attempt to state in the most meaningful and artistic way I can what it is to live . . . to be aware of the importance of birth, and to be terribly, acutely aware of the death that marks the end of that passage, and to try to live life in that awareness. I see my life as like a very complicated piece of lace or a snowflake. My path toward art therapy and the present imagery in my work is like threads of connection between my birth and the present. Through the conditions that deter- mined my childhood, my early adulthood into middle age, and now approaching older age, there are threads extending out that are not yet looped and linked into the whole and won't be until I die."

Musick has few illusions about the world, but she remains an idealist, and she quotes Robert Kennedy: "One individual can reach out and touch another individual— and that person another—and another, until the touching circles the globe. Then great change can take place." From her existentialist worldview, she has arrived at a prophetic vision of hope that we can create goodness and beauty through our own actions.

P A T R I C I A   B R O W N

*A*t various stages in writing
this book, I have had to pause
and wait for guidance.
This happened in the winter of 1992 when the book required that I meet
more seers, but I had given myself the restriction that each
life I recorded had to touch mine in a natural way. I did not know
where I was to meet other sages. I had just completed a time-
consuming project for SLMM when I realized I was free to get back
to the book. While I was stuffing packages in a tote bag
on the way to the post office, I sent out a silent request for help.
The phone rang. It was Patricia Brown. She had asked Michael Naranjo's
wife Laurie whether she knew a writer who was interested in spirituality.
Laurie gave me as a reference. "When I heard your name, I had a little
tingle," she said, "and I knew I should call you first." The timing of her call was
so uncanny for me, I felt it was an immediate answer to my prayer.

WE TALKED LONG ENOUGH for Patricia Brown to explain that she is a practicing clinical psychologist. In an extraordinary way, she spontaneously and unexpectedly receives lyrics and melodies which she tapes and then writes.

Patricia mailed me her published libretto for a musical, Songs from Ave: A Mystic Muse. *She writes in the Introduction, "In 1986, I bore witness to an outpouring of music and lyrics from a heretofore unknown part of myself. That I knew nothing of music construction made the process all the more joyous and mysterious. These songs came as a prayer and an invocation to a healing longed for deep within, particularly in the realm of the divided feminine, the chthonic and the celestial. The songs accompany a script which plays out this polarity in the drama of the Christ and the women who loved him, most importantly Mary, the virgin mother, and Mary Magdalene, the prostitute. Arising from a place of psychological struggle commingled with a deep commitment to spiritual application, these songs came forth as a healing response from a deeper layer of myself. That Christ, as God-man, loved the breadth and the depth of the feminine is the redemption. That his disciples, as men, did not is the contemption."*

I was the one who received the tingle on reading these words. Here was a woman's experience lit by professional knowledge of psychological theory, dealing with a theme I had long pondered—the great gulf between Christ's acceptance and support of women and the distorted relationship between the Church and women. I read into her words the historical, outward split between the patriarchy and the experience of being a woman. Patricia Brown, as I later discovered, suffered deeply from an interiorized split between the masculine and feminine aspects of herself. To heal this division is the purpose of her spiritual journey. The wisdom she shares derives from this inner core. Recording the story of her process has given me a broader view of my own struggle with boundaries.

Patricia Brown is a fragile brunette with very light skin contrasting with dark hair and light-catching eyes. Her expression is wistful. She was friendly and easy to talk with, so our rapport grew rapidly.

I called on Patricia Brown at Rancho Ancon north of Santa Fe, the four and a half acre estate Patricia's husband Gip Brown inherited from his aunt Agnes. The couple were given half of the property in 1974 soon after their marriage, with the proviso that they would be family to Agnes, a task they endured until her death in 1988.

Agnes James was widowed at a young age and her only son had died. She was a tough, self-sufficient business woman in Santa Fe during the 1940s, and her outer manner was hard and dominant. She sought to replace her son with Gip. The newlyweds felt her invasive presence from her home only a few yards away. As she aged, she remained independent, but she demanded fealty. Her effect on Patricia Brown was similar to living with a difficult mother-in-law who treated her as a rival. To get along with the situation, Patricia Brown relied on meditation and metaphysical studies. Looking back, she thinks

Agnes was a spiritual influence. She quipped, "My Auntie-Guru, Anti-Guru!"

PATRICIA BROWN: HEALING THE HEALER

Patricia and Gip Brown have set aside their 250-year-old main hacienda as a conference center. Their property includes several rentals plus the home where Gip and Patricia live with their children, Keegan and Amiya (Sanskrit, meaning the immeasurable). Artworks on several outer walls and statuary in the garden pay homage to the Virgin of Guadalupe, Kuan Yin and also to Native American divinities. A feeling of sacred space pervades their land. Just over the wall outside the property is a burial mound.

We met in the small house Patricia uses for her office. No clinical or office-like appurtenances were in sight. She conducts sessions with clients in a living room setting where two comfortable armchairs turn toward each other. Or she does oral psychological testing at a dining table beside a galley kitchen. We sat there to talk through the day, well into the afternoon.

Patricia Brown, whose original name was Irene MacDonald, was born in Sendai, Japan, in September 1947. Her father was an Army Engineer colonel. Her religious heritage was nonspecified Protestant, but when she was eight years old her parents enrolled her in a Catholic school in Rome, where her father was stationed. The frequency of spiritual practice in daily mass, the prayers and the atmosphere of the school brought back a vision she had had when she was three years old. In a kaleidoscopic moment, she had looked ahead through the length of her life, watching it unfold like a movie. Everything she has experienced since, she feels, has been a follow-through on that preview in childhood.

The marital difficulties of her parents affected Patricia's self-image at increasingly more disastrous levels. She relates that she was already anorexic in Rome. Her mother had just given birth to a second son. At the same time, her father had fallen in love with someone else.

"I was the Little Princess when I was young. I was very attached to my father and I clung to him," she says.

The MacDonald's home life was strained not only by her father's affair, but also by his severity and by the alcoholism that fueled his outbursts of temper. Patricia still describes him as a brilliant, disciplined engineer—and a demanding mentor. She admired him and wanted to please him. His intellectual standard was responsible for Patricia developing the capacity to concentrate as long as necessary to achieve academic success.

In the MacDonald household, Patricia's mother kept the peace by apologizing to her husband, although she had committed no wrongs. Patricia followed her mother's example. At home, to appease her father and mimic her mother, she practiced being noncompetitive. At school, she had to compete and excel to win her father's "partial praise."

When Patricia was 16 years old her father returned from an unaccompanied tour to

Korea. A year later, during her freshman year of college, her father returned to Korea at his own request.

"Even though he knew he might never see me again, he could not even hug me," she remembers.

The MacDonalds soon divorced, and Patricia's father married a Korean woman. While just beginning her undergraduate studies at the University of Texas, Patricia absorbed into her own psyche her mother's Hera-like rage at men. She also deeply felt the distrust her mother had of younger women, particularly pretty women like herself who might steal a husband.

Mrs. MacDonald's situation, as a divorced, former officer's wife, was uncommon at that time. She struggled to raise her younger son who was still a child, but the divorce actually released her unrealized strength. She enrolled in college, completed a four-year degree and developed a career.

The fracture of her family in Patricia's late teens sowed the seeds for an inner fracture which led to a long and painful struggle with identity, gender and self-worth.

"The implicit message I heard from my mother at that time when she had been rejected was that to be a whole woman, a valued woman, you had to have a man.

"At the same time, I also sensed that I, as a pretty young woman, could be threatening. I interpreted this as 'Don't be a young woman.' My college years were a period of dark, existential alienation. I acted the good daughter, the good girl who had to do everything perfectly, but I was never able to deal with my own problem of growing into womanhood and finding my own identity. I felt that the sexual part of myself, the chthonic, fertile part, was bad, evil and harmful to other women.

"It was devastating. I had nowhere to go with my young adult crisis. I knew I needed to find a career, like my mother was doing, because I couldn't depend on a man once I'd lost my looks."

Through the five years following her parents' divorce, Patricia lived out her confusion by strenuously studying and partying.

"Outwardly, I made the best of my looks. Underneath, I was consciously defective." She did not really believe she could be sufficient unto herself.

Meanwhile, her mother became a medical technologist and happily remarried. Her father divorced his second wife and married an even younger Korean woman. Patricia did not see him from 1969 until he lay dying in a coma in 1987. His influence on her life, however, was disempowering.

As a student, Patricia suffered from test anxiety, irregular menses and fear of public speaking. At the same time, she succeeded in the most masculinized, analytical gauntlet many women face—the university system.

To celebrate her graduation, she went on a long car trip through Europe with a girl-friend. "For the first time, I enjoyed freedom from my family. I felt happy just being myself, on my own."

She entered graduate school at the University of Texas in clinical and community psychology in a more independent state of mind than ever before. She stopped going home as often and lived a more Bohemian life. Her mentor was Ira Iscoe, a distinguished scholar in her field of study. Though inwardly rebellious against the doctrinaire codification of psychology, Patricia squelched the creative side of her personality and played to win the academic game.

"I did well academically, but I paid a heavy price for it. I had to give up a lot," Patricia admits. She put aside, for example, the strong interest in drawing and painting which she had pursued most of her life.

During her second year of graduate school, she discovered Krishnamurti's writings on the tyranny of institutions, the cruelty of ideologies and the false personality. He promotes simple love, simple caring. "Krishnamurti rang more true about life than anything else I had found to that time," she says.

"I've never been personally ambitious, but I have wanted to be of service," she says. She found Krishnamurti's philosophy supportive of her attraction to clinical practice, rather than psychological research. Although she was well prepared to continue as a research psychologist, the cerebral and detached nature of laboratory work did not suit her inner sense of direction.

On spring break in 1972, during her second year in graduate school, she took a trip with friends to Santa Fe. At the La Fonda Hotel, she was introduced to Gip Brown and went with the group to stay on his aunt's estate. Although they were both from Austin, they had not met before. They soon found they shared some of the same hardships as children of alcoholics.

"I felt it was destined when I met my husband. Gip was administrative director of the New Careers Poverty Program, working on the east side of Austin, Texas, among impoverished Blacks and Hispanics. He and I have similar ideals."

After earning her Ph.D. in 1974, newly married to Gip Brown, Patricia moved to New Mexico with high expectations. It took them longer than expected to find employment in the Land of Enchantment because the state attracts many qualified people. For a year, Patricia taught psychology at a community college. She then became director of mental health with the Indian Health Service in the Santa Fe Service unit that cares for fourteen tribes of Utes, Apaches and Pueblo Indians. The most frequent referrals to the clinic were related to alcoholism and the abuse that accompanies it. "This job was very appropriate for me," she says.

Brown is a confident and tenacious professional. In clinical practice, her feminine instinct for nurturing reveals itself, but she also says, "I can be objective enough to be nonpersonal. Although I am not aggressive, I can be very crusading for a cause. While I directed the mental health program, we expanded from 12 to 22 staff members."

Brown's Native American patients were sent to her by doctors and nurses, or occasionally by social workers and law enforcers. "I have no problem believing Indian people who tell me they feel a spiritual threat, perhaps from black magic. I approach all clients in basically the same way, to affirm them, to ask them how they cope with stress and to help them preserve their sanity."

Soon after moving to New Mexico, Brown read Yogananda's *The Autobiography of a Yogi,* and she was so devoted to his principles that she underwent an initiation at the Yogi Center in Los Angeles.

"Yogananda prescribes a systematized practice, but I became militaristic in my approach to Transcendental Meditation and yoga," Brown says. Because of her habit of zealotry, she treated the recommended yogic exercises as a required regime. Such a fixated attitude did not resolve her continuing problems with the inner feminine/masculine conflict that still tormented her.

"I had a lot of negativity about my body. Nothing would grow around me, and I had a hard time getting pregnant. I felt there was an evil part of my own being destroying my fertility. For two years I couldn't conceive, and I had to take fertility drugs to become pregnant. When Keegan was born, I didn't want him to look at me for fear he wouldn't like me. Luckily, he didn't open his eyes, and by the time he did I was absolutely in love with him."

After her pregnancy, Brown was anemic, and Keegan had frequent ear infections. Despite rounds of antibiotics, regular medicine did not seem to help. She looked for an alternative healing method. On that quest, she visited Dr. Srikrishna Kashyap, an ayurvedic doctor then practicing in Santa Fe, informally known as Dr. Shyam.

Shyam solved Brown's physical problems with homeopathic methods. He soon started a meditation group, and she attended with the expectation that she could apply his principles to her practice of psychology. He became her teacher as well as her healer. She consulted with him once a week about herself and her patients.

After Amiya's birth, when Gip's aunt Agnes demanded that two-year-old Keegan be given to her, the couple had to face how seriously degraded Agnes' psychological condition had become. Everyone they brought in to help, Agnes drove away. She remained physically strong, but her condition worsened, and the strain of living near her increased. Nonetheless, the Browns fulfilled their promise to look after her.

"I felt a karmic need to stay," Patricia says. But, with two babies at home, she decided to give up her job and devote herself to motherhood. It was not long, however, before she was rehired on contract by the Santa Clara Pueblo and the Indian Hospital in Santa Fe on a part-time basis. She also opened a limited private practice in an office away from the ranch. Eventually she wove together a complicated work schedule that allowed her to put her main attention on her children at home.

Brown's private crisis was her feeling of being fractured. She was more comfortable with her outer public persona than with her nurturing, feminine side. "In my work as a psychologist, I was outer directed. Motherhood is inward. I was feminine, but I still felt I shouldn't have been.

"I've worked with a lot of dark issues: murder, L.A. gangs, sexual abuse and torture. So, I've had to go deep in human misery. In 1984, at one point, I felt that a client was a threat to me. He had sexually abused his children. In this person's presence, I could feel heat on one side of my forehead, and I had a great fear that he would rape me."

Brown turned to Dr. Shyam for aid. He believed her patient was indeed a real threat to her and, uncharacteristically, he gave her a mantra, which is a personal sound pattern to use as a meditation device. He told her to repeat it for two weeks and not to see the client during that time. Repeating a mantra aloud, singing it or saying it silently is a form of yoga, the union of sound and spirit. "Nothing is as effective and calming for me as mantra yoga," Brown says. She followed Dr. Shyam's advice and had no further problem with the client.

In due course, Shyam gave Brown a Sanskrit name, Gayatri. It means the primal sound in the universe as well as the first light of dawn. She has identified herself with this spiritual name, and it has served as a way to by-pass her sense of being separated from her true nature.

The connection of Gayatri with sound relates to the central mystery in Brown's psychic life. She said:

"There was a full moon on the summer solstice of June 21, 1986. It was a breathtaking New Mexico night. We had been to a party where there was a strange energy. I spent much of the evening talking with a physicist about his cynicism. When we returned, I was too wound up to sleep, and I went outside and sang mantras for two hours under the full moon. I felt a sense of radiant peace and flowing energy like a fountain of limitless lovingness, pouring freely as if it would never end. The dam inside myself was breaking. That's when, for the first time, a song came to me—a devotional song. I went inside and sang it into a tape recorder.

"Afterwards, whenever I had deep emotions—positive or negative as long as they were intense—a song would come. Somehow the spiritual practice of the mantras and the yearning for transcendental contact to bring harmony set up a pattern for this creativity."

After years of denying her own creativity, Brown was forced to confront it. Music and poetry flowed from her in complete form. Melody and lyrics arrived together in one piece. She did not labor over the notes and words. She describes her supercharged connection with creativity as "an aspect of human consciousness." Through creativity, she could get beyond her everyday life into another dimension. In 1988 she wrote: "The artist engrossed in the creative act is at that moment renouncing the world and thereby can give the world a gift that emerges from the core of life. Because artists touch that essential core, they are in a position to experience the essential matrix of being."

Most of Brown's creative breakthroughs happened after 10:30 at night. Her habit is to stay up at least until midnight. "I have so many duties that I build up a charge and then I need to discharge. I meditate in the evening in the living room. During the day it is like a gymnasium where the children play."

For two years, songs wakened her in the wee hours before dawn. "I lived in two worlds. For ten years, I had lived here, working with a population in which machismo and Catholicism have the effect of splitting Hispanic women. They become codependent upon abusive men."

Browns's clients exemplified, in terrible terms, the division she felt internally between the feminine and masculine aspects of herself. She dealt with young girls trying to be sexy to attract men, and abused older women whose men acted out the Rambo image. One of the songs she received is titled *Macho*.

Drugs were a serious problem in her neighborhood. Drug addicts, she says, can no longer produce endorphins, and they have no natural joy. They take their pleasure from fighting, so it is hard to keep them out of jail. In a single week, six heroin addicts died close by her home from a bad shipment of drugs.

One evening fairly late, she had the fearful thought, "I'm all alone in my office and I could be killed. I could be dead." By focusing on the protection of her spiritual name, Gayatri, Brown kept her fears of the addicts at bay. She realized later that she had used the name for protection instead of a tool to heal her internal sundered feelings. The name then became a symbol of her strength, rather than a reminder of her weakness.

Music still comes to her, but Brown's extrasensory experiences entered a new stage around 1988. She now has frequent ecstatic moments in an altered consciousness. Using Indian terminology, she says, "Samadhi describes absorption states, and Nirvana refers to total enlightenment. They are deeply blissful states. No other thoughts interfere. Time collapses during an altered state."

One such experience happened during a visit to New Orleans. Brown slipped into a state of bliss and had this dream:

"I saw a Being on a golden throne. What struck me was that I remembered
the vision I had at three. Now at 42, I was experiencing the vision I had

previsioned. It continues to unfold. I'll have an experience and recognize it as part of the childhood vision as if it had already happened. I feel that my life, and everyone else's, is in a container. I am living out a story that already exists. After that experience in New Orleans, I wrote this poem."

On the Wind

I have dreamed my life
Long ago
Down to the last stitch and safety pin.
I have gazed on every face
With the longing for the Beloved.
In the wholeness of all,
I have dreamed myself
And stood still, at peace,
Sustaining the majesty of ten thousand stars.

Brown's self-healing required more than a good marriage, motherhood and creativity. She had to integrate the masculine side of her nature. In this effort, she had the advantage of being a psychologist, able to interpret the images arising in her own psyche.

"In meditation, I had an image of a handsome young man with a mustache putting on his boots. I saw him in a mirror and I heard a carriage door slam. Then, I looked up and saw some spires that looked Russian. I felt healed when I saw that I was that man.

"I've had a vision of a Samurai lord, a horrible person who was abusive to women, ruthless. He made guttural sounds. Two years ago, I recognized that person in myself. The vision helped me release my father. Whatever people do to other people, they do to themselves. In releasing my father, I released myself."

In a more recent vision, Brown has seen another Asian male wearing a flat hat. He is a dancing Shiva holding a sword. Through him she could see "stars and galaxies moving in eternal change." She feels it means, "It's all coming around and will come out right."

As Brown became more aware of herself in the guise of a male, perhaps in another lifetime, she could better reconcile with her present life as a woman. The inner struggle she has faced is relevant to many of us today as we become aware that we have both masculine and feminine aspects of our nature.

In her private struggles, she has had the steadfast support of her husband Gip. "He's a rock," she says. Her trust in Dr. Shyam has led to her new role as lifetime managing director for Wisdom Wave, a nonprofit spiritual organization founded by followers of Dr. Shyam that is headquartered at Rancho Ancon. She has been taking notes about his teachings for ten years.

Brown says:

"Shyam is more like Krishnamurti than Yogananda. He does not promote a belief system. Gip explained that Shyam's message leads to dropping away of ego barriers that prevent our having a clear perspective on reality. He's speaking words of wisdom of pure consciousness from a common source. It resonates as true. Shyam is the model for a "style of philosophical inquiry related to that of Krishnamurti, who calls for a relentless self-awareness. I love his teaching. It's a great joy. I let it wash over me and try not to intellectualize or set up any barriers. He knows the whole thing—I only know pieces." She views Dr. Shyam as both her mentor and her father figure.

Dr. Shyam, who holds a master's degree in psychology, graduated from the London School of Homeopathic Ayurvedic Medicine, but he also earned a doctorate in divinity in India. He is a spiritual teacher and healer. Shyam promotes a nondogmatic metaphysical system. His advice is to live life the best way you can. The god he describes resembles Satchitananda—Absolute Truth, Consciousness and Bliss. He bases his ideas in the Vedas and the Buddhist principles of truth, law, justice, mercy and love.

Shyam is a holistic thinker. About the word romance, he has said, "It is the venturous force or energy behind creation, permeating each and every abstracted mood or mode, occurring constantly in nature as well as in living beings. If one is scientific-minded, one can observe this romantic trend in elementary particles, atoms, cells, organs, individual beings, structures, musical notes, arts, and primal forces. To think of romance is to think of the veiled factors of grandeur in oneself."

Brown believes, "My mission is to be an intercessor. I have to stand on my own and to recognize the creativity in myself. I've totally changed my life style. We were living like yuppies. Now, we have created a spiritual sanctuary. My concrete work is to raise my children. I want to share with many people by communicating Dr. Shyam's wisdom through poems and music. Shyam doesn't want discipleship. He allows me this special relationship, but he resists exclusivity and adulation."

Each Sunday evening at Rancho Ancon, Gip and Patricia Brown hold meetings to sing, pray and chant in ritual celebration of the divinity as each person sees it.

Both Shyam and Patricia Brown realize that she is in need of a feminine source of wisdom as well as a masculine. Some years ago, when they met, he gave her prayer beads that were a gift to him from the late Anandamayi Ma, Mother Bliss Incarnate, Ever Blissful. Patricia found herself drawn to pictures of Anandamayi Ma who became a model for her of unconditional mother love. Another feminine sage of India, Mother Amritaniji, meaning Eternal Life, is also a source of feminine strength for her. "Shyam fulfills my needs for a father and my intellect's need for truth. Anandamayi Ma and Amritaniji fulfill my need for a mother, for the embodiment of femininity and divinity."

Brown's work in community psychology brings her in contact with highly stressed people for whom ritual sexual abuse, incest, rape and murder are common. They suffer from Post Traumatic Stress Syndrome every bit as severely as Vietnam veterans. She feels the psychological difficulties that plague her have given her insights into their broken spirits. "My own experience has been like an internal siege. I've encountered those who become cynical and despairing. They've lost something precious, and innocent. I want to share with them that we go through these experiences in order to give some beauty back to others."

Brown ends her chapbook of poetry with a work titled *Echo*. An excerpt from it makes a fitting end to this story as well:

Upon each heart
Is placed a sacrificial stone,
A sacred trust
To the hidden unseen law.
Each one at an appointed time
Comes to place upon that stone
An offering for life or death.

To offer death brings life.
To offer life brings death . . .

I say to make the gift
One dies to the delusion
That life may be our own . . .

PLATE 7

"The Suicide"
Bruce Lowney

*Y*ears ago I dropped by Peter Rogers' studio one day on an errand,
and he introduced me to his visitor, the artist Bruce Lowney. The two men
seemed to have something in common, not only a kinship of physical fitness and
similar size, but a glint of a dream in their eyes. Some weeks later when I saw
Lowney's haunting work, I felt that he had created a language of symbols that
perform like a dictionary. Each symbol stands for a cluster of meanings.
I interviewed Lowney with that idea in my mind.

A VISIT WITH LOWNEY reveals a man of deep emotional tenor. In his art, he expresses an air of solitary suffering, and he suggests our profound need is for relationship with each other and with nature. Yet he chooses fierce words to describe himself. "I am an integral, uncompromising, heterosexual man, insistent on my own vision and resolute in defense of my soul space. All I have ever wanted is to live in peace and do a few good works before I die. Time is running out."

Lowney told me he did not think the word prophetic applied to him, but I have found that the imagery in his paintings and lithographs is filled with prophecy. He seems to be warning his viewers that we are nearly at the end of the wrong trail, and beyond the immediate place where we stand as a human race there is impending doom unless we change course. I think of his work as a visual and contemporary form of the Hopi prophecy that the world is out of balance.

For a long time, Lowney's art dealt with trees that seemed human in form and meaning. Anthropomorphizing the tree allowed him to say things that he felt would be too emotive if the figures were human.

Bruce Lowney walks to a different drumbeat than most people. He is a mature artist whose art is finely wrought with classical finesse—a style not often found today. The term he applies to himself is symbolist, a maker of symbols.

BRUCE LOWNEY: MODERN SYMBOLIST

In Bruce Lowney's most celebrated lithograph, a single tree falls from a cliff. Its fragile roots are lifted upward. Its branches hurl downward. A raking light on the warm face of the cliff casts an ominous shadow, doubling the impact of the tragedy. The solitary drama is silent and fraught with questions. Did the tree slip from the broken ledge? Was it pushed away through pressure from the other trees? Did it throw itself off? The artist's title, *The Suicide*, seems to provide an answer, yet his conception retains its mystery.

What is it that makes a dying tree so touching? Lowney acknowledges that the tree is anthropomorphic. Trees are "upright and reaching for the sun," he says, "of trunk and limb, a man-symbol."

Lowney tells about his life by remembering the trees in the places he has lived. The first trees of his childhood were in the apple orchards near Watsonville, California, where he grew up. When he lived in Carmel, he was surrounded by firs and cypress. His memories of trees flowered in black and white lithographs that he did while working on his Master of Art degree at San Francisco State University. At first he drew forests, but these changed into symmetrical, sometimes twelve-branched Trees of Life, like living menorahs. One of his comments about living in New Mexico was that the deciduous elms were a welcome contrast to the evergreens of California.

Lowney is a tall man with blue eyes and a fair, ruddy complexion. He is physically strong from prolonged outdoor work as well as the muscular effort required in stone lithography. His features reflect his father, the descendant of Irish forebears who sailed around the Horn to San Francisco. He is in his fifties, but he seems younger, in part because so much of his conversation deals with his plans. Success, in his eyes, has to do with commitments to his family and to his art. He speaks of future generations and his desire to leave behind a positive contribution to their welfare.

I drove out to Lowney's Peace and Quiet Ranch to begin our interviews and my friend Suzanne Caldwell, a collector of his work, went with me. The ranch is an especially beautiful 160-acre parcel of trees and rocks in a forested area west of Albuquerque and south of Grants, New Mexico, off a state road that leads to the El Moro Monument, near the Continental Divide, at an altitude of 7,600 feet.

The place is a testament to Lowney's innovation. The basic structure of his living space is a railroad car that he bought and transported to a prepared slab. Growing from that building are a second floor, a wing of garages, and studio areas. There is an outdoor cooking pavilion and patio for occasional barbecues, plus storage buildings and enclosures for animals that he raises. And there is yard upon yard of running stone walls.

Lowney greeted us with utmost courtesy and welcomed us into his narrow quarters. We talked while sipping the wine and eating the cheese and crackers he had prepared. He soon mentioned the walls along the road and pathways of his property and told us he had built them while in the depths of depression over the breakup of his long marriage. Building the walls, he told us, required a massive output of energy that helped him deal with a sense of abandonment by friends he and his wife had shared for years. From that revelatory moment when Lowney brought our attention to the walls, I have felt that two forces operate in him: an exceptionally deep emotional nature and an objective self-scrutiny laced with irony.

In the course of that long afternoon, Lowney expressed his lasting regret over the failure of his first marriage to the mother of his son Ben. He is close to Ben, but for many years he saw him only during summer vacations. Ruing that separation and feeling responsible for it have cast a shadow on Lowney.

I felt a great sadness in him that day. The impression I took away from our interview was of a master artist in the midst of transformation. Today he looks back at that time and says, "It has taken me years to get over the totality of my mid-life crisis of which the divorce and other relationships were only parts. I am a different man today, and my work is different, but *I am the same artist.*"

The key to Lowney's work, I think, is the modern crisis of alienation. In tribalism, we can still observe the identity of the social group, but twentieth-century civilization has brought with it a fracturing of community. Lowney addresses that separation of people from one another and from nature.

Lowney believes that all art, his own included, is essentially autobiographical. He says, "I have always been an artist and have always used art as my vehicle of personal expression. My interest is in illustrating *ideas*, rather than making *Art*." The conflict he has suffered at different times in his life comes through in his images.

Lowney first lived in New Mexico in 1966 while teaching and taking post-graduate work with the well-known master of color lithography Garo Antreasian at the University of New Mexico. As a result working of with him, Lowney added color to his own prints.

Lowney became a permanent resident of New Mexico in 1972 when he was trying to put his life back together after his first marriage ended. He moved to Placitas, which is now an upscale bedroom community. In those days, it was a tiny, out-of-the-way village, a difficult thirty miles away from the university and other artists. In *The Hill*, the first color lithograph he did after his return, Lowney captured the landscape of the area north of Albuquerque near the town. His print projects the mood of lonely vastness that makes any visitor to rural New Mexico sharply aware of the distance to the nearest source of water and gasoline. *The Hill* established Lowney's reputation as a printmaker of note. The Albuquerque Museum bought it, and it was reproduced in color by *Art in America* in 1973.

Although he seeks close companionship, paradoxically, Lowney likes solitude. He has an aversion to the destructive mania of civilization and to its pervasive development at the sake of the environment. In 1986 he revisited the idea of a solitary knoll in his enigmatic lithograph titled *The Last Hill*. Here, a mound stands alone, half carved away, on a bleak, empty plain. He, too, has felt at times like that hill, only half of a whole. *The Last Hill* is in the art collection of the Albuquerque International Airport.

In his somber icons, Lowney juxtaposes recognizable subjects in surrealist ways to pose questions about mortality and the human condition. He is drawn to isolated artifacts which remind him that all we see will eventually pass away in the ceaseless maw of time. Lowney does not necessarily trust that life will get better, but he clings to the hope that it will. Underlying his images is a strong sentiment in favor of life's continuation and meaning.

In the last decade, he has turned more often to painting, reversing his earlier preference for lithographs. After many years of practicing printmaking in an exacting manner, he finds a release in the subtle potentials of painting as well as its larger scale. "I couldn't bear to draw any more leaves in those solitary trees," he said with a wry grin.

Although his moments of inspiration often come in a flash, Lowney's creative process is a long one, the antithesis of spontaneity. He records quantities of notes in the form of pencil sketches on scraps of paper. To retain his insights, he saves them for future reference. Later, he translates selected sketches into 8" x 11" drawings. Lowney invests these notes with the same importance others might give to stocks and bonds. He calls them his "visual dictionary," and he stores them in his "bank account." He compares them to "the retention of dreams, caught before they evaporate." The images he commits himself to depend equally upon contemplation and intuition. It might be years before he actually uses one of his ideas in a print or a painting.

In a long and exacting art education as a printmaker, Lowney only had one semester of studio painting, and it was taught by an artist who was devoted to nonobjective art. In the years since, Lowney has worked out his own painting methods.

"I reacted against the instruction because it had no personal meaning for me," he said. "To do a painting or a work of art, I need a reason, an allegory, or something to give it a purpose."

In the late eighties, Lowney painted scenes that stretch far away into the distance. These are dreamscapes, not portraits of the woods and mesas of western New Mexico, but they do reflect the sense of endless spaces you can see from his ranch.

In his painted vistas—he calls them attempts at Beethovean landscapes—he thrusts the background into the deep distance by means of ever more delicate color transitions, lightening toward the far horizon. These paintings of infinity are his metaphors for the unity of time and space.

Lowney's prints and paintings are recognizably smooth on the surface, and they have a linear clarity reminiscent of the Northern Renaissance. All his work displays meticulous craftsmanship; precise drawing; tight control of the medium; strong, formal modeling and an emphasis on perspective. He projects a sense of quiet drama, and he stages his work with authority, but his work is often eerie.

Shadows invade the scenes in unpredictable ways, adding to their mystery. He seems to prefer untenanted places in the desert, on the plains, in cities, forests or ruins. Into these vacancies, he frequently injects architectural elements, with an emphasis on their angles and curves, to remind us that man's intelligence affects the environment everywhere. One of his most ironic devices is to picture living plants as though they were forced into geometric forms by a tyrannical human will.

In his lithograph *The Overgrowth*, a pyramid is entirely covered by green plants indistinguishable from those that cover the adjacent plain. The plain and pyramid form a single mass against a distant horizon and a cloudless sky. Man's presence has been effaced; only plant-life remains. In this way, Lowney considers the possibility that mankind might disappear and that more primitive forms of life will start the evolutionary process over again.

Lowney intends to convey a message in his work. He wrote to me that he thought, " . . . the best critic would be a seven- to twelve-year-old child who isn't conditioned yet. And if that child has to ask, 'What does it mean?', there is something wrong with the image. They ought to be able to see it, although not upon the surface. My images are meant to be looked *into*. I work within the tensions of form and idea. The pictorial surface is the window to that experience."

More than many of us, Lowney has had his share of difficulties dealing with the duality of masculine and feminine attributes. The female nature is noted as the seat of intuition and emotion, the male nature as one of action and rationality. Lowney commented on this age-old polarity in a pair of small paintings he calls *The Stumble*. The first panel shows a man's foot hitting what seems to be a rock, but when more closely examined, it proves to be a brain. In the companion painting, a woman's foot collides with a heart. He said he wanted to achieve a "throbbing between recognition and disbelief." My first reaction to the pair was recognition: ah, yes, women wear their hearts on their sleeves, entirely too vulnerable. And men's problem is that they get trapped by their intellect. But then, I smiled at Lowney's low-key sense of humor, poking fun at himself and at us.

Like the French Symbolists of the late 1800s, Lowney is engaged in a continuous inner dialogue and reflection upon currents that are gradually transforming science, art, mysticism and philosophy. "There's a little osmosis at that center [of myself], between the scientific and the mystical," he said.

Though reticent, Lowney is an articulate man. Of his own work, he writes:

"My images come together like a poem, from fragments of visual memory, from pieces of reality that focus some association of personal thought and feeling. I then work to consciously arrange that resonance of meaning in a context, with as much fullness of idea, form and dimension as I can. It becomes a possible reality. I rarely depict a human being in my work; the human element is the viewer whom I try to engage in responsive involvement.

"My ideas are of two types: single allegorical, emphatic images with a symbolic meaning on the one hand, and on the other, far-horizon landscapes in which I express yearnings for the peace and sublimity of space. Both are based on my respect for the paradoxes of life and the conflicting and converging of inner and outer worlds in the human experience."

There is a happy ending to Lowney's story. He met and patiently wooed a lovely young woman, Kelley Jones. Their wedding on the Peace and Quiet Ranch in the summer of 1990 was held under the trees in an elevated clearing. His son was there and many of Kelley's relatives. A harpist played down below as they recited their vows. It was a romantic event, a ceremonious new beginning.

Just before he and Kelley were married, Bruce wrote to me demurring from any intention to be prophetic. He said he just wanted "to live a purposeful life." Yet the images he makes reach out beyond his ranch and the privacy he guards so well, into a larger arena. For the viewer of his work, a lasting, thought-provoking ghost image remains in the mind, much as the ghost of a print remains on a plate after it has run through a press. The image of a tree committing suicide leads us to speculate that nature has its own despair and might be seeking mercy. Perhaps the earth is suffering from our human activity with feelings of its own. Because of our actions we are heading into a time of increasing chaos.

Lowney seems to be saying that what we do has consequences for all species and the planet itself.

In July 1992 Bruce and Kelley Lowney left for a two-year stint with the Peace Corps in New Guinea. "Art seems like a self-centered activity. I think we should try to help other people if we can," Bruce explained.

His letters from New Guinea indicate that he was disenchanted with his art before he left, but he has felt a renewed energy and vision in the mountain province where he has been engaged in gardening, helping the local villagers with building projects and painting. Back home, Ben has kept the ranch going and used his dad's studio to work on his own sculpture.

I think of Bruce Lowney as a man who has visualized the sense of impending waste-land that pervades our twentieth-century consciousness. In a doleful tone, he has pictured the earth as a place potentially devoid of life and of love. Nonetheless, he retains his faith in the future. Despite the personal dislocations and disappointments he has faced, he seems to have an unquenchable spark of optimism that we can move forward to a better way of living. His response to our end-of-the-millennium angst is to remain loyal to his talent and beliefs and to be a good steward of the land. He commits himself to bonding. I find that prophetic. From the fractured state we are in, it seems to me that Lowney's ideals can serve as a guidepost to a more holistic, caring world.

Bruce thinks we may be facing a social as well as an ecological cataclysm. He has had a vision of an Apocalyptic event. In this image, which has affected his inner sense of direction, he saw a glowing light breaking overhead. He interprets his vision as an affirma-tive and upward-moving symbol.

"There is always that foil, the dramatic situation of tragedy and comedy, dark and light. To know the one, we have to have its opposite."

first met Gilah Yelin Hirsch at The Rim Institute, high in the mountains of northern Arizona in September 1988, and there I was again in late May 1990, sitting in a canvas yurt, talking to her hour after hour. She was at home in the woods. I was not. All the time we talked I was conscious of that, of my being an alien "out there" and of her being comfortable. She had lived through the harsh winter in the uninsulated office cabin. Now her nest was in the yurt. She was summer artist-in-residence and coordinator of the conference On Knowing offered by The Rim a few months later in August. She told me:

"My life is very magical in so many ways, yet I am the first to say I don't believe in magic. It's a question of patterning, of being sensitive to delicate nuances of pattern. It's delighting but not surprising how the events of my life anticipate each other and move in a line that certainly makes for an unusual life."

GILAH YELIN HIRSCH, in her late forties, is of medium stature, with fine, fair skin, luxuriant Titian-red hair and orange-brown eyes. Even in the mountains she wears softly feminine clothes. Gilah, a scholar, an artist and a feminist, said, "I'm very happy that I am a woman—a female, feminine woman. I've never had any idea of myself as a man. Anais Nin, whom I admire, was beautiful and always dressed in feminine clothes. She was proud of being a female, she was articulate in what she did and said, and she had dignity." In the early 1970s Gilah was among the founding members of the women's art movement in Los Angeles, a group that stressed feminism at the sake of femininity. Anais Nin observed the consciousness-raising groups which had sprung up at the time, women supporting women; and she advised Gilah, "Whatever happens, you're going to have to do it alone. People who make changes work alone, not in groups." The radiance of self-containment, clear-headedness and attentiveness which Gilah sensed in Nin can be felt in the energized, centered space around Gilah herself.

GILAH YELIN HIRSCH: PERCEIVING PATTERNS

An only child, Gilah Yelin Hirsch grew up in Montreal's Jewish community, which she describes as one of the most intensely intellectual in North America. Her maternal grand-parents, the Borodenskys, came from Chernobyl, Russia. The Yelins were from Poland. Her mother, Shulamis Yelin, is a poet and story writer. Her father, Ezra Yelin, was an intellectual Talmudic scholar, more atheist than believer. "My father was an Old World man. He was 45 when I was born." When he was 53 years old, he was the victim of a traffic accident that left him an invalid. From the age of eight, Gilah was his nurse-companion, constantly exposed to his atheism and his wish to die. "When he died at 66, it was a question of celebrating his death. He hated his ignominy," Gilah said.

Gilah's frame of reference is that of a world citizen, a pattern of thinking which began in her childhood. She said, "I grew up learning four languages—French, English, Hebrew and Yiddish. As an adult, I have learned Spanish, Italian and German, as well as Latin. I have an ear and a curiosity about language. When I was three, emulating my mother, I wrote stories and 'speeches' in Yiddish and English and some of them were published. I wanted to be a writer and psychologist. I had a sense of world responsibility early in life. Other children came to tell me their problems, but I had no one to tell my thoughts to."

Gilah attended a school, founded by her mother and others, where teaching was done in Hebrew and Yiddish. Her class in the Torah, written in Hebrew, was conducted in Yiddish by an Orthodox Jew. Gilah noted that Hebrew pronouns for God are interchange-ably male or female. "The words have no gender, only a syntactical relevance, singular or plural. I questioned the teacher, 'If it is written here, isn't it therefore true?' 'Yes', he said.

'Then how come we have only been taught of God as a male?' The man grew apoplectic. He grabbed my hair and threw me out of the class. My question had rocked his foundation. I became my father's daughter then. I questioned everything."

When Gilah was 10 years old she wrote a letter to Einstein. "I asked him, 'How is it that you, a scientist, can not only believe in God, but the wrathful God of the Old Testament?' My mother found the rough draft of my letter in the trash. She kept it. She asked me, 'You wrote to Einstein?' A week later the answer arrived. 'Always form your opinions according to your own judgment. You have shown in your letter you are able to do so. Sincerely, A. Einstein.' He died a week later. I still think of him as my pal, my friend." Einstein did not really answer her question, yet in an uncanny way his words were appropriate advice.

"I had no childhood. We lived in a tiny two-bedroom apartment, lined floor to ceiling with books that were an intellectual's library of the time. I know no children's literature, but I had the benefit of beginning to read the Great Books at six years old. At eight, I read Freud's Interpretation of Dreams, and I understood it enough to argue with it as being a narrow system."

"My mother gave me creative resilience of soul. My father gave me analytical ability." Gilah's mother lectured and wrote a book of poetry, Seeded in Sinai, and Shulamis: Stories of a Montreal Childhood which is well-known in Canada. She continues to write extraordinary poetry.

Gilah said, "My solace was writing, not art. I loved writing stories. I began school at four. At 14, on a scholarship, I took a trip to Israel with a group for leadership training. I began McGill University at 16, then I took my second year at the Hebrew University in Israel, and traveled the following summer in Europe on my own."

Gilah was engaged to a Montreal doctor, but she met Ed Hirsch in Israel and married him when she was 19. They lived in Cambridge, Massachusetts, until Ed graduated from Harvard, and she took one term at Boston University. For her sake, they moved to Berkeley in 1964, during the height of the Free Speech Movement, and she enrolled at the University of California. She graduated in 1967.

"I was shy and sheltered, but I found myself in a maelstrom of political radicalism. I was tear-gassed on several occasions. For the first time I saw the power of the people and the relationship of the individual to suffering. I was an English major at Berkeley. I didn't know yet that I was going to be an artist. My only art classes had been in high school and again at Boston University. At Berkeley, I found art history fascinating because it mirrors the history of other disciplines, so I took a double B.A., in art history and English. I began writing art criticism for publication, but I knew so little about making art firsthand that I took some beginning courses in drawing, painting and printmaking. I found an unexpected creative home, so I was compelled to return for graduate studies in art. On the strength of my portfolio from these early courses, I applied to graduate school at UCLA and was accepted. After a year of instruction I became a teaching assistant in drawing and painting, and I had a solo show at the Lytton Gallery in the Los Angeles County Museum. While Ed worked on his doctorate in educational research at UCLA, I received an M.F.A. in pictorial arts specializing in painting, in 1970."

In 1972, the Hirsches' marriage ended.
Gilah joined the faculty of California State University at Dominguez Hills, where she was given tenured status in 1978. Her life is a balance between teaching and being a professional artist.

"My paintings reflect my thought process at the moment. My work is sometimes called visionary, but it's accessible. I perceive color as a layering of frequencies. To give the impression of depth, I paint many, many layers of frequencies in varying values of hue and intensity. I think that if I put enough into my painting it will evoke a response in the many layers of the observer. My imagery has gone through five distinct periods since 1968, varying in subject matter and painting styles. I am not what is called a mainstream artist, but I have exhibited and been well reviewed in mainstream galleries and publications."

From the first painting she did at UCLA in 1967, Gilah's work has been assertive and marked with a definite style. Always pictorial, her first series consisted of elements taken from architectural environments reconstituted as patterns of light. Such a painting is *Intent*, based on the experience of looking through an open tent-flap. At an early age, she painted a series of photo-realistic images, of foods and "kitcheny" things exaggerated in scale. Without prior graphic experience, she was an artist-in-residence in Albuquerque at Tamarind Institute, which is devoted to lithography. Around 1974, she began painting tondos of complex design, resembling the intricacy of Celtic knots. From the precision of this style she turned to the expressionistic landscapes she has painted since 1981.

Gilah received international coverage in 1978 for curating the show Metamagic. It was the first national exhibition of the spiritual in art to be housed in a prominent university art gallery. The subject was personally relevant to her. She has had many numinous experiences—perceptions beyond the ordinary, beginning in childhood.

"At 14, I had my first major simultaneous cognition, involving my aunt Dena, my mother's sister, who had cancer. I resemble her physically and psychically in my personality. I was very close to her. I was in school playing basketball when I struck a light fixture with the ball. The lights went off and suddenly I recalled a book in which all the candles were suddenly extinguished in a church when a general had died in battle somewhere. I thought 'Dena died at 4:00.'" When she got home, Gilah said something to this effect, and it turned out to be true. Her mother witnessed this very real extrasensory experience. "I had quickly associated several ideas. I threw the ball. I darkened the light. I felt guilty thinking maybe I caused her death. I've had many synchronous telepathic cognitions since I was a little girl."

In 1974, Gilah had a strange experience with synchronicity. Unconscious, almost frozen, in the snows on the upper slopes of the Sierra Nevada, she wakened to see looking down at her the face of a former lover whom she had last seen two years before in Los Angeles. He dug her out of the snow bank and saved her life.

Another extrasensory episode saved Gilah's life during the nadir of the winter of 1989. She had decided to spend the entire season at The Rim, which is a spiritual center during the summer months. It is high in the mountains of Northern Arizona. Gilah stayed in the uninsulated office cabin. Affected by leaking propane fumes, in the depths of solitude and depression, she went to bed in the freezing cabin and succumbed to the idea of simply dying. She was dozing when she "saw" the same man who had rescued her sixteen years earlier. He was standing beside the bed. "You will have to get through this one in the snow, too," he said.

"I understand the episode better now as a lucid daydream. It was not a vision. I know that I manufactured an alter-ego to save myself again. I was drawing on an imprinted pattern already there, leaning toward joy. I wanted to live more than I wanted to die. The psyche has an astonishing capacity."

In 1979, soon after Gilah returned from a year as artist-in-residence at St. Martin's School of Art in London, she had a major psychic and physical episode.

"I became paralyzed on the left side of my body—I felt a blue numbness and pain. I was misdiagnosed as having multiple sclerosis. In trying to work with the paralysis, I had someone draw around my naked body with a pencil on each of two blank canvases, five and one half feet by two feet wide. For a year, I painted horrendous nightmarish images of demons inside that body form. Sometimes I held my hand over my eyes because the images were so dreadful. I felt compelled to go through color regeneration of my pictured body many times. Finally, it grew green with growth seeds. I called it *Through Generation*. On the second canvas, I worked with the regeneration of my spirit and called it *Surge*."

Painting helped Gilah surmount her physical problems, which were never explained. Soon thereafter, she was a guest of the Dorland Mountain Colony (the only resident art colony in Southern California) where she took refuge in nature. Walking through the woods, she noticed how frequently nature repeats the forms of crossed lines, Y-shaped lines, curves, serpentines and single lines; and she took dozens of photographs of them. Later she noticed relationships between these natural forms and varied alphabets. She then intuited that early humans must have had a kinesthetic reaction to linear forms in nature. First, they began drawing them and then they invested them with meaning. She formulated a theoretical morphology of alphabet, illustrated with many of her photographs. She has given slide-lectures on this subject at a number of symposia and written a book to explain the theory she calls Cosmography.

"In 1981 I attended the Menninger Foundation's annual conference in Council Groves, Kansas, to present a slide survey of my paintings as they reflect my philosophy of life. I gave another presentation there in 1985 of my work on Cosmography, to explain that what we perceive echoes the physiology of the cognitive process."

I commented on the range of activities she engages in, and Gilah said, "What I do in the world is far in excess of what I was trained for. I am asked to do these things on the basis of experience." The home that she created from a downtrodden duplex in Venice, California, has brought her acclaim in architectural circles and invitations to speak on the subject. The place has become almost a temple, attracting politicians, scientists, theologians, philosophers, film makers and artists. The natural pond at Dorland Mountain inspired Gilah to build a self-sustaining pond on her property, stocked with water lilies and koi, neither of which she has ever had to feed. The beauty of her home draws her back, but she also feels a force attracting her to distant responsibilities.

"Many years ago in the early 1970s I remember saying to a visitor that I would like to meet someone who could speak Tibetan so well he would know its slang." Gilah's casual mention of Tibet alerted my "trigger word" reaction. I was especially keen to know more about her relationship to it.

The allure of Tibet has called out to Gilah since childhood, and that fascination underscored her grant application in 1985 to the National Endowment for the Arts. She sent four slides of paintings from Dorland Pond for consideration by the NEA and was awarded $15,000—no strings attached. On a paid sabbatical from her university, she used the money to make a 10-month trip through fifteen countries in Asia, hoping to find answers to the question, What is considered sacred? On the journey, she found a commonality in Asian belief systems—a reverence toward nature and natural sources often worshipped in the embodiment of deities. The trip started on September 1, 1986, led her to Japan, Hong Kong, China, Mongolia, Tibet, Nepal, India, Sri Lanka, Bangladesh, Burma, Thailand, Sumatra, Java, Bali and ended ten months later in Singapore.

"When I travel I always take only what I can carry. I learn a great deal this way, because I am able to communicate with gestures and empathy. I am writing a fictionalized docu-novel about my experiences in Asia, called *Lone Monkey in the Forest*. Two of the characters who appear pervasively have the same name—

Amiel and Amielle. If I had had a child, that is the name I would have chosen. This character stands for indigenous friends I meet who tell me their stories. The genuine human soul who suffers grief, love, fear and abandonment is the same in every culture. Joy is more culturally determined, whereas grief *always* comes from loss of contact, separation or abandonment.

"The timing of my trip to Tibet was so precise that I feel I was meant to be there during those exact six weeks. Afterward, the Chinese literally closed Tibet to tourists. From Lhasa I shared a jeep and driver with three others. We traveled through Tibet to Katmandu in Nepal. I was profoundly moved by the plight of the Tibetans. It is a unique place at an average altitude of 12,000 feet. In the village of Tingri, I looked across the field and saw the top of Mount Everest like a little hill under the full moon. The country has been trashed by the Chinese. Tibetan language and culture are altogether different from Chinese. Tibetan physiognomy closely resembles the Navajo. Navajos and Tibetans are nomadic shepherds, and both people wear silver and turquoise jewelry.

"On the Tibetan plateau, a woman might marry all the brothers in a family. Conditions are so hard that one husband might be out with the sheep or selling sweaters, while another brother stays at home to protect the family. The greatest blessing in Tibet is to have five daughters who are considered to be the embodiment of the five sacred Tibetan mountains—one of which is Chomolung (Mt. Everest). The mountains are the Mother Goddesses.

"The first night I spent in Lhasa I dreamed of being a black-haired French nun of the 17th century, wearing a brown habit. I was looking for souls of Lost Travelers who had fallen into holes in the Snow Mountains. I dreamed an entire topography, a kingdom, and its architecture. The dream was so vivid it has stayed in my mind."

In November, after leaving Tibet, Gilah attended an international conference in New Delhi that dealt with space—anything from astrophysical to metaphysical space—where she presented her theory of Cosmography. A Tibetan abbot among those in attendance invited her to visit Dharamsala, India, home of the Dalai Lama in the Himalayas and the site of the Tibetan government-in-exile. She accepted. Gilah arrived in Dharamsala in December, and she stopped to ask the information officer about conditions in Tibet. A man named Narkyid N. Kuno called over to her, "I want to talk to you." He had lived for some time in the United States and when he heard there was a newly arrived American interested in learning about Tibet, Kuno was eager to return the hospitality he had received in the States. Gilah had finally met the man who knows Tibetan slang. In that moment, she bonded her life to the welfare of Tibet through friendship with Kuno.

Kuno's life is a storybook tale. Since 1983, he has been the Official Biographer of the

Dalai Lama. Now in his sixties, Kuno was educated at the Potala Palace in Lhasa to be a monk official. In 1952 he was among a small group of rising civil servants sent to Beijing for five years to learn the Chinese language, culture and way of life. While there, he resisted Maoist indoctrination and managed to return home just in time to avoid the effects of being blacklisted by the Chinese government. Two years later, during the Chinese military invasion of 1959, he helped defend the Joghang monastery before escaping in a grueling two-month trek through the mountains into India. Kuno has held ministerial posts in the government-in-exile. After earning a master of art degree in education from Western Michigan University at Kalamazoo in 1979, specializing in linguistics and cultural anthropology, he has served on several university faculties in the States. At Gilah's request, I met Kuno myself in July 1990, when he gave a workshop at The Rim. Several weeks later, Kuno visited with my husband and me. He is an extraordinary person who is dedicated to the Dalai Lama's plan for world peace.

"Kuno and I have talked ever since we met," Gilah said. "When I told him my dream of being a nun, he recognized the landscape I described as the Snow Mountain from the lore of Bon, the animistic religion that preceded Tibetan Buddhism." One of the first links between Gilah and Kuno came from her interest in the morphology of alphabets. The Tibetan language is believed to have come from the Brahmic. Gilah does not know Tibetan, but she believes the written Tibetan alphabet is related in form to the Gupta, a language from northern India. Kuno, who has a major interest in linguistics, has reached a similar conclusion through an historical perspective. Only a few months before meeting Gilah, he had presented a controversial paper at a linguistics conference in Vienna in which he related Tibetan to Gupta. He appreciated her agreement with him on this issue, and this intellectual concurrence helped establish their friendship.

Gilah invited Kuno to be her house guest in California. She asked many friends to hear him make the case for Tibetan survival. Her discussions with him of Tibetan philosophy, amplified by further study, have profoundly affected her thinking. She respects Kuno deeply, and says, "His behavior is characterized by compassion and intelligence. He is perpetually checking his motivation and is a constant reminder to me of how to be a refined, meticulous, caring human being."

One of the questions I ask of artists is, "What is your primal image?" Not surprisingly, Gilah's primal image has to do with relationship. It is permeated with Tibetan Buddhism. "My primal thought was originally, 'All things are in duality.' One must be a witness—i.e., be aware—of the Self, to acknowledge the presence of duality. To integrate the duality is, I believe, a triangular system. There are the two poles of the duality as well as the third element which is the witness. We can call that consciousness. You can be stuck in one aspect or the other of the duality, but if you can gain enough perspective you see both aspects at the same time. That is the perspective of 'the other,' the perspective of consciousness."

I was curious about where Gilah places this witnessing consciousness in her thoughts, and she said:

"I think it fluctuates. I'm going to have to say that which I know comes from experience, and I am someone who has followed experience more than any other teacher. I have felt it necessary to discover for myself what is real and relevant to me.

"Having examined many systems, the one that is closest to me is a certain quality of Buddhism which deals with the interdependence of all things. Nothing exists on its own. All things exist in relation to one another. All things come from cause, are the consequence of cause. In Tibetan Buddhism cause and effect, i.e., karma, goes on from lifetime to lifetime to lifetime.

"Tibetan Buddhists believe in an essence, an unstainable essence, that can appear as an animal, a plant or a person. The Dalai Lama says that all things are impermanent, including death. When you look at time in that way there is no question of beginnings and endings. There are just different states. From my perspective I would say form is a parenthetical aspect of a state, or a possible evidence of a state.

"I believe in nature. I believe there is something so vast, so exquisite in the multiplicity of patterning in nature that I need nothing more. I am perpetually dazzled by its complexity and adaptation. The source of this patterning is incomprehensible. We were about to discuss whether we have one or many lifetimes. I try to think like a mountain. A mountain does not seem to change, yet changes do occur over eons. Causal changes of a mountain have far-reaching effects. I believe that my choices of behavior have a very long range of consequences, an infinite ripple effect.

"Lately, I've been thinking, 'I have earned this moment. What is the very best that I can do with it for the greatest good?' That thought has come through this year of being in isolation for so long. I've changed this winter. As a woman in the forest alone, I was living with wild animals, in the dire circumstances of high mountains and high snow. I had given up everything that used to define me, my house, my job, my studio, my friends in the community, my public schedule, my private life—everything was gone. During the winter, I synthesized these five ideas: 1) There is no future; the past is a disputable memory. 2) The moment is all that is real, and it is a tripartite constellation of information, sensation and emotion. 3) Operate from heart/mind. 4) Live to give the greatest good to the greatest number for the longest time. 5) The baseline is one of joy. Life is the greatest gift.

"My beliefs are relational, not theistic. Our responsibility is to live consciously and responsibly with each other. I think we are all interwoven with one another for

PLATE 8

"Toward the Source of Triangulation"
Gilah Yelin Hirsch

one lifetime, or for eons, depending upon how you believe. I can be considered psychic. I am aware of more patterns simultaneously than others might be, but I don't believe in magic.

"Kuno sent me an invitation back in September to visit Dharamsala. When things got so dire here in February—I was melting snow for survival, there was no water, no power, I was physically stranded, I was freezing, I couldn't do any work—I decided to go to India, but Kuno did not know I was coming. I went from one Himalaya to another. I had no idea I would get there just two days before the Dalai Lama was to give his oral transmissions of ancient sacred initiations and teachings. When I arrived, monks were everywhere. There was no place to stay in Dharamsala, but Kuno finally found a room in an old Tibetan apartment house down the mountain.

"Let me tell you a karmic aspect to the story. In 1987 I had given a little short-wave, battery-operated radio with earphones to the monk translator of the Dalai Lama's Namyal monastery. When I discovered that the teachings would be given in Tibetan, with a simultaneous translation into English for the handful of Western-ers with FM radios and earphones, this same monk, now the secretary of the monastery, returned the radio I had given him, giving me access to the transmis-sions.

"During the teachings, the Dalai Lama was seated on his throne within the temple, not visible, and yet the trance we were in was so deep because of the information he was imparting and the way he was teaching, that not seeing him didn't matter. The weather was continuously awful: snow, rain, sleet, hail, winds. We sat outside on concrete in the cold, day after day. And that, too, didn't matter.

"For the first time I understood what they meant by transmission—*trance/ mission*. We were entranced and it was his mission to impart the information to the best of his ability. Every couple of days I would report to Kuno what I was getting out of it. Even he and other highly enlightened Tibetans didn't feel they were worthy of receiving these initiations. He said to me, 'What if I were unclean in a past lifetime?' And I said, 'Certainly, I'm being presumptuous to be hearing these.' He told me, 'No, you are karmically supposed to be here.' The Dalai Lama re-peated this in his transmissions. 'You are destined to be here and to use this knowledge to the betterment of all sentient beings—people, animals, plants—all life.'

"The Dalai Lama is believed to be the incarnation of the Avalokiteshvara, the male deity embodying fully enlightened compassion. In Dharamsala the towns-people say, 'I'm going to hear the Buddha speak today.' At a certain point, when I had spent five hours a day every day for two weeks listening to this unstoppable, thoroughly intelligent, life/mind-changing teaching, I began to think maybe this is the Buddha, because the information is so deeply penetrating on a positive level that it seems right.

"My feeling is that my experience at The Rim had reamed me out on an emotional, psychic, intellectual level and reduced me to a purely elemental state of survival. Everything I knew before was out the window. In a state of emptiness I went to the other mountain top and was filled with primal information that stuck to my insides like mother's milk.

"The Dalai Lama trained us to prepare for death. He imparted the process of dying, what to expect and what to do just after dying. As an essence, he said, you continue living in a discarnate state until your rebirth. He taught the theological science of visualization, a series of techniques which enables the practitioner to be in total control of mind and body in life as well as during the dying process.

"In 1987, when I came back from my year in Asia, I had this revelatory dream: I am about to start on a slalom and the markers are made of Tibetan chortens. The chorten is a funerary stupa made of gold [found at burial sites]. I'm at the front edge of the slalom course and I'm feeling I'll never be able to do this one. Then a voice coming from the end of the slalom booms at me over and over again, 'You are protected from the incongruities of life.' Over and over again. I woke up in an incredulous state wondering where those words had come from.

"In Dharamsala on this trip I dreamed I was sitting in a darkened auditorium, in the first seat on the right of the front row in a huge audience. On the illuminated stage, standing behind a lectern, much like I have been in the past, a person was fumbling, trying to get a point across. The person next to me whispered, 'You know you're the one who is supposed to be up there.' I said, 'Oh, no. How can I be up there and be humble at the same time?'

"One of the last things Kuno said to me, and he said it over and over again, was 'There are thousands and thousands of artists in the world. Nobody sees like you. Nobody thinks like you. You must concentrate on your generative work.' His idea of generative work is 'all your original ideas in every way you make them and produce them.'

"My generative work is not only teaching, painting and writing; it's also counseling people. People have always come to me for counseling appointments. Word of mouth brings them to me. I am a Universal Life Minister and, legally, I do weddings."

Before Gilah left India, Kuno gave her a beautiful gift, a book titled *The Aim of Life*. He had calligraphied Tibetan seed syllables for body, speech and heart/mind and inserted this page adjacent to an illustration of a painting showing the back of a red-haired woman. The figure wears clothes of the colors Gilah happened to be wearing that day, wine and purple, and raises her right hand and index finger in the teaching position. The painting indicates a person in the act of teaching, relating to the world. Kuno's gift symbolizes Gilah's role as teacher, not only at the university but wherever in the world she is called upon to share her knowledge.

After they had lunch together the day she was to leave, Kuno and Gilah went outdoors and shared an astonishing experience.

"The weather had been terrible for a long time, but on the last day I was there the sun came out. Then there was a tremendous hailstorm with golfball-like hailstones which went on for twenty minutes. Suddenly, zillions and zillions of white butterflies seemed to emerge from the vanishing hailstones. If a surrealist film maker had done this we'd have thought, what a great mind, what a great artist. The mountain top was suffused with these white butterflies, an unheard of rarity in March in the Himalayas.

"I planned to leave late that night of the full moon on the 9th of April, and I went to the temple one last time. It was the beginning of a 16-day ritual, the oldest, most primal of all the Tibetan rituals. I sat on the stage where there are many raised altars and the throne of the Dalai Lama and the various High Lamas, and witnessed the whole ceremony going on below the dais. The rituals and the music are mind-altering. After two and a half hours, masked dancers came in wearing enormous masks of various deities which are manifestations of different aspects of the self.

"In the Tibetan view, the personality is made up of 54 personae, plus one. The one is the watcher. Buddhists have studied the mind for 2,500 years. The Dalai Lama wants us to understand that his Gelugpa lineage is analytic, not animistic or shamanic. The Tibetan concept of interdependence constitutes a way of life. It is a code of ethics and moral behavior. I've studied the Kabbalah. I find a parallel between the code of ethics in Tibetan Buddhism and in Judaism. They both believe that the relationships that matter are between human beings. Buddhists extend their respect to all sentient beings."

Attractive as she finds Tibetan Buddhism, Gilah says as a person raised in a Jewish background she cannot practice it because she could not prostrate herself to another person. Kuno advised her to simply be herself when she met the Dalai Lama and other High Lamas. He assured her she has no obligation to act differently from the way she feels. She has never practiced any religious system, but she believes that the philosophical tenet of Tibetan Buddhism, to live from heart/mind, to live from compassion and wisdom, has the power to change the world. "The Chinese invasion forced the Tibetan culture out into the world from its former isolation. Maybe this is a karmic event leading to world peace," she conjectures.

Tibetans have a procedure for discovering the incarnations of deceased High Lamas. Gilah learned something of this tradition in Dharamsala. "There are many High Lamas. All of them have incarnations. On this last trip I met a four-year-old incarnation of the Dalai Lama's junior tutor who died as an old man five years ago. This child has been on the High Lama's throne for two and a half years. I was taken to be blessed by him and also to photograph him. He was surrounded by his teddy bears as venerable, elderly High Lamas prostrated themselves before him. The child took me into the next room to see his predecessor who is embalmed with his eyes open, sitting in a teaching position in a little shrine room, full of flowers and deities. His body will eventually be gilded and preserved in the Palace where the Dalai Lama currently lives."

Kuno has given Gilah access to the inner life of Tibetans. In knowing Kuno, Gilah has become "close to the closest." I suspect she might herself be a reincarnation, born in a country far distant from Tibet. She does not reject that idea out of hand.

"I have seen that reincarnation certainly works for the Tibetans. My own idea is there is too much energy in any essence or soul to be snuffed out entirely. So my belief is that there is an ongoing essence which continues from lifetime to lifetime. The form of the incarnation depends on our actions while living, but our present lifetime is our precious opportunity to act positively in all relationships.

"Once you have some experience with the Tibetans you can't pull yourself away. I have been drawn to Tibet since I was a very young child."

Acting on her concern for Tibet, she has made applications to foundations for help in bringing sanitation to Dharamsala. Even before her recent contact with Tibetan wisdom, Gilah was involved with an effort to convince political leaders that Tibet is a global asset and the world should adopt the country in order to save its culture, religious heritage, flora and fauna.

Gilah's own name holds patterns connected with Tibet. In its entirety, her name is Hassia (refuge) Gilah (joy) Yelin (deer) Hirsch (deer). On every Tibetan temple are two deer, messengers of the Buddha. Buddha preached in the Deer Park at Sarnath. To become a Buddhist, you "take refuge" with the Buddha, the Dharma and the Sangha. Dharma is the practice of the spiritual path in daily behavior. Sangha is the community. In her case, she has been taught directly by the Dalai Lama, and she serves as a teacher for others. "I think the most important thing I teach, in all contexts, is, 'Question everything. Do not take anything at face value.' I was really confirmed in this view when the Dalai Lama asked, 'How do you pick a teacher?' and said it might take up to seven years before your scrutiny of that teacher's behavior will convince you the person is worthy of being your teacher."

Though Gilah is a professor of art, she sometimes teaches students who are not art majors. "I know that art is often peripheral to my students. There were years when I would become resentful of students' apathy to what was important to me. In a moment of frustration, years ago, I once said, 'Painting and art are my altar. If you don't want to be here, leave.' However, times have changed. Now I find a much greater and deeper interest in the quest for self-expression and making that spiritual practice evident through art."

In truth, it might be Gilah herself who must leave in order to function at a wider level. She is already discovering that as her public life becomes greater she must work to preserve her privacy, but she believes she no longer requires the isolation of the wilderness. "I have learned from it all I can."

Kuno has told her, "You are already in history." Such a comment from him and others puzzles her. She wonders how to concentrate on being herself and still accept the responsibility that Kuno has implied she is to assume. Whatever happens, she will remain an artist.

"I am a creative person. When I experience a trigger of some sort, it initiates a process, leading to an accumulation of associations which become creative productions. I have a very sharp awareness on many levels at one time. I've often wished for a partial lobotomy so I could close down my openness because I can retain too much information. Yet, I have an incessant curiosity in seeing more aspects of the pattern, and I'm endlessly fascinated by new information, which makes the grand pattern denser."

My purpose has been to discover the prophetic message in Gilah's life, not only in her art, but in all that she does to link people together through her extensive travels, exhibitions, lectures and writing. She told me that she believes her message has to do with "relational integrity and the sense of interdependence. I feel we are all creatures, like all the other creatures." I teased her then, saying the word "creatures" seemed to refute what she had said about not believing in a deity or cosmic mind. To me, "creature" implies Creator. Her answer was, "The theory of evolution suggests things come from each other. I don't think the source is a persona. The thread that runs through my thinking is relatedness. Nothing is the responsible cause. All is cause and effect of the other."

Through my relationship with Gilah Yelin Hirsch, I, too, have had a meaningful exchange with Kuno. He presented me with a traditional white silk scarf and then draped it across the arm of our life-size folk carving of Jesus. The unifying incongruity of it delights me. This extension of my life toward a country I have relished in my mind for decades seems inevitable, yet I could not have expected it even six months before. From one experience to another, all is cause and effect, just as Gilah says. In our post-Einsteinian world, her relational philosophy seems entirely apt and endlessly validated.

*W*hen a friend mentioned she was going to see a Toltec healer named Miguel Angel Ruiz, I thought of Michelangelo and of Archangel Michael. I thought Miguel must be a significant connection between art and spirit. And it proved to be so. I made an appointment to see him briefly in Santa Fe a few days later.

Across a footbridge on the small porch of Miguel's house were two doors, each with a beveled glass insert, and a woman who introduced herself as Maureen. We quickly discovered we each had four o'clock appointments, hers for a healing for severe arthritis in her hips and knees, and mine to get acquainted. After waiting a few minutes, she knocked and Miguel's wife Gaya came to the central door.

Gaya is a tall, friendly, attractive brunette. When I met her, she was wearing Nikes and a warm-up outfit, watching "Oprah" on television in a formally decorated, Southwestern-style room. Miguel appeared on the raised hallway, came down the two steps to the living room and gave me a big hug. He is a small, strong,

dark-skinned man who reflects his Indian heritage. When I first met him, he had long hair, a mustache and a beard. He has absolutely intense, shiny wet brown eyes. Gaya explained the two appointments and I asked, to my own surprise, if I could observe the healing. Maureen agreed. We entered a well lit room whose door also adjoins the porch. Maureen was nude under a sheet and blanket on a healing table. I sat on a couch. Miguel explained that he contacts the "seed" and opens himself to do what he is guided to do.

TAKING CARE not to uncover his client, he administered a deep massage with scented oil, probing two fingers in and around each joint. Maureen gasped when he worked on her knees and hips. She had already told me the treatments felt as if her inside of her bones were being scraped of accumulated mineral deposits, but they had helped her so much she was eager to continue them. The massage took about 40 minutes. Occasionally, Miguel held his right hand up a split second as if receiving a scalpel. Later, he said that was his way of channeling. He was intent on his task and worked very fast. He clearly exerted considerable energy.

After the healing ended, Miguel joined me in the living room on a carved fruitwood love seat. He took my hand while talking quickly. Although I was only able to speak with him for twenty minutes, I realized that he is an artist of the spirit. He told me that emotions fuel our thoughts and create reality. Our reality, he said, is a dream that has been built from fear; but we are really love. We made three appointments for a month later, when he was due to return from San Diego and Teotihuacan. The materials I brought home to read gave me an introduction to his and his mother's teachings.

Miguel is the thirteenth child of Sister (or Mother) Sarita, an 80-year-old psychic healer, medium and seer who lives in San Diego. When she was 60 years old, after experiencing a visionary healing of her heart and liver, she dedicated her life to healing. Her visions continued. She spent five years in Mexico City preparing for mediumship. Her father and grandfather, and generations before them, passed down the Toltec tradition of wisdom and methods of healing. They are called naguals, rather than shamans. Toltecs are not a separate racial group. Miguel told me that the word, properly used, refers to those who have achieved mastery of inner knowledge.

Sarita has become well known. In 1971 she used her garage in San Diego as a healing temple. By 1973 she needed a larger property in the Barrio Logan. In 1990 she opened Nueva Vida, Spiritual Teachings and Healing Institute where she teaches and treats clients. Sarita studies auras. She sees a "beautiful light" on the right side of a person's body if a healing is possible. Auras are in all the chakra colors. A purple light is peace, tranquillity, love and faith. Gray means the person believes himself to be sick, "but really it is their own negative thinking that is creating this sickness." Each morning at 3 a.m. she prays and meditates for two hours. Sometimes she sees herself doing a healing and later learns that the person saw her in a dream.

Miguel Angel Ruiz was born in Guadalajara in 1952 and raised from age seven to age fourteen in Tijuana. He was educated in Mexico City where he became a general surgeon. In the early 1980s Sarita received the wisdom that she was to accept 21 apprentices, among whom was Miguel. During the time he apprenticed with Sarita, he practiced surgery with his brothers, Carlos, a neurosurgeon, and José Luis, an oncology surgeon, in Tijuana. Each Sunday, for up to 12 hours, he trained with his mother. She transferred her knowledge by telling stories and by passing along techniques as well. After three years, Sarita told Miguel and two others they had become masters and they were ready "to share the esoteric knowledge that for centuries has been kept secret. This is happening all over the world and is being called the New Age." Miguel could not speak English, but he learned the language while teaching his first classes. He says, "My five years of teaching have been five years of transformation of myself." He now has over thirty apprentices, some in San Diego and others in Santa Fe.

Although Miguel teaches the Toltec way of knowledge, he says, "The conclusions are the same all over the world, if you go deep into a system of knowledge . . . The purpose of the classes is to become aware of what we really are, why we are here and what happens to us when we die. The most important goal is to be aware that we can clean the minds we have been programmed to have."

Sarita and Miguel do healings, psychic surgeries and individual teaching sessions in San Diego. Miguel has taken groups of his apprentices to Teotihuacan, the City of the Gods, near Mexico City. He makes ceremonies amid the pyramids there on a visionary journey from hell to heaven, beginning at the Pyramid of Quetzalcoatl, down a long straight thoroughfare through a series of plazas. At the Place of Recollection the participants imagine an "etheric double" to which they transfer all their memories of who they are. Then they close their eyes and walk through this plaza to the Place of Sacrifice. On the altar, the etheric double is ceremoniously sacrificed. A big release and pulsing energy is felt by each person. They sit on the Pyramid of the Moon and move, at last, to the Pyramid of the Sun, where they climb to the top and leave a gift in a final ceremony. The purpose of the pilgrimage is to face and dissolve fears.

MIGUEL ANGEL RUIZ: MASTER OF INTENT

Miguel Angel Ruiz says his life has been divided into seven-year cycles, except for a major disruption during his twenties when he had a nearly fatal car accident. His family was poor and so spread out in age that he did not meet his older sisters until he was seven years old. They were already married and living in Tijuana with children of their own older than he.

With disarming simplicity, Miguel describes his first seven years as blissful, "I had no fear." His mother Sarita's energy was devoted to helping her family survive when, at times, they did not have enough food. She made the decision to enroll her husband and three oldest sons in the army. They lived in Mocorito during the three-year enlistment. Her action saved them. In his memory, Miguel's first moment of awareness is of that house in the village. He can still "see" the floor, the stairs, roosters, cats and dogs, and he can remember feeling happy there. "I recognized my brothers as giants. I never thought of yesterday or tomorrow. Everything was a toy to me."

The family was Catholic, but Sarita always had people coming to her for a Toltec healing. Even as a girl she was known as a healer. Her father Leonardo Macias and grandfather Eziquiel Macias, who lived to be 117 and worked until the day he died, were Toltec naguals.

In 1959 Sarita and her husband José Luis moved with nine of their children to Tijuana to live with her parents. When Miguel started school, his second seven-year cycle began. "I know how fear came into my life when I first judged myself," he recalls. He was having a fight with a boy of his own age when he suddenly became aware that his grandmother was watching and laughing. "I feel ashamed because she judged me, and I feel embarrassed, and then I feel fear. I know this because of The Inventory, a spiritual review in which I deal with the emotions that I have created. While doing The Inventory, I came to this memory. I started doing The Inventory in 1980."

The Inventory is a process of going back to objectively watch your own life unfold. It is a discipline and a meditation, and its purpose is to deal with the energy of fear. Once revealed, fear is released, and one experiences freedom without judgment for the first time since early childhood. The technique does not require a hypnotist or an outside agent. Miguel's apprentices are learning to do this for themselves.

"Normal is happiness, but we lose that in the process of our education. We learn to be unhappy. We learn to judge. This increases the power of our mind to think. Our abstract mind begins to grow. This is the normal process in every human. The Inventory releases the sickness that is left in the mind from education." Fear comes from the domestication we receive from our parents, teachers, religion and society itself. The belief system we have is not what we ourselves have invented, but what is passed on to us. We learn from all elders. "The system passes on pain, and we are simple followers."

Children are domesticated in the same way as animals, Miguel explains, by punishment and reward. "After judging came into my life, I rebelled. All children rebel. I rebelled against fear, but they made me afraid anyway. I looked for different ways to escape the pressure, and I found I could get behind my mother and use her for protection."

Miguel's deepest fears, apparently, were directed towards the discipline exerted by his older brothers who were determined he should adopt the macho style and become tough. "What scared me was judgments. Most judgments were about my behavior. To be macho, a man should be very strong even as a little boy. I had a lot of sensitivity, but I learned to be macho from my older brothers. I rebelled but, during my second seven years, my main goal was to be accepted by my brothers."

Miguel began to hunt for his own identity and to worry less about what his brothers thought of him when he was 13 years old. The family's finances were improved enough for the last four sons to achieve higher education in Mexico City, due to the sacrifices of both their parents. In college and medical school, Miguel did not feel the pressure to be tough. He had an excellent memory and was a good student. Although he lived in the family home, he felt he was alone because his mind was independent.

When he was 21 years old, Miguel married Socorro, a fellow student. Two years later they had a son, Miguel Angel, Junior. In September 1978, Miguel and Socorro had another son, José Luis.

Sarita had, by this time, moved back to Tijuana where she began her practice as a professional healer. With only one year left in medical school, in January 1978, Miguel and fellow students went to a party some miles away from Mexico City where they all drank heavily. Driving home from this party, he had a life-changing accident.

Three times during the weeks prior to the event, Miguel had dreams of being in a car crashing into a wall. Just before his actual accident, as though he were looking on from outside the car, he saw himself at the wheel asleep and heard his companions screaming. In his vision, he reached across, opened their door, and pushed them out. Then he broke the front windshield and folded his arms around himself. In fact, he drove straight into a wall and demolished the car; but his companions were safely outside on the ground before the car struck. Doctors x-rayed Miguel and found he had no injuries. Later, he could not remember spending the night in the hospital.

Someone called his older brother, who was still living in Mexico City. He came, signed Miguel out of the hospital and drove him home. During the next few months of his life Miguel's experiences were not normal. He felt he was floating instead of walking. His body did not feel like his. He began to have visions, and he could leave his body at will. He saw auras around people like "an egg" of light. "Everything I believed in was gone. I became very quiet, inward, and not interested in politics anymore." He missed a semester of school while he came to grips with his new self. Looking back upon that cataclysmic change, Miguel says, "I died then." He believes it was his "real me" who pushed those men from the car and saved all their lives. "I was no longer Miguel."

Mexican medical education requires a preparatoria, followed by four years of medical school, one year of residence and a final year of public service. Miguel finished his year of residency and earned his degree in medicine in 1979, the same year that Socorro graduated in dentistry.

As soon as he had the opportunity, Miguel asked his mother's father for help in understanding what had happened to him. Leonardo Macias, acting as a nagual, introduced him to a colleague, a discarnate teacher. During the next year Miguel was required to do public service. He lived alone in the Sonoran Desert and practiced at a small village clinic, while his wife and children lived in Tijuana; and Socorro started her practice of dentistry. This isolated year was vital to Miguel's development. At will, whenever he had a few moments to himself, he could withdraw, close the door and leave his body. In the "other" dimension, he met his grandfather's colleague whom he visualized as a skinny old man with a white beard. From this discarnate, he learned many elements of inner wisdom that have been passed down for centuries.

Miguel's exchanges with this teacher caused him to remember the times he had spent with his grandfather Leonardo and the stories he had heard from him. Although his cousins were afraid of their grandfather, Miguel was playfully at ease with him. Leonardo always told Sarita that her son Miguel would be special, but as a child Miguel paid no attention to this prognosis. Now he realizes his grandfather's stories were a form of training, and he was learning the ancient tradition from Leonardo even then.

At the end of his service year, Miguel joined his brothers Carlos and José Luis in surgery practice in Tijuana. In 1983 his marriage ended in an amicable divorce, and he entered apprenticeship on weekends with his mother. Socorro eventually gave up her practice, and she too works with Sarita.

By 1986, Miguel faced a painful decision about how best to be a healer. After three years of training with his mother, she had declared him to be a "Master of Intent." In the Toltec tradition, there are three forms of mastery: 1) A Master of Awareness knows what God is, what position we are in as humans on earth, where we are and where we are going. 2) A Master of Stalking specializes in transformation. 3) A Master of Intent deals with the spirit.

"Intent," Miguel explains, "is that part of the universe that puts everything in order so that everything exists. Intent is the expression of the Will. The Will is Spirit. Spirit is Love. The name of God is Love." The naguals from whom Miguel descends were all Masters of Intent.

In his medical practice, Miguel had come to realize, gradually, that most of the patients who came to him for illnesses were involved in a form of self-punishment, a by-product of a mind sickened by fear and judgment. "Ninety-nine point nine percent of people have succumbed to fear. It is a strong disease in human minds. The symptoms are unhappiness, anger, jealousy. Anger is fear with a mask. I discovered that people were suffering from symptoms of mental disease." Miguel chose to stop working on their bodies alone and to use his Toltec knowledge to work directly on their fear-ridden minds.

"When I knew I could heal the mind, I stopped being a medical doctor. I give people awareness and help them face their own fears, and I have wonderful results."

Miguel started teaching and seeing clients at his mother's center. His spiritual work was helpful to him.

"I was healing myself and I was happy again. After my car accident, I discovered that this [the world] is not real. It is nothing but a dream. It is not true, but it is a dream that has structure and continuity. This dream was made by humans over the centuries for thousands of years. Humans create the mind of the planet. The function of the mind is to dream. We are dreaming twenty-four hours a day.

"We think with the mind. The mind is not matter. It is not the brain. Yet, the mind was made by the brain, by the nerve system of the body and by what we call the soul."

Each person goes through a pattern of development from a fearless state to a fearful one in response to those fears set into the mind by the surrounding culture. Fear is necessary, according to Miguel, in order for us to learn to think abstractly, as opposed to simply knowing things. In his own case, he could remember facts very well, but he says he did not think until he had learned to judge and to be fearful.

The paradox in what Miguel teaches is the relationship of fear and ignorance to thinking. Without becoming fearful, we cannot learn to think. Without overcoming our fears, we cannot be happy. He uses the notion of giving a man a gun to explain the stages of fear and ignorance: "Give a gun to an ignorant person who is afraid and he will kill. Give a gun to a fearful person who is not ignorant, and he will only use it in a dire case. Give a gun to an ignorant person who is not afraid and he will only use it by accident. Give a gun to a person without fear who is not ignorant and he will throw away the gun."

Miguel shared some basic components of his beliefs: "Humans are now at the stage of transformation. There are gurus all around the world whose purpose is to bring light and reduce fear. One of the blockages to transformation is the effort of those in power to stay in power by keeping society ignorant and in fear. Drug use is the direct and deliberate result of actions by people in power who use fear and ignorance to keep others in thrall."

Miguel's work is part of a worldwide transformation, and it rests entirely on the notion of Love. The opposite of love is fear rather than hate. He says pure love has seven characteristics: "Love has no expectations. Love has no obligations. Love has respect. Love is patient. Love does not pity. Love is detached. Love is kind."

In my interview with Miguel, I sensed that his transformation had been interiorly dramatic, something more dynamic than just seeing auras. When I saw him again, I asked about his visions. He told me this story:

"I saw a gigantic snake which swallowed me. In the process, I was in the body of the snake. I was transforming. I had no body, but I kept my perception. I felt no fear and everything was clear. My state of mind was one in which I understood everything without words.

"It was like a long tunnel. When I first entered the snake, I saw demons and I was afraid, but the deeper I went into the tunnel, the more I could see that the demons weren't real. I had a clarity of mind and I grew stronger. I was just Will, with tenderness. I loved everything.

"At a certain point, I went out of the snake's other head, on the other side. When I went out of the other head, I was everything, but I was me also. Everything is alive. Everything is a living being. We are one being. But, each of us is also a little being. We are living energy. We are Will.

"Being in the snake was a kind of digestion. It was eating me. I was the result—the real me. The mortal parts of me died."

The accident jogged Miguel's memory of earlier times in his life when he had visions without realizing it. He was around 12 years old when the family television set stopped working. In all innocence, Miguel opened the back to see what was wrong and plunged his screwdriver into an area where he should have suffered a fatal shock. Nothing happened to him, but the television was destroyed. "I saw a sword of energy, a blue light, that went out from me below the navel." He believes the blue light disconnected the electricity, with the intent or will to save his life.

Today, this light comes as a force during a healing session. He feels the light emerging from below his navel, his eyes, his hands, and, in lectures, his voice. "When I give a lecture to a crowd, that part of me which has connections with that part in the people . . . my love . . . activates the love in them. Emotions are very contagious, especially love. All emotions are like the light. Love is infinite, containing billions and billions of emotions. It is a vibration like light."

While living in Sonora, his guide, the discarnate old man, told him about love. Miguel said:

"Long ago when my teacher put a flame in my heart, it started to grow, and it touched all my selves. All of me grew until I had a need to share. I shared with the trees, and the trees loved me back. My love grew, and then I decided to share it with the water, and the water loved me back. Then my love grew more and I decided to love every animal, and they loved me back. My love grew bigger and I decided to love every crystal and every stone in the earth, and they loved me back. My love kept growing and I decided to put it in the air, and the air loved me back. Then, I looked at the stars and I saw the moon and the sun and I decided to love them, and they loved me back. Finally, my love grew so big, I wanted to love every human, and they loved me back. Now, wherever I go, I put that flame in your heart."

When I told Miguel about Michael Naranjo's concept that he had been the spirit of the wind in the canyon, that he had lived as a tree and then as every kind of tree, and then as each of the animals, and as every kind of person, Miguel smiled his agreement and interest.

"After a certain level, all masters are the same. In the earth, there is a circle of masters, but they have no body. They live here and they love the earth. Heaven is here also, not just hell. There is one living being and we are part of that. The whole universe in all its dimensions from matter to spirit is a single being.

"God does not come down to reach humans. Humans go out to God, both inside and outside also. When our love is big enough it is easy for us to find love everywhere in nature. When it is not big enough we only sense human fear. We perceive fear from other humans, and it prevents us from feeling the emotions of the trees and the rocks. Every living thing—including what we call the inanimate—is moving. All the atoms in the rock are moving. The rock is of the earth, and the earth is a living being. Everything is in motion, in an unfinished chain of creation.

"Sometimes I call the wind, and it comes. Our planet is a living being and each part is an organ in the living being. Every tree has a specific function, just as humans are here to have emotions and to dream, to have imagination. The dream goes all around the earth. It is the result of what humans dream. We have an inside and an outside dream. So the dream of the planet has continuity. Our emotions can affect the whole world.

"As we become clear and direct our intent, we can connect with other organs on the planet. With intent, we can make it rain or snow. We can stop a hurricane. We are connected with our planet. It is easy to understand that this is the explanation of miracles. The earth is alive.

"Whatever happens in our body goes to our brain and affects all of our organs. This happens in the earth, too. What we do to the earth, to one of its organs, affects the whole earth, but there is no way that humans can destroy the planet."

Miguel's vision substantiates that of Dr. Frank Alper, who believes the earth is transforming from a 5.5 vibration to a 6. Miguel even concurs with Alper's channeling that Earth will not remain a planet of transformation as it is today. The Toltecs, from whom the Mayan/Aztec calendar was derived, say that the light from the sun gained a new quality in 1992, and we entered the sixth world at that time. According to the Mayan calendar, the old world ended in 1991.

"Our tradition teaches that we have had five humanities before. We began our sixth world on January 11, 1992. The quality of light has changed, and it will affect the planet Earth and the whole universe," Miguel explains.

The center of the galaxy is like the brain of a living being. Miguel says there is an exchange of information from star to star, just as there is among our own neurons and cells. The light is the messenger, and messenger means angel. The earth receives information from the center of the galaxy. The galaxy has its own metabolism and homeostasis—a state of physiological equilibrium—and so does the earth. The metabolism of the earth will change in reaction to the light changes. Already there is more violet in the sunsets. This violet does not come from volcanic ash. Volcanoes erupt as the result of information received by the earth from the galaxy. The same information affects humans. Humans must create emotions of a better quality because the dream of the planet must change.

"The dream puts humans to work, just like ants. Because of the change in the quality of the light, humans will change from fear to something nearer to love," Miguel says.

Miguel believes his greatest vision is that he is no longer a separate identity; he can see himself in other people, and he knows that we are all one.

I asked Miguel, "What is self-love?" He told me that self-love is to be aware of what you really are, and to know that everyone is really love.

Then I asked him, "So, what about narcissism?" He said, "Narcissism comes when we create an identity and attract attention to our importance. It is a false identity. We are pretending to be best, strongest, most important. We project an image and then we love it."

In the Initiation of Death, he says, the part that dies is the false part that makes us suffer and weakens us.

Miguel introduces the concept of the Angel of Death to his apprentices. His first intention is to help them realize they are living in hell.

"A part of their mind is judging what they do and what they do not do, what they feel and think and what they do not feel and think. They have the need for punishment because a part of their mind is the judge. All of us acquire this part during our domestication when we learn what to believe from the dream of the planet.

"Another concept I introduce is that we started to die from the moment we were born. The Angel of Death is the owner of the dream, including our own body. We don't own anything. We just participate in the dream. The Angel of Death is the Messenger of God, yet she is also God because everything is God. The Angel of Death is responsible for life. It is the Eternal Change, like a two-sided coin of Life and Death.

"We can suffer for every loss that we have, or we can surrender to the Angel of Death as our greatest teacher, because the Angel of Death will teach us to live.

"From the point of view of the body, we are not immortal. The Angel of Death can take our body at any moment. Today could be the last day of our life. This gives us two choices: We can suffer because of what we are losing, or we can enjoy every moment and live until the last moment.

"Death takes everything we have little by little before we die. This is a benediction because it allows us to experience the joy of the new. If you are a warrior, the Angel of Death is always behind you, taking away every moment back into herself. If she does not take the past, there's no way to live the present or to reach the future."

As an example of loss and opportunity, Miguel points to the day we graduate from high school. "We feel nostalgia for our teachers and old friends we have made, but we look at the future as something potentially great. At such a moment, we can see both loss and gain."

The conclusion to all this is that nothing belongs to us. The Angel of Death can claim it at any time. We suffer from each loss as long as we are attached to those we love and our possessions. Eventually, we have the possibility of becoming aware that we own nothing. The problem for humans is that our mind is so powerful and it wants to live in the past, to cling to the dream. As long as we allow ourselves to live in the past, we have no opportunity to live in the present.

Apprentices who are working on The Inventory must learn to let go of their past. It is dead. Whatever happened in the past cannot be used as an excuse to punish oneself and be unhappy. The rule is, let it go and live in the present. If, however, you review the past with "old eyes," that is the eyes of the judge and the victim, then a visit to the past will revive old fears and you will suffer guilt and self-punishment again.

Miguel teaches, "To change the eyes, to see without judgment, is to love whatever was in the past. Then you don't feel pain. You are cleaning whatever garbage was in the past with the fire that does not burn, but purifies everything it touches." During The Inventory, apprentices are preparing for their own death, "changing from the inside until they are bigger than the judge in their mind."

The apprentice alone knows when the moment has arrived to go for the Initiation of Death. At that stage, he or she can see that the dream of the planet is ruled by fear, controlled by the judge and the victim. The dream is nothing but hell. It is impossible to build a safety zone within this dream-hell, but everyone tries to build such a place, either through the home, the family, a career, or whatever becomes important to the dream identity.

Miguel compares the human state to that of "monkey mind." Hunters will put a narrow ring in front of a monkey and behind the ring will place a banana for temptation. The monkey reaches through the ring and grabs the banana. Because he will not let go, the hunter easily captures the monkey who has literally trapped himself in desire. This is what people do with their possessions. All that is required to leave hell behind and enter heaven is to let go of our possessions and be happy. "Happiness is not to be afraid," says Miguel.

Once a person has been through the Initiation of Death, he or she does not belong to hell anymore, but neither does he nor she have heaven. This between space is the Place of Temptation. The temptation is to go back into the dream. However, the initiate does not have the option to return to the dream. The change has already taken place, and the only way is to keep transforming until heaven is reached and freedom is achieved.

The dream is one of polarity, separation, good versus evil; but at a transformed level of consciousness, there is only One. This One is a living being. Miguel comments that most scientists do not consider the universe a living being. They consider the creation of the universe a mystery. He claims that it is not a mystery, but is easily understood through a study of the microcosm of human procreation. "The sperm and the ova coming together create new life. In the macrocosm, the original sun was created in this same fashion. It divided millions of times to create the universe. If we go directly to the spirit we see that everything is one, but it is always, eternally in reproduction," he says.

To paraphrase Miguel, we can see in Teotihuacan the whole earth up to the time humans created the dream of the planet. Humans need to find God. They have projected many Gods out into the dream according to the level of hell they were in. The Romans created a different God from the Greeks, one that would conquer the world for them. Their heaven was for the warrior who died in war. As their ambitions grew, God grew, and they succeeded in conquering the world. Then their God decayed as they talked of justice.

And what about the Judeo-Christian tradition? Miguel says that Jesus, during his lifetime, ran into a wall of negativity and rejection of his prophecy. His contemporaries were in bondage to Rome, and they treated Jesus harshly because of their fear. When the Holy Roman Empire co-opted Christianity it turned the name of Christ into a demon and set in motion the conquest of Europe. In this hemisphere, the name of God, and of Jesus, was used to kill Indians and to conquer territories.

We are now witnessing the end times of this process as the pure spirit of Christ is returning. In the present period, Miguel says, the prophesied second coming of Jesus has already come true, through all who understand what he originally came to give. "Now we are again creating God, and Jesus is part of it. He was always a human, but he reached the level of consciousness where he became God."

Miguel prophesies, "Nothing is new. Now is the time to bring back the best from the past and to make the prophecies of the past come true. We are bringing the Kingdom of Heaven to Earth. Jesus and Buddha shared the tools of transformation with us, but the process of the Initiation of Death has been known for centuries. In Ancient Egypt, the initiate spent three days in a sarcophagus as he journeyed into death. Wotan hung in the Tree of Wisdom for three days. And Jesus died for three days before the Resurrection." In the new transformation, Miguel is certain that Jesus will take part because "he is the best we know, the best there is."

For Miguel, the Initiation of Death occurred at the time of his car accident. Today he guides others through this process in less traumatic ways, and he says, "It does facilitate the Initiation of Death to be in Teotihuacan, the Place of Hell, because the dream is alive there."

Gaya, who went through the Initiation of Death in Teotihuacan during the spring equinox of 1992, says it was the most awesome experience of her life. The moment she stepped into that area, she felt the energy of the ancient Toltecs. She felt as if she, too, "knew everything, but without words."

HAVING COME this far, through prolonged connection with other people's lives, I know that I have been on a shamanic journey into their memory banks. Events in their lives are as vivid to me as imagery from my own life.

I can "see" the star shower in Los Angeles with the boy Serge King while simultaneously sensing the flow that carried him to Africa and then to Hawaii. There the pictures fuse with being on Kauai myself as his student. What King taught through guided shamanic exercises has stayed with me. Over time, I have learned to recognize that shamanic wisdom is infiltrating life upon life.

Pat Musick looking into the abyss is such a strong image that I feel as though I am slightly to her left with a full view of the kitchen cabinets behind her. As He Who Sleeps at the Foot of the Horse lies on his couch in exhaustion, I watch the ceiling open and the bird of prey swoop down to attack. I join the group at Ayer's Rock when Linda Tellington-Jones instructs them in automatic writing, but I also recall seeing her sitting on a table in Santa Fe's El Dorado Hotel while healing a cat.

I have an indelible mental picture of Peter Rogers in the crowded corridor of the night train from Edinburgh: he is hearing the words, "The illusion of separateness. The understanding of oneness." Every so often, I revisit the rice paddy in Vietnam and look into the eyes of the Vietcong who throws the fateful grenade at Michael Naranjo. Counterbalancing that image is the actual memory of seeing Michael on film as he touches the lips of Michelangelo's *David*, a privilege that lit his face with joy.

With Richard Newman, I feel the succubus warning of impending death and my own answering curiosity about the process of dying. I think of Melissa Zink, in her home off the beaten path by the Rio Grande river—drawing, sculpting, reading, writing, using her computer—thriving on freedom. I imagine Patricia Brown outdoors in the moonlight, awestruck by the inner music and lyrics she is hearing for the first time. In my vision of Miguel Angel Ruiz, I see him hurtling through the car window, unhurt, and then watch the process of his becoming a nagual.

Afraid as I am of the wilderness and the unknown, I walk beside Gilah Yelin Hirsch in the forest while she discovers primal forms of alphabet; and I picture a snowy day in the Himalayas listening to the Dalai Lama. Of all the possible fates that I would not have wanted, cloistered life in a convent has to be among the most dreaded; yet, I sometimes look into Stanhope Abbey to find Meinrad Craighead still in her nun's habit thinking of the Mother God, feeling the urgency to leave. My favorite image of Bruce Lowney is the day of his wedding to Kelley, under the pine trees on his land; but, I remember my first visit with him there when he was starkly alone. We spoke of paradoxes.

Barbara Hand Clow's unrestrained accounts of previous lives in ancient temples elicit my own shadowy fantasies. Frank Alper's shamanic excursions to Atlantis reveal a familiar world to which I sometimes go for information. I occasionally catch a glimpse of Mary-Margaret Moore, years ago, sitting on her meditation stool in the Santa Barbara garden, thinking, "It shouldn't be this hard."

Mary-Margaret, in her monthly visits to Albuquerque, announced that the end of her service to the Bartholomew energy will come in early 1995. Her intensity has stepped up several notches as this ending draws closer. The essence of Bart's wisdom—"This is IT!"—is narrowing like a laser beam to a single prescription for a spiritually engaged life. "BE. NOW." In the moment of full awareness s/he promises we will find the open channel to our higher selves. It is possible at any such moment to contact the Divine.

Since I believe this to be true, I try to live "on the rim." To one side is material reality, the stuff of daily living where the clock and calendar, plans, lists, action, obligations and pleasures are teeming. On the other side is the numinous darkness with its central corridor of light, usually blue, that calls me. Whenever it enters my mind to do it, I visit that half-lit blueness to see if there is a message waiting—something like checking the celestial mailbox. Often as not, there is a brief note in the form of a partial understanding ready for pickup.

I am never surprised if I receive a mental memo related to a book. Three people in one week recommended James Redfield's adventure story, *The Celestine Prophecy*, which is rapidly rising in popularity, and so I bought it with the certainty it would relate to my work. The lean plot projects a search in Peru for an ancient book containing nine insights that sequentially lead a seeker toward spiritual transformation.

Redfield's first insight is that we must pay attention to the coincidences in our lives. Seemingly uncoordinated meetings, words, and intuitions will suddenly seem related and hint at an organized level of meaningful activity beneath everyday life. Another insight is that the basic stuff at the core of the universe is pure energy, which Redfield says is on the same continuum as beauty. To awaken to this essential energy one must develop an appreciation for beauty wherever it is found. Focusing on the energy of beauty has an active effect on the observer and on what is observed. Of all Redfield's insights, these are most relevant to what I have experienced in discovering *artists of the spirit*. It is no accident that I have responded to the artists/shamans I have met, nor to the presence of beauty and mystical meaning in their stories. I assume these meetings were purposeful.

The creative people who drew my attention have gradually acquired wisdom during their highly focused lives. Despite all their traumatic incidents, they are propelled forward on a path of learning and spiritual growth. Something initiates their journey. A visionary moment, as experienced by Peter Rogers and Richard Newman, or a long series of severe tests, as undergone by He Who Sleeps, led to their sensing a cohesive order existing in tandem with chaotic reality.

The shaman is one who is attuned to the moment by moment images within his/her own mind. These artists/shamans are especially respectful of their own process. Amid the shifting episodes in their lives, they remain committed to their creative source. In varying ways, either in artwork or through ways of healing and teaching, they give creative form to their knowledge. The very process by which they create is the integrating mechanism of their lives. They have a dual focus, ever scanning the inner world as it yields fragments of visionary memory while remaining more than normally attuned to the outer world's kaleidoscopic possibilities. Their struggle to integrate the inner and outer nature of their vision has been the field of my concentration upon them—and it has validated my own process.

Seeing another person's life as a pattern, made up of related segments, emphasizes the importance of the parts to the whole. If nothing that has led to the present moment for any of us is an accident, then nothing earlier than the present moment can be safely discarded or impugned. We seem called upon to find our shadows and embrace them for they, with our lightest moments, combine into our wholeness.

Joan Halifax tells of a great heron who reminded her that "... storytelling is a kind of root medicine, a way for us to enter our depths and derive nourishment from the fruitful darkness." (*The Fruitful Darkness*, p.111.)

In all of these stories I have told, darkness has eventually proved fruitful for these wounded healers and insightful artists. The quality of darkness marks each life in a separate way. He Who Sleeps' story stands out from the rest for the misery of the personal, inimical destruction visited upon him by those he expected to trust. His extraordinary healing gifts have not eased his lonely life, nor have they safeguarded him from further wounds.

Michael Naranjo's war wounds were so devastating they forced him to rely upon the latent inner vision that fuels his art; yet, within his fruitful darkness he has been surrounded by a loving family he has always trusted.

Barbara Hand Clow's abandonment and abuse in infancy have darkened her life, but she admits that within the shadow she has discovered multiple paths to wisdom.

By telling a story, we are staging a drama. As witnesses to the drama, we are especially curious about the heroine's or the hero's response to challenge, for in their response we find models for ourselves.

The adage "When the student is ready, the teacher will appear" promises we will always discover knowledge as we need it. So today, as our traditional sources of wisdom are shattering around us, it is no surprise to find ourselves in a Golden Age of Prophecy.

Our psyches are being flooded with prophetic information propelling us toward a holistic worldview. While I have been following my intuition that artists and healers are similarly gifted, Robert Jay Lifton has studied the multiplicity of *The Protean Self* and John Briggs has built up a research base for the study of genius in *Fire in the Crucible*. The protean self and the genius have points in common with *artists of the spirit*.

Lifton writes, "In a time of fragmentation and trauma, proteans can awaken our species belonging, our species self. We can assert our organic relationship to each other and to nature. That assertion, for symbolizers like ourselves, is a matter of the psyche, of the imagination. We can come to feel what we *are*: members of a common species. We are multiple from the start . . .

"In style, the species self incorporates premodern holism and spirituality, the modern quest for the universal, and the pluralism that has come to stamp the postmodern." (*The Protean Self*, p. 231.)

Meanwhile Briggs offers the term "omnivalence," which he links with moreness and otherness. To be ambivalent is to be of two minds. To be omnivalent is to be aware, all at once, of many possibilities and potentialities.

"In the 'more'ness of omnivalence also lurks the circular paradox that the act of expressing one's vision is an act of discovering what it is . . . The step is not a long one between the omnivalence in a creator's vision, and the mystical and quasireligious pronouncements dotted here and there like exotic flowers in the biographies of most creative geniuses." (*Fire in the Crucible*, p. 118-119.)

Lifton reminds us that "The symbolizing self is *developmentally* sensitive to influences from early childhood but never entirely 'determined' in outcome by any of them. The evolving self, in constantly recreating all such influences, traumatic or otherwise, becomes itself causative and always prospective or forward moving." (*The Protean Self*, p. 29.)

The artists and seers I have come to know have led protean lives. By way of their intensely focused creativity, they have constantly recreated themselves and, in the process, gained access to their shamanic ability.

We are acting shamanically whenever we follow through on a creative idea. First, we enter into our imagination and wait. A thought appears. Then we formulate an intention, which can be an image. Finally, we carry it out in whatever medium is our forte. The creative process is our applied shamanic ability.

Jesus was the most masterful shaman the world has ever known. He could affect matter by changing water into wine. He could heal through his intention. He could teleport, appearing in more than one place at a time. It is possible that he could, through his advanced shamanic skills, still his bodily processes to die and then return to life. Jesus had the mission to awaken us to our spiritual nature. When he said that what he could do, we could do also, it could have been an urging to use our innate shamanic ability to create reality with our minds. For whatever reason, his mission did not succeed at the time, but the memory of his life has been cultivated and preserved. Today, in the midst of social chaos, we are remembering bits and pieces of shamanism.

Shamanism is practical spirituality. A person can use his imagination as a path to a higher dimension of reality than the one we experience everyday. In this zone of awareness, everything affects everything else, and our thoughts are catalysts for creation.

Shamanism has been steadily practiced in the cultures that Douchan Gersi, in his *Faces in the Smoke*, refers to as "People of Tradition." Gersi is a modern voyager into the cultures of those who live in a sacred world inhabited by many spirits and who still practice the rituals needed to maintain it.

Like Carlos Castaneda, Fred Alan Wolf and Serge King, Gersi goes into the mental and spiritual spaces of shamanistic tribes to bring back for us an updated account of other realities. He tells the story of living, as a child, in Africa, where nearby Belgian missionaries gave his parents a flat, black, shiny stone. The stone can remove venom, poison and infections from wounds. An Indian medicine man taught them how to make it from plants and carbon compounds. The black stone saved Gersi's life more than once when he was bitten by snakes. He has seen these stones among Saharans and Afghanistanis. Gersi also lived among the Tuaregs of the Sahara Desert and relates that in their creation legend they are the descendants of those who were trading along the African coast when their own country, in the middle of the Atlantic Ocean, disappeared. Gersi's future life was accurately foretold by a Tuareg shaman who read the idle marks he told Gersi to make within a square of flattened sand.

"What is impossible for us remains impossible as long as we live in the cultural world that formed our perceptions. Thus each culture creates its own limitations and its own limitless possibilities," Gersi writes. I propose that *artists of the spirit* and others like them are here to change our sense of what is possible.

Deepak Chopra is a medical doctor from India whose scintillating books, tapes and personal appearances are heralded for their wisdom. Basing his guidance on a synthesis of quantum physics, ayurvedic and allopathic medicine, plus an Olympian view of human potential heavily influenced by Eastern philosophy, Chopra exhorts us to drop all of our self-imposed limitations. He promotes a shamanic turn of mind, and says we have the ability to heal ourselves through creative visualization as well as life-affirming thoughts. He repeatedly refers to our spiritual nature as a useful aid in keeping ourselves balanced, youthful and happy. Chopra is one of the new leaders who bridges disciplines in a holistic way.

An apparent forward impulse in human affairs is leading us toward a change in consciousness. Outbreaks of spiritual wonder are bursting forth around the world. José Arguelles dreams of and catalyzes the Harmonic Convergence. The Berlin Wall falls. The Cold War ends. The PLO and the Israeli government try to work together. Crop formations appear in the fields all over the world as visible proof that an unknown energy is active on the planet. Books containing shamanic exercises as a means to good health are proliferating. In the popular culture, images of angels are a "hot item" with wide appeal for people of all religious persuasions, and for people without religious affiliation. Teachers of meditation, alternative medicine and self-help are found everywhere, even in Russia.

Something is afoot.

Matthew Fox asks, "What meditations . . . lead to fuller living and deeper spiritual celebration of both pain and joy?" He answers, "art as meditation." (*Original Blessing*, p. 190-192.) To take spirituality seriously means taking art seriously, Fox says. "Not art for the sake of art . . . but art as prayer . . . Only art as meditation reminds people so that they never forget that the most beautiful thing a potter produces is . . . the potter."

Artists of the spirit have made a vocation of their gifts. Their gifts are their way-showers. Fox believes that the spiritual dimension of the artist's journey is to create the artist. We are all gifted. We are all, to some extent, artists, and all of us are creating ourselves.

Redfield's insight is that we must become aware of beauty. Joseph Campbell has written an exhilarating chapter on "The Way of Art" in his book *The Inner Reaches of Outer Space: Metaphor as Myth and as Religion.* Campbell presents Thomas Acquinas' three requirements for beauty: integrity, or a sense of wholeness; harmony, which refers to the relationship of parts to the whole; and radiance, a supreme quality of "whatness," which leads the mind to a blissful silence. Campbell tells us, "One's heart is waked, not by the form of the work, but by its content . . . (p. 130.) "Like the priest, the artist is a master of metaphorical language." (p. 121.)

Beauty and content are not limited to gentleness. A work of art, like a life, can be both beautiful and harsh. Gilah Hirsch's passionate canvasses, Pat Musick's assembled sculptures and Meinrad Craighead's haunting archetypal figures bring us face to face with raw power. They also demonstrate that the eight visual artists I have selected are not ones that fit the prevailing mode of marketplace art. All the artists I have featured create art that communicates. Although created as the fruit of intense self-scrutiny, their art is not preoccupied with the self. It speaks a universal language that appeals to the level of mind on the same energy continuum as beauty.

The structures of wisdom created by the eight sages in the book are also works of beauty. Miguel Angel Ruiz teaches a way of dying in life to the fears that entrap us. Such ancient knowledge applies to everyone. Barbara Hand Clow approaches her work as a ritual maker by going around the earth to awaken sacred sites. In doing this work, she believes she is restoring to our shared memory the information held in sacred places. Linda Tellington-Jones can blend with the life force of animals and people, to soothe them and heal them with touching. Patricia Brown draws upon her inner conflict of masculine and feminine energy to counsel her clients, while at home she derives her spiritual practice from an Eastern belief in oneness. He Who Sleeps withdraws his consciousness from the present to the reptilian age and finds the source of an illness, which he then is inspired to treat shamanically. They are all creating oneness from diversity, and they are achieving integrity, harmony, and radiance.

Our limitations in modern Western culture are outgrowths of divisive polarities. We usually favor one aspect of a pair of opposites over the other. God is good. Satan (the designated enemy, illness, drugs, crime, etc.) is evil. Winning is good. Losing is not.

Maleness outranks femaleness, although we are beginning to acknowledge the injustice of this notion.

Fear-driven divisiveness is shattering neighborhoods, cities and states. One need not be a sociologist to see that Western civilization is close to the breaking point.

Some contemporary prognosticators predict that a cataclysmic change lies ahead, yet the prophecy we can harvest from the stories I have told here is that change occurs as an evolution in our thinking rather than as a physical disaster. Essentially, these *artists of the spirit* have turned their traumas into the stuff of art and life.

Pat Musick learned that negatives can be turned into positives. Frank Alper has channeled that we are vibratory beings resonating at certain frequencies and the entire vibratory rate of humanity is accelerating. Living people whose vibratory range of perception is prodigious are signals that our consciousness is evolving rapidly.

In his *The Holographic Universe*, Michael Talbott explicates the idea that the universe is a holograph and so are our brains. Each particle of a holograph reflects the whole. The holographic paradigm attests to the wisdom of "as above, so below." From this grounding, Talbott spreads his net widely to address the mind/body developments in medicine. He discusses Dr. O. Carl Simonton's successful work using visualization techniques to help patients self-heal from cancer. The book is a who's who of those among us who are on the edge of their fields. The message of the book is: everything connects.

Talbott's account of the Near-Death Experience (NDE) research by Kenneth Ring led me to Ring's *Heading Toward Omega*. Even the title has a messianic tone, and it harks back to Teilhard de Chardin's writing. The Omega point is the peak toward which evolution, according to de Chardin, is striving. Ring tells us what those who have nearly died report when they return. For my purposes, I have selected a few of his findings: 1) In the midst of dying, the experiencer "may find himself in a state of dual awareness," able to perceive the physical scene around him and another reality drawing him toward it. 2) The death state is free of time and is nonlocal. The concepts of time and space as we know them become meaningless. 3) The dying person may enter a "world of light and preternatural beauty." (p. 37.) Experiencers say the light communicates a feeling of pure, unconditional love that is so overpowering, they do not want to return to life.

Dying, Ring believes, "involves a shift of consciousness away from the ordinary world of appearances into a more holographic reality of pure frequencies." (*The Holographic Universe*, p. 245.)

The brief NDE experience has a permanent transformative effect on the person's nervous system, "so as to activate latent spiritual potentials." (p. 245.)

Talbott and Ring, like Teilhard de Chardin, Marilyn Ferguson, Fritjof Capra and others who have inspired my thinking, end their books with prophetic projections. They suggest that a metaevolution is underway in which, as Ring says, "A new race of human beings is coming into existence which could transform the planet." (*Heading Toward Omega*, p.259.)

Ring also says that perhaps the process we are witnessing is "the shamanizing of modern humanity." (*The Holographic Universe*, p. 299.)

My original goal in writing this book was to show that certain artists and seers think and behave in a similar way. I now see that there is a wider implication in linking wisdom with creativity. Our human creative faculty, our imagination, is our spiritual channel to holistic consciousness. Therefore, shamanism is related to creativity and the imagination. If we are witnessing the shamanizing of humanity, and I agree that we are, I believe the evolutionary aspect of ourselves is our creative imagination.

I have featured here a small sampling of thousands of prophetic artists and seers around the globe. These gifted ones among us have become aware of a cohesive order operating in the universe that reveals itself in the most fragile coincidences of our lives. Their holistic insights serve as catalysts. Each of them affects a number of others, who then spread their awareness mind to mind, slowly changing the content of the noosphere and the direction of human evolution. In this way, the future is mediated through our own minds.

While concentrating on a selection of people who are both wise and creative, I feel I have been watching the process of evolution work itself out in the lives of individuals who are the seedlings of a new humanity. Archaic shamanism was and is practiced by a chosen few: As shamanism reemerges in our imagination, everyone will have access to it. Everyone will be an *artist of the spirit*.

BIBLIOGRAPHY

Alper, Frank. *Exploring Atlantis, Vol. I - III.* Phoenix: Arizona Metaphysical Society, P. O. Box 44027, Phoenix, AZ 85064, 1982 - 1986.

Universal Law. Phoenix: Arizona Metaphysical Society, 1986.

Arguelles, José. *The Mayan Factor: Path Beyond Technology.* Santa Fe, NM: Bear & Company, 1987.

Bancroft, Anne. *Weavers of Wisdom, Women Mystics of the Twentieth Century.*, London: Arkana, 1989.

Barrett, William. *Irrational Man: A Study in Existential Philosophy.* New York: Anchor Books, 1962.

Bartholomew, Alick, editor. *Crop Circles-Harbingers of World Change.* Bath, U.K.: Gateway Books, 1991.

Berman, Morris. *Coming To Our Senses.* New York: Bantam Books, 1990.

Berry, Thomas. *The Dream of the Earth.* San Francisco: Sierra Club Books, 1988.

Bly, Robert. *The Little Book of the Human Shadow.* San Francisco: Harper & Row, 1988.

Boissiére, Robert. *The Return of Pahana: A Hopi Myth.* Santa Fe, NM: Bear & Company, 1990.

Bolen, Jean Shinoda. *Goddesses in Every Woman.* New York: Harper & Row, 1984.

Borysenko, Joan. *Guilt is the Teacher, Love is the Lesson.* San Francisco: Harper & Row, 1990.

Briggs, John. *Fire in the Crucible:The Alchemy of Creative Genius.* New York: St. Martin's Press, 1988.

Brommer, Gerald F. *Transparent Watercolor.* Worcester, MA: Davis Publications, 1973.

Brown, Betty Ann and Arlene Raven. Photographs by Kenna Love. *Exposures: Women & Their Art.* Pasadena, CA: NewSage Press, 1989.

Campbell, Joseph, Editor. *The Portable Jung.* New York: Penguin Books, 1981.

The Mythic Image. Princeton, NJ: Bollingen/Princeton, 1974.

The Inner Reaches of Outer Space: Metaphor as Myth and as Religion., New York: Alfred Van der Marck, 1985.

with Bill Moyers. *The Power of Myth.* New York: Doubleday, 1988.

Capra, Fritjof. *The Tao of Physics.* New York: Bantam Books, 1977.

The Turning Point: Science, Society, and the Rising Culture. New York: Bantam Books, 1983.

Carlson, Richard and Benjamin Shields. *Healers on Healing.* Los Angeles: Jeremy P. Tarcher, Inc., 1989.

Cerminara, Gina. *Many Mansions.* New York: New American Library, 1988.

Chopra, Deepak. *Unconditional Life: Mastering the Forces that Shape Personal Reality.* New York: Bantam Books, 1991.

Ageless Body, Timeless Mind. New York: Random House, 1993.

Creating Affluence: Wealth Consciousness in the Field of Possibilities. San Rafael, CA: New World Library, 1993.

Christ, Carol. P. and Judith Plaskow, Editors. *Womanspirit Rising.* San Francisco: Forum/Harper Books, 1979.

Cirlot, J. E. *A Dictionary of Symbols.* New York: Philosophical Library, 1962.

Clow, Barbara Hand. *Eye of the Centaur: A Visionary Guide into Past Lives*. St. Paul, MN: Llewellyn Publications, 1986.

Heart of the Christos: Starseeding from the Pleiades. Santa Fe, NM: Bear & Company, 1989.

Chiron: Rainbow Bridge Between the Inner and Outer Planets. St. Paul, MN: Llewellyn Publications, 1987.

The Liquid Light of Sex. Santa Fe, NM: Bear & Company, 1991.

Signet of Atlantis: War in Heaven Bypass. Santa Fe: Bear & Company, 1992.

Craighead, Meinrad. *The Mother's Songs: Images of God the Mother*. New York: Paulist Press, 1986.

The Litany of the Great River. New York: Paulist Press, 1991.

Cranston, Sylvia and Carey Williams. *Reincarnation: A New Horizon in Science, Religion and Society*. New York: Julian Press/Crown Publishers, 1984.

Davies, Paul. *God and the New Physics*. New York: Touchstone/Simon & Schuster, 1983.

de Chardin, Pierre Teilhard. *The Phenomenon of Man*. New York: Torchbooks/Harper & Row, 1965.

The Future of Man. New York: Torchbooks/Harper & Row, 1964.

Hymn to the Universe. New York: Colophon/Harper & Row, 1965.

Letters From a Traveler. New York: Torchbooks/Harper & Row, 1962.

The Divine Milieu. New York: Torchbooks/Harper & Row, 1960.

De Saint-Exupéry, Antoine. *The Little Prince*. New York: Reynal & Hitchcock, 1943.

du Nouy, Lecomte. *Human Destiny*. New York: Longmans, Green & Company, 1947.

Eisler, Riane. *The Chalice and the Blade*. San Francisco: Harper & Row, 1987.

Eliade, Mircea. *Shamanism: Archaic Techniques of Ecstasy*. Princeton, NJ: Bollingen/Princeton, 1974.

Myth and Reality. New York: Torchbooks/Harper & Row, 1968.

Symbolism, the Sacred and the Arts. New York: Crossroad Publishing, 1988.

The Myth of the Eternal Return; or, Cosmos and History. Princeton, NJ: Bollingen/Princeton, 1974.

Erdman, Erika and David Stover. *Beyond a World Divided: Human Values in the Brain-Mind Science of Roger Sperry*. Boston: Shambala, 1991.

Ferguson, Marilyn. *The Aquarian Conspiracy*. Los Angeles: Jeremy P. Tarcher, Inc., 1980.

Editor. *New Sense Bulletin, Brain/Mind Bulletin*. Los Angeles, CA.

Fortune, Dion. *The Mystical Qabalah*. New York: Ibis Books, 1981.

Fox, Matthew. *Original Blessing*. Santa Fe, NM: Bear & Company, 1983.

A Spirituality Named Compassion; and the Healing of the Global Village; Humpty Dumpty and Us. Minneapolis, MN: Winston Press, 1979.

The Coming of the Cosmic Christ. San Francisco: Harper & Row, 1988.

Gadon, Elinor W. *The Once and Future Goddess*. San Francisco: Harper & Row, 1989.

Galland, China. *Longing for Darkness: Tara and the Black Madonna; A Ten-Year Journey*. New York: Viking, 1990.

Gersi, Douchan. *Faces in the Smoke*. Los Angeles: Jeremy P. Tarcher, Inc., 1991.

Gettings, Fred. *Dictionary of Occult, Hermetic and Alchemical Sigals*. Boston: Routledge & Kegan, Ltd., 1981.

The Occult in Art. New York: Rizzoli, 1979.

Gimbutas, Marija. *The Language of the Goddess*. San Francisco: Harper & Row, 1989.

Goldenberg, Naomi R. *Changing of the Gods: Feminism and the End of Traditional Religions*. Boston: Beacon Press, 1979.

Greeley, Andrew M. and Mary Greeley Durkin. *How To Save the Catholic Church*. New York: Elizabeth Sifton/Viking, 1984.

Halevi, Z'ev ben Shimon. *Kabbalah: Tradition of Hidden Knowledge*. London: Thames and Hudson, 1979.

Halifax, Joan. *Shaman: The Wounded Healer*. London: Thames and Hudson, 1982.

The Fruitful Darkness: Reconnecting with the Body of the Earth. San Francisco: HarperSanFrancisco, 1993.

Hall, Manly P. *The Secret Teachings of All Ages: An Encyclopedic Outline of Masonic, Hermetic, Qabbalistic and Rosicrucian Philosophy*. Los Angeles: Philosophical Research Society, Inc., 1975.

Harman, Willis and Howard Rheingold. *Higher Creativity: Liberating the Unconscious for Breakthrough Insights*. Los Angeles: Jeremy P. Tarcher, Inc., 1984.

Global Mind Change; The Promise of the Last Years of the Twentieth Century. Indianapolis, IN: Knowledge Systems, Inc., 1988.

Harner, Michael. *The Way of the Shaman*. San Francisco: Harper & Row, 1990.

Hartshorne, Charles. *A Natural Theology For Our Time*. La Salle, IL: Open Court, 1989.

Hastings, Arthur. *With the Tongues of Men and Angels: A Study of Channeling*. Orlando, FL: Holt, Rinehart & Winston, Inc., 1991.

Hillman, James. *Re-Visioning Psychology*. New York: Harper & Row, 1975.

Inter Views. New York: Harper & Row, 1983.

Anima. Dallas: Spring Publications, Inc., 1985.

Head, Joseph and S. L. Cranston. *Reincarnation: The Phoenix Fire Mystery*. New York: Julian Press/Crown Publishers, 1977.

Holiday, F. W. *Creatures From the Inner Sphere (The Dragon and the Disc)*. New York: Popular Library, 1973.

Huxley, Francis. *The Way of the Sacred*. New York: Laurel/Dell, 1974.

Hyde, Lewis. *The Gift: Imagination and the Erotic Life of Property*. New York: Vintage Books, 1983.

Institute of Noetic Sciences. *Bulletin*. Sausalito, CA.

Jamal, Michele. *Shape Shifters: Shaman Women in Contemporary Society*. New York: Arkana, 1988.

Jaynes, Julian. *The Origin of Consciousness in the Breakdown of the Bicameral Mind*. Boston: Houghton Mifflin Company, 1976.

Jung, Carl G. *Man and His Symbols*. New York: Doubleday & Company, 1964.

Modern Man in Search of his Soul. New York: Harcourt, Brace & World, 1933.

The Undiscovered Self. New York: New American Library, 1961.

Jung, Emma. *Animus and Anima*. Dallas, TX: Spring Publicactions, 1989.

Kandinsky, Wassily. *Concerning the Spiritual in Art*. New York: Dover Publications, Inc., 1977.

Karagulla, Shafica, M. D., *Breakthrough to Creativity*. Santa Monica, CA: DeVorss & Company, Inc., 1972.

King, Serge Kahili. *Imagineering For Health*. Wheaton, IL: Quest Books, 1981.

Kahuna Healing. Wheaton, IL: Quest Books, 1983.

Mastering Your Hidden Self. Wheaton, IL: Quest Books, 1985.

Urban Shaman. New York: Simon & Schuster, 1990.

Earth Energies. Wheaton, IL: Quest Books, 1992.

Klimo, Jon. *Channeling: Investigations on Receiving Information From Paranormal Sources*. Los Angeles: Jeremy P. Tarcher, Inc., 1987.

Kubler-Ross, Elisabeth. *On Death and Dying*. New York: Macmillan Publishing, 1977.

Kuhn, Thomas S. *The Structure of Scientific Revolutions*. Chicago: University of Chicago Press, 1970.

Kung, Hans. *Signposts for the Future: Contemporary Issues Facing the Church*. New York: Doubleday, 1978.

Leonard, George. *The Silent Pulse*. New York: Bantam Books, 1981.

The Transformation. New York: Delacorte Press, 1971.

LeShan, Lawrence. *Alternate Realities: The Search for the Fully Human Being*. New York: Ballantine Books, 1977.

The Medium, the Mystic, and the Physicist. New York: Viking, 1974.

and Henry Margenau. *Einstein's Space and Van Gogh's Sky*. New York: Macmillan Publishing, 1982.

Lipsey, Roger. *An Art of Our Own: The Spiritual in Twentieth Century Art*. Boston: Shambala, 1989.

Lemkow, Anna F. *The Wholeness Principle: Dynamics of Unity Within Science, Religion and Society*. Wheaton, IL: Quest Books, 1990.

Levi, Primo. *The Periodic Table*. New York: Schocken Books, 1984.

Lusson, Michelle. *Creative Wellness*. New York: Warner Books, 1987.

What Is Wholism? Self-published. 1982.

Matanovic, Milenko. *Lightworks: Explorations in Art, Culture, and Creativity*. Issaquah, WA: Lorian Press, 1985.

Mella, Dorothee L. *The Language of Color*. New York: Warner Books, 1988.

Stone Power II. New York: Warner Books, 1987.

Michell, John. *The New View Over Atlantis*. San Francisco: Harper & Row, 1983.

Mitchell, Edgar D. and John White, Editor. *Psychic Exploration, a Challenge for Science*. New York: G. P. Putnam's Sons, 1974.

Monroe, Robert A. *Journey Out of Body*. New York: Anchor/Doubleday, 1977.

Far Journeys. New York: Dolphin/ Doubleday, 1985.

Montgomery, Ruth. *Aliens Among Us*. New York: Fawcett Crest, 1985.

Moody, Raymond A, Jr., M.D., *Life After Life*. New York: Bantam Books, 1976.

Moore, Mary-Margaret. *I Come as a Brother*. Taos, NM: High Mesa Press, 1986.

From the Heart of a Gentle Brother. Taos, NM: High Mesa Press, 1987.

Reflections of an Elder Brother. Taos, NM: High Mesa Press, 1989.

Muck, Otto. *The Secret of Atlantis*. New York: Quadrangle/The New York Times Book Co., Inc., 1978.

Neumann, Erich. *Art and the Creative Unconscious*. Princeton, NJ: Bollingen/Princeton, 1974.

Nelson, Mary Carroll. *Michael Naranjo; The Story of an American Indian*. Minneapolis, MN: Dillon Press, 1975.

Connecting: The Art of Beth Ames Swartz. Flagstaff, AZ: Northland Press, 1984.

"Layering: Approaching the 'Layer' as a Formal Element and a Significant Metaphor in Artmaking," *Leonardo*, vol. 19, Pergaman Press, Berkeley, CA, 1986.

"Meinrad Craighead: The Litany of the Great River," *Southwest Art*, Houston, TX, December 1991.

"Michael Naranjo; Visionary in Bronze," *New Mexico Magazine*, Santa Fe, NM, October 1975.

"Peter Rogers: Journeyman Artist," *American Artist*, May 1976.

O'Leary, Brian. *Exploring Inner and Outer Space*. Berkeley: North Atlantic Books, 1989.

Paladin, Lynda, ed. *Painting the Dream: The Visionary Art of Navajo Painter David Chethlahe Paladin*. Rochester, VT: Park Street Press, 1992.

Piper, Raymond F. and Lila K. Piper. *Cosmic Art*. New York: Hawthorn Books, Inc., 1975.

Rank, Otto. *Art and Artist*. New York: Agathon Press, Inc. 1975.

Redfield, James. *The Celestine Prophecy*. Hoover, AL: Satori Publishing, 1993.

Reep, Edward. *The Content of Watercolor*. New York: Van Nostrand Reinhold, 1983.

Regan, Georgina and Debbie Shapiro. *Healers Handbook: The Step-by-Step Guide to Developing Your Latent Healing Abilities*. Shaftesbury, Dorset, England: Element Books, Ltd., 1988.

Regier, Kathleen J., Editor. *The Spiritual Image in Modern Art*. Wheaton, IL: Quest Books, 1987.

Ring, Kenneth. *Heading Toward Omega: In Search of the Meaning of the Near-Death Experience*. New York: Quill/William Morrow, 1984.

Roberts, Jane. *Seth Speaks*. Englewood Cliffs, NJ: Prentice-Hall, Inc., 1972.

The Education of Oversoul Seven. Englewood Cliffs, NJ: Prentice-Hall, Inc., 1973.

The Nature of Personal Reality. Englewood Cliffs, NJ: Prentice-Hall, Inc., 1974.

The Worldview of Paul Cezanne; A Psychic Interpretation. Englewood Cliffs, NJ: Prentice-Hall, Inc., 1977.

Roman, Sanaya and Duane Packer. *Opening to Channel*. Tiburon, CA: H.J.Kramer, Inc., 1987.

Rogers, Peter. *The Painter's Quest: Art as a Way of Revelation*. Santa Fe, NM: Bear & Company, 1987.

Rucker, Rudy. *Infinity and the Mind: The Science and the Philosophy of the Infinite*. Boston: Birkhauser, 1982.

The Fourth Dimension; Toward a Geometry of Higher Reality. Boston: Houghton Mifflin Company, 1984.

Samples, Bob. *The Metaphysical Mind*. Reading, MA: Addison-Wesley, 1976.

Sanford, John A. *The Invisible Partners*. New York: Paulist Press, 1980.

Dreams: God's Forgotten Language. New York: Harper & Row, 1988.

Satprem. *The Mind of the Cells, or Willed Mutation of Our Species*. New York: Institute for Evolutionary Research, 1982.

Schlemmer, Phyllis V. and Palden Jenkins. *The Only Planet of Choice*. Bath, U.K.: Gateway Books, 1993.

Shlain, Leonard. *Art and Physics: Parallel Visions in Space, Time and Light*. New York: 1991.

Sinnott, Edmund W. *The Biology of the Spirit*. Los Angeles, CA, Science of Mind Publications, 1973.

Spangler, David. *Revelation: The Birth of a New Age*. San Francisco, CA: The Rainbow Bridge, 1976.

Emergence: The Rebirth of the Sacred. New York: Delta/Merloyd/Dell, 1984.

Stearn, Jess. *Edgar Cayce: The Sleeping Prophet*. New York: Bantam Books, 1969.

Steinsaltz, Adin. *The Thirteen Petalled Rose*. New York: Basic Books, 1980.

Sylvester, David. *Interviews With Francis Bacon*. New York: Thames and Hudson, Inc., 1980.

Talbott, Michael. *The Holographic Universe*. New York: HarperPerennial, 1991.

Tellington-Jones, Linda. *T.E.A.M. News International and other publications*. Santa Fe, NM: Animal Ambassadors International, P.O. Box 3793, 87501-0793.

with Sybil Taylor, *The Tellington Touch*. New York: Viking Publishers, 1992.

Thompson, William Irwin, et al. *The Findhorn Garden*. New York: Lindisfarne/Harper & Row, 1975.

Imaginary Landscape: Making Worlds of Myth and Science. New York: St. Martin's Press, 1989.

Tompkins, Peter and Christopher Bird. *The Secret Life of Plants*. New York: Avon Books, 1973.

Trungpa, Chogyam. *Cutting Through Spiritual Materialism*. Boston: Shambala, 1987.

Tuchman, Maurice et. al. *The Spiritual in Art: Abstract Painting, 1895-1985*. New York: Abbeville Press, 1986.

Vaughn, Frances. *The Inward Arc: Healing and Wholeness in Psychotherapy and Spirituality*. Boston: New Science Library/Shambala, 1986.

Velikovsky, Immanuel. *Worlds in Collision*. New York: Doubleday, 1950.

Villoldo, Alberto and Stanley Krippner. *Healing States: A Journey Into the World of Spiritual Healing and Shamanism*. New York: Fireside/Simon & Schuster, 1987.

Von Däniken, Erich. *Chariot of the Gods*. New York: Bantam Books, 1973.

White, Stewart Edward. *The Unobstructed Universe*. New York: E. P. Dutton, 1940.

The Betty Book. New York: E. P. Dutton, 1977.

Waldo-Schwartz, Paul. *Art and the Occult*. New York: George Braziller, 1975.

Whitton, Joel L., M.D. and Joe Fisher. *Life Between Life*. New York: Warner Books, 1986.

Wolf, Fred Alan. *Star Wave: Mind, Consciousness, and Quantum Physics*. New York: Macmillan Publishing, 1984.

Parallel Universes. New York: Touchstone/Simon & Schuster, 1988.

The Eagle's Quest. New York: Summit Books, 1991.

Zink, Dr. David. *The Stones of Atlantis*. New York: Prentice Hall Press, 1990.

Zink, Melissa. *Water Dog's Tale*. Silverton, CO: Finn Hills Arts, 1983.

We at Arcus Publishing hope you have enjoyed reading *Artists of the Spirit*. Here is information about our other books:

The Tarot Handbook: Practical Applications of Ancient Visual Symbols by Angeles Arrien is an original, inspiring work that brings Tarot out of the fortune-telling context by exploring the symbols from a psychological, mythological, and cross-cultural perspective. Visually attractive and thoroughly informative, it appeals to the novice as well as the serious Tarot student. Many readers consider it an essential resource on the subject and use it daily.

The **Thoth Tarot Deck** is featured in detail in the book; we offer the deck for sale as a convenience to our readers.

Signs of Life: The Five Universal Shapes and How to Use Them, also by Angeles Arrien, won the 1993 Benjamin Franklin Award for New Age Book of the Year. This book demonstrates the historical and cross-cultural use of the five universal shapes: the circle, the triangle, the spiral, the cross, and the square, each symbolizing a specific inner process to which all people attribute similar meaning. An amazingly accurate and powerfully insightful guide, the book includes the Preferential Shapes Test that identifies current tendencies, conflicts, and resources that can assist one's personal growth and integration. Beautifully designed and illustrated, it is a joy to own and a marvelous gift for someone special.

A Change of Heart: The Global Wellness Inventory by **Meryn G. Callander and John Travis, M.D.**, is a series of self-evaluations that stimulate the reader to come into better attunement with the environment. Beautifully illustrated, the book encourages the re-examination of our day-to-day thoughts and actions and offers new directions for effecting change in our global consciousness.

Each of our books can be found in bookstores across America, and in some shops in Australia, Great Britain, and Europe. Should your local bookstore not have the one(s) you want, they can special order for you upon request.

If you prefer, you may order any of our books directly from us and we will pay the postage and sales tax, if applicable. Your order will be on its way to you within two working days after we receive it.

A Change of Heart	$15.95	Call, fax, or write:
Signs of Life	16.95	
The Tarot Handbook	25.00	Arcus Publishing Company
The Thoth Tarot Deck	14.00	P.O. Box 228
Artists of the Spirit	25.00	Sonoma, CA 94576
Shipping and Handling	No Charge	1-800-248-9123 – Visa/MC
State Sales Tax (CA)	Pre-paid	Fax – 1-707-996-1738